Practice and Performance
An Assessment of Ambulatory Care

health
administration
press

PRACTICE AND PERFORMANCE:

An Assessment of Ambulatory Care

by
Ruth Lyn Riedel and Donald C. Riedel
University of Washington

Library of Congress Cataloguing in Publication Data

Riedel, Ruth Lyn.
  Practice and performance.

  Bibliography: p.
  Includes index.
    1. Ambulatory medical care—Connecticut.
  2. Ambulatory medical care—Connecticut—Evaluation.
  I. Riedel, Donald C., 1935—   joint author.
  II. Title.
RA395.A4C87   362.1'2   78-31776
ISBN 0-914904-29-9

Health Administration Press
The School of Public Health
The University of Michigan
Ann Arbor
1979

Acknowledgements

This monograph is based on the activities of a project that spanned eight years and involved the efforts of hundreds of individuals. While we cannot present each of their contributions here, we would like to identify a few whose participation was vital to the successful completion of the study.

Our colleagues and co-principal investigators throughout the course of the Study were: Dr. James E. C. Walker, Professor and Chairman, Department of Community Medicine and Health Care, University of Connecticut; and Dr. Frederick C. Weber, Jr., private practitioner in Internal Medicine and Past-President of the Connecticut State Medical Society. The Study could not have been started, let alone completed, without them. Dr. Walker provided the leadership in helping the Medical Society clarify its interests in and commitment to self-evaluation. His boundless enthusiasm for the goals of the project was contagious, and helped brighten many a dark hour. Dr. Weber made things happen. His perseverance and even-handedness were responsible for the smooth working of the Advisory Committee and his personal integrity helped assure objectivity of the inquiry. Together, they provided invaluable assistance in the interpretation of the analyses.

The study was funded by several sources: The Connecticut Regional Medical Program, the Division of Regional Medical Programs, and the Bureau of Quality Assurance. Two individuals in particular should be acknowledged for their far-sightedness and continuous support: Edward Morrissey and Royal Crystal. Support services of various kinds were generously provided by the University of Connecticut, Yale University, and the University of Washington.

Responsibility for oversight of the scientific merit of the study rested with the CACS Advisory Committee. Members of the Committee spent numerous hours dealing with a wide range of issues and problems, and were condemned to many evening meetings over cold cuts and cold chicken. Special thanks go to Drs. Norman Alisberg, Joseph Cullina, David Grendon, and James Root for their help and support.

Under the wing of the Advisory Committee were a number of other special committees and panels: for the construction of criteria; for the design of specific components of the project; for the development of field instruments. Our thanks to the dozens of physicians, administrators, and social scientists who gave unstintingly of their time.

And the project staff, especially: Dr. Daniel Hamaty, who was project director during the early phases; Richard A. Guzzo who did the basic work on the scoring mechanisms and the factor analyses; Gerrit Wolf who provided advice on analytic strategy and the analysis of the leadership data; Ellen G. Fine who developed and administered the physician interview schedule and who assisted in the project management and recruitment of sample physicians; Drs. Natasha de Leuchtenberg and Dirk Sostman who provided expert medical consultation and developed the clinically oriented scoring mechanism.

Finally, we wish to thank Berkeley Parks and Claire La Voie for their patience and assistance in editing and typing this manuscript.

However, try as we might, we cannot share responsibility for any errors or misinterpretations contained in this book. They're all ours.

To the Memory of
Johannes Frederick Pessel, M.D.
(1894–1977)

TABLE OF CONTENTS

LIST OF TABLES

LIST OF FIGURES

1

Introductory Note and Overview

Over the past decade we have witnessed a mammoth increase in the volume of medical care services delivered on an ambulatory basis. The *National Ambulatory Medical Care Survey* (NAMCS) reported recently that during the year 1975 567,600,000 visits were made to office-based physicians in the United States (*Advance Data,* 12 Oct. 1977). Well over half of these visits were made to primary care physicians. General/family practitioners were credited with 41.3 percent of the visits, internists with 10.9 percent, and pediatricians with 8.2 percent. This represents more than four times the number of visits recorded for hospital outpatient departments and emergency rooms by other sources for a one-year period.

The rapidly increasing volume of primary care delivered in private and hospital practices partly explains why recent investigation has been focused on problems of access, barriers to utilization, and, to a lesser extent, the cost of services provided. However, studies on the *delivery* of ambulatory care are few in number. Those directed toward the clinical content of care have used a variety of approaches, but none has addressed the critical questions surrounding management effectiveness in practices outside of institutions.

DEVELOPMENT OF THE CONNECTICUT AMBULATORY CARE STUDY (CACS)

The variety of quality review programs that were beginning in other parts of the country in the late 1960s and early '70s soon aroused the interest of organized medicine in Connecticut. A growing number of physicians seemed ready and willing to assume responsibility for the evaluation of patient care in this area. The need for a study that would document the quality and patterns of care provided in ambulatory settings was expressed by representatives of the University of Connecticut, Yale University, and the Connecticut Regional Medical Program (CRMP). In the fall of 1971, at the invitation of representatives of the Connecticut State Medical Society (CSMS), they met to discuss areas of mutual concern. The idea for the Connecticut Ambulatory Care Study (CACS) grew from a shared belief that a well-documented study was essential to establish a foundation for future activity by the agencies responsible for the delivery of health services in Connecticut. It seemed especially important to learn more about provider characteristics and organizational factors that affect the quality of services.

After several informal meetings to determine the feasibility of an evaluative study, representatives of the CSMS, the University of Connecticut, Yale University, and the CRMP successfully negotiated a contract with the federal government to undertake the Connecticut Ambulatory Care Study.

The objectives of this study were:

1. To determine the applicability of methods for patient care evaluation developed in other geographic areas and other outpatient settings;
2. To develop standards and techniques for monitoring the quality and appropriateness of ambulatory patient care in Connecticut;
3. To evaluate the effectiveness of alternative organizational devices for primary health care delivery;
4. To construct mechanisms which would best serve the educational needs of practicing physicians in ensuring the quality of health care.

An Advisory Committee representative of ambulatory practice and the collaborating organizations was formed to assume responsibility for: (1) ensuring the scientific quality of the study; (2) assisting in the selection and orientation of physicians participating in other study advisory groups; (3) recommending and recruiting experts from both private and academic medicine to form a Technical Committee which would choose diseases or problem areas for study and design the strategy for the construction of evaluation criteria; and (4) reviewing all decisions made by the Technical Committee and its subcommittees.

As part of the process of forming the Advisory Committee, the eight hospitals and five multi-specialty group practices in the study areas were formally invited to participate in the study. After lengthy discussions and meetings with representatives of the respective institutions and groups, all of the hospitals agreed to participate. However, only one multi-specialty group was willing to take part in the study. These refusals precluded the possibility of making three-way comparisons, and therefore the study was modified to concentrate on differences between private and hospital ambulatory care. Another early objective of this Connecticut study was to provide measures of the cost of care so that quality could be viewed in relation to cost. However, funds were not available to undertake that component of the project.

SUMMARY OF CONTENTS

The following chapters describe the different phases of the Connecticut Ambulatory Care Study as it pursued the objectives stated above. After the development of the Advisory Committee, a Technical Committee was formed to select topics for study and to oversee the panels which developed specific criteria of care for each disease or problem area. Nearly 100 physicians were involved in this early stage of the study, which is described in Chapter 2 along with the development of standards for evaluation, including the model employed for the decision-making process and the instrument used to validate the results.

Chapter 3 elaborates the process of criteria development in terms of rater reliability and the manner of subdividing criteria for the purpose of attaching quantitative scores to physician performance.

Chapter 4 examines the distribution of physicians throughout the state of Connecticut according to primary specialty, practice setting, and geographical area. A stratified random sample of 162 solo practitioners was selected from all primary care physicians in greater Hartford and greater New Haven. These geographical areas contain nearly three-fourths of all internists, pediatricians, and general practitioners licensed to practice in Connecticut. Five hospitals with comprehensive outpatient services in greater Hartford and greater New Haven were chosen for comparative purposes. Samples of patients were selected from both practice settings. One hundred and ten private practitioners and 167 hospital physicians were finally included in the study.

Personal interview schedules were administered to the participating physicians in both practice settings. These were geared to elicit information on personal and professional attributes. Chapter 5 presents the relevant findings in relation to major variables such as setting, specialty, and number of years in practice.

Relevant attributes of the organizations which deliver health care were determined by means of another instrument. This interview was conducted with either the physician or a senior staff member in 100 of the private practices, and with administrators and clinic chiefs in the hospital sites. Chapter 6 presents the results of these interviews. Comparisons are made according to the major variables of setting and specialty, with number of years in practice and the size of private practices included for some attributes.

The results of the performance analyses presented in Chapter 7 show the extent to which physician performance was congruent with individual criterion items and the relative importance of selected variables in explaining differences in care.

The final chapter summarizes the results of this investigation and addresses its implications for physician training, quality monitoring programs, and future research agenda.

2

The Development of Standards for Evaluation

The early 1960s marked the beginning of a serious debate between the proponents of precess and outcome evaluation of ambulatory care. The literature has been summarized by Christoffel and Loewenthal (1977), Brook et al. (1977), Shortridge (1974), Lewis (1973) and Donabedian (1968). Brook et al. (1977) have reviewed problems in using outcome criteria. In many situations, the information on patient outcome is not available or would require such extensive follow-up that project resources would be overtaxed. The use of disability measures is problematic because it is "heavily influenced by intervening factors such as genetic make-up and physical and social environment" (Brook et al. 1977). Indicators of outcome, such as death or restoration of normal function, may occur years after the onset of treatment.

On the other hand, the use of explicit process criteria in evaluating care has long been criticized for weaknesses resulting from the assumption that physician performance does make a difference in patient outcome. This underlying assumption has been questioned by Fessel and Van Brunt (1972), Brook and Appel (1973), and Brook et al. (1977). Missing data or inconsistent recording of tasks or procedures is also a complicating factor and has recently been offset by using multiple methods of data collection. For example, it was personally communicated to the authors in 1978 that direct observation of the physician has been used by several research teams of the National Board of Medical Examiners as a validity check on records data.

The Connecticut Ambulatory Care Study was initiated in order to assess performance and provide feedback on deficiencies to the practicing physician. In view of the special needs of this study, which was conducted under the auspices of the state medical society, investigators and advisors decided to concentrate project resources on process measures with concomitant emphasis on structure, i.e., the amount and type of resources used in the provision of care (Peterson 1956; Clute 1963. A series of workshops were also planned in which immediate feedback was to have been provided to sample physicians on their performance and followed by a period of restudy. These feedback sessions never took place due to various political and budgetary constraints.

ORGANIZING THE TECHNICAL COMMITTEE

The first step in the development of standards for evaluating ambulatory care was the formation of a committee which would be responsible for choosing diseases or problem areas for study. The Technical Committee was created to function as a parent committee which would subdivide into panels after the selection of the diseases or problem areas, and then serve as a linking mechanism for these groups. Its additional responsibilities included:

1. Overseeing the development of criteria within the panels;
2. Reviewing criteria as presented by the panels;
3. Proposing alternative methods to be used in collecting data for the appraisal of the cost of care within various practice settings; and
4. Nominating members for working committees to suggest methods for assessing cost of care and collecting data for other components.

Figure 2.1 shows the organization of the committee's structure.

The Advisory Committee began the process of selecting a Technical Committee by providing project staff with a comprehensive list of nominees. The nominees were contacted and asked to express an interest in serving. Eighty-six physicians responded favorably to the initial contact and their names, together with information on specialty, hospital appointment, and organizational affiliation were assembled and put on a rating form. The form was circulated to members of the CACS Advisory Committee and the CSMS Statewide Medical Planning Committee. Rating of the candidates was done on a scale of one ("best choice") to four ("try to do without"). After all names with ratings of four were dropped from the list, a group of thirty-four candidates with substantially higher rankings were chosen by this process.

From this group of thirty-four, staff assigned the physicians with

FIGURE 2.1
Committee Structure

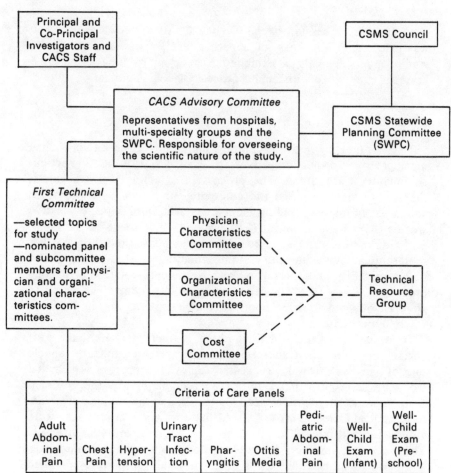

specialties other than general/family practice, internal medicine, or pediatrics to a Technical Resource Group which was designed to advise the Technical Committee on questions relating to subspecialty areas. These same physicians later served on the criteria of care panels. The Technical Committee itself was composed of thirty members selected according to the following major criteria:

1. Practice setting: equal representation from private, multi-specialty group and institutional outpatient practice settings;
2. Specialty: family practice, internal medicine, and pediatrics;

3. Geographic area of the state: an attempt was made to have equal numbers from the greater Hartford and greater New Haven areas.

After the first session of the Technical Committee, a chairperson was selected on the basis of apparent level of enthusiasm for the study, leadership skills (as exhibited in the group meetings), and some previous experience with similar processes such as utilization review.

SELECTION OF TOPICS FOR STUDY

The first meeting of the Technical Committee was used to introduce members to the project objectives and basic design of the Connecticut Ambulatory Care Study. The process of selecting topics began at the second meeting when the committee members were presented with a list of diseases and problem areas used in previous evaluative studies (Payne and Lyons 1972, Kessner 1973, Kroeger et al. 1965). The Committee was asked to choose candidate study topics that represented both acute and chronic conditions, were cared for by both generalists and specialists, and were representative of a large proportion of the care provided to ambulatory patients. The members were encouraged to draw upon their own experiences, in practice, where appropriate.

To assist the Technical Committee in their deliberations, staff consulted a number of sources in an attempt to establish a reliable rate of incidence for the suggested topics. Information was culled from the series of studies by Kroeger et al. (1965), the National Drug Therapeutic Index (NDTI 1970, 1972), and the National Ambulatory Medical Care Survey (1973). At that time, certain problems were anticipated with regard to abstracting data for some of the diseases. These observations were assembled, along with other relevant issues and skills to be considered for each topic, and lists were compiled for the committee members.

Eventually fourteen topics were selected as representative of four broad areas of medical practice: Chronic Disease, Acute Disease, Problem Areas (i.e., Chest Pain, Abdominal Pain), and Special Skills (such as ECG interpretation). Problem Areas were included for several reasons. The sampling plan for patients (as described in Appendix A) called for a cross section of the patient population seen during a selected two-week period. Since this would include first contacts as well as repeat visits for acute and chronic conditions, it was expected that a working or final diagnosis would not be available for a sizeable

FIGURE 2.2
List of Topics with Screening Criteria

Topics	Description
Adult Abdominal Pain	Applies to all cases where the patient is 18 years of age or older and the initial complaint is abdominal pain, abdominal distress, or abdominal cramps. This must be the primary complaint identified by either the patient or the physician. Other complaints may be present, but they must be secondary in importance.
Chest Pain	Applies to all male patients between the ages of 35 and 65 who have been under treatment for chest discomfort or chest pain for at least two months. (In those cases where the patient had not been followed for that amount of time, staff returned to the office or clinic after a two-month period had elapsed to complete all items.)
Hypertension	Applies to patients between the ages of 17 and 65 who, on the first visit with this complaint, had a blood pressure systolic reading of 160 or greater, or a diastolic reading of 95 or greater, or a combined reading of 160/95 or greater, or had a previous diagnosis of hypertension from another practice.
Urinary Tract Infection	Includes all adult females with symptoms or signs referable to the urinary tract.
Pharyngitis	Includes both adults and children where the initial complaint is sore throat.
Otitis Media	Includes only children 12 years of age or younger with an initial or recurrent episode of earache or middle ear pain which is substantiated by the physician.
Pediatric Abdominal Pain	Applies to all cases where the patient is 17 years of age or younger and the initial complaint is abdominal pain, abdominal distress, or abdominal cramps. This must be the primary complaint identified by the patient, the accompanying adult, or the physician. Other complaints may be present, but they must be secondary in importance.
Well-Child Examination (Infant)	Includes all children from birth to 2 years of age appearing for a check-up with this physician (clinic) for the first time or for a scheduled periodic check-up.
Well-Child Examination (Preschool)	Same as above, for children between the ages of 2 and 7.

portion of the sample. It would have been impossible to evaluate the care received by these patients if diagnostic categories were the only topics chosen. Furthermore, the inclusion of problem areas provided an opportunity to evaluate the diagnostic acuity of the practitioners, especially the appropriate use of resources and the length of time taken to arrive at a diagnosis.

Five of the original fourteen topics had to be eliminated during the pretest period. Arteriosclerotic Heart Disease was dropped because of the marked similarity of the criteria to those developed for Essential Benign Hypertension. Diabetes Mellitus was excluded because an average of six hours was required to abstract the patient record. Adult and Pediatric Obesity were eliminated because of problems which arose in constructing criteria, i.e., in one of these panels, physicians could not agree on the need for height, weight, and blood pressure readings. ECG Interpretations were ruled out because tracings could not be obtained without the permission of the sampled patient.

Figure 2.2 presents a final list of the nine topics selected for study and a brief explanation of the parameters established for each disease or problem area.

CRITERIA DEVELOPMENT

For the next stage of the project, the Technical Committee divided itself into nine subgroups, one for each of the selected topics. Additional members for these criteria of care panels were recruited by means of a nomination process similar to the one used in forming the parent committee. An appropriate mix of specialties, practice settings, and geographic locations was again sought, and likely candidates were contacted by phone. A total of seventy-three physicians agreed to serve on the panels and participate in developing criteria for the nine study topics.

Phase I

After the panels had been assembled, every member was interviewed by a senior staff person, either the medical director, the research director, or a senior research assistant. The interviews were conducted to elicit suggested criteria for each topic according to broad components of care: History, Physical Exam, Laboratory Procedures, Special Procedures, Medications, Treatment Goals, Instructions (provided to the patient or family), and Follow-up. All interviews were taped so that a physician could be consulted on medical terminology and logical construction. The resulting lists of criteria were compared with those generated by other studies to ensure that there were no glaring omissions. The lists were then circulated to all panel members who were asked to review the material prior to the first group meeting.

Phase II

These panel meetings were held in several locations to accommodate physicians who were practicing in different areas of the state. Some of the panels were able to complete their criteria selection in one meeting, others required two or three sessions. Members were given careful instructions to discuss each criterion item on the combined list and to consider its importance and usefulness for evaluating care in each practice setting (see Figure 2.3 below). They were asked to revise or eliminate items where appropriate in order to facilitate the work of the abstractors who would be responsible for collecting data from the records. Few additional criteria were generated during these meetings.

After the panel had discussed the proposed criteria and agreed on designations, a condensed list was assembled on a worksheet and circulated to panel members. At a subsequent meeting, the groups were asked to designate each item on the list as Essential (E) or Optimal (O). An *Essential* criterion was one that had to be complied with in every case and could not be waived due to the pressure of time or other situational constraints. An *Optimal* criterion was one that did not have to be complied with in every case but could be left to the discretion of the individual physician. An example of an Essential criterion for Pharyngitis was "throat culture for every patient presenting a sore throat." An Optimal criterion for the same disease would be explaining to the patient why such a culture was necessary. Panel members were asked to exclude criterion items

FIGURE 2.3
Task Instruction Sheet for Panel Members

GROUP TASKS

I. Discuss each item considering its importance and usefulness in each setting. The same items will be used to evaluate quality of care in all three settings.
II. Try to eliminate items where possible so that abstractors will have a manageable job, ensuring reasonable accuracy; i.e., no more than 10 items if possible.
III. *After* condensed list of items has been developed, rank each item according to Essentiality (E) and Optimality (O) on worksheets. (Worksheets will be collected by Staff.)

INDIVIDUAL TASKS

After the group tasks have been completed, a weighting sheet containing all items listed by the group will be mailed to each panel member. Ranking will be done on a scale designed to measure the importance of each item (weighting each from 0 to 100). Data on ranking sheets will provide a distribution indicating a convergence of weights rather than "consensus" in each item. A final determination of convergence will then be made by a statistical measuring technique.

whenever possible in order to get the list down to a manageable number.

Phase III

In the literature of group decision making (especially Dalkey 1967), it has been shown that forcing consensus within a limited amount of time will cause group members to conform very quickly. In other words, the members of a small group will arrive at an answer that is agreeable to everyone at the expense of their own beliefs. For example, a physician who does not believe that it is necessary to take the temperature of every patient presenting with abdominal pain might agree with a strong chairman and one or two other members of the group that the item is Essential. When the additional step of polling the individual members of the group is added, opinions tend to converge to one answer. Obviously, the right or correct answer is not known in a study of this nature, but a convergence toward one particular solution is a more accurate indication of group beliefs than a consensus which is fast and premature.

In his dissertation research, McClain (1970) noted the phenomenon of premature consensus in a group of hospital physicians who were making final determinations of criterion importance. He suggested that items should be rated outside of the group setting on a scale sensitive enough for the rater to work with. He used a range of 0 to 50 which he felt, in retrospect, was not sufficiently sensitive. This work influenced our decision to offer panel members a range of 0 to 100. The convergence achieved when this method was used in the present study enabled staff to determine statistically which were the Essential criteria using the weights assigned by the individual physicians when away from other group members.

During Phase II it was evident that group members arrived at an early consensus through a series of compromises. In order to offset this behavior, another step, similar to McClain's was added to the decision model. Lists of the Essential and Optimal criteria selected by panel physicians were mailed to all group members one week after their last meeting. Each person was instructed to assign weights to every criterion using a range of 0 (for least significant) to 100 (for most significant). These quantitative scores exhibited patterns different from those derived from the previous designations of Essential versus Optimal (see Table 2.1).

Table 2.1 shows the individual ratings of Pharyngitis criteria assigned by panel mambers. The first column of ratings includes designations

DEVELOPMENT OF STANDARDS FOR EVALUATION

of Essential (E) or Optimal (O) made during a group meeting. The second column shows the numerical weights assigned by the individual panel members privately. Results show how difficult it was for the group to make a decision either in the group setting or away from it. Raters in this panel tended to use the high end of the scale (raters 1, 2, 4, and 5). Rater 3 displayed a behavior pattern which was common in other panels; he bounced back and forth between 50 and 100.

Generally speaking, items on which the committee had difficulty in achieving consensus were given low ratings. The criterion item "History of Smoking" is a good example of this behavior. Raters 2 and 4 were so puzzled by this item that they were unable to assign a value during the meeting. Rater 1, who apparently wanted to exclude "History of Allergies" and "Previous Illness," changed his mind when he was alone and gave them a weight of 80. He both raised and lowered his judgments of importance throughout, except for "Temperature Reading" which he weighted 20.

The panel chairman tabulated the individual designations of group members noting a final panel consensus on one part of his work sheet. That consensus appears in the column so labeled. The panels had difficulty reaching consensus on almost all items that proved troublesome to the medical records staff later on.

Rater 2 lowered his evaluation of several items, especially, "History of Allergies," which he had previously designated as Essential. Rater 3 made two categories of Essential items, high Essential (100) and low Essential (80s). Like his colleagues, he used the higher end of the scale; thus, a 50 probably meant that he wished to exclude the item altogether. Overall, his score was also lower when he was away from the group. Rater 4 was fairly consistent in his behavior across settings (i.e., both in the group and in private). The exception was his approach to "History of Allergy" and "Previous Illness," the same items that bothered Rater 1.

Rater 5 liked everything and did not discriminate very much among items. However, he showed his good judgment when he gave a resounding "0" to a poorly worded criterion item: "A definite statement as to whether bacterial or viral etiology, if infections." If only he had expressed these feelings during the panel meeting, he would have earned the gratitude of all of the staff for getting rid of this troublesome item. Another difficult item was the negatively stated "use of ampicillin" in relation to "mononucleosis." It would have been very helpful if Raters 2 and 4 had expressed their true feelings about the negatively stated criterion in which ampicillin was contraindicated when mononucleosis was suspected in adults. Unfor-

Table 2.1
SUMMARY TABLE
Group and Individual Weightings of Pharyngitis Criteria

Criterion Items	Group Ratings Raters 1	2	3	4	5	Consensus	Individual Ratings Raters 1	2	3	4	5	X̄
The date of onset	E	E	E	E	E	E	100	100	100	100	80	96
Presence of cough and fever	E	E	E	E	E	E	100	100	80	100	100	96
Check for Rheumatic fever in the past, anywhere in the record	E	E	O	X	E	E	100	50	100	90	100	88
Smoking history, if recurrent pharyngitis (LTA)	E	—*	O	—	E	E	85	90	50	70	70	73
History of allergies	X	E	O	O	E	none	80	20	100	70	100	74
Similar previous illness	X	E	O	X	E	E	80	70	50	80	100	76
The presence of rhinorrhea and hoarseness	O	E	O	O	E	O	85	100	50	70	100	81
The occurrence of vomiting (LTC)	O	E	O	O	E	O	80	40	50	60	70	60
A detailed description of the pharynx and tonsils	E	E	E	E	E	E	100	100	100	100	100	100
The appearance of the tympanic membranes and ear canals	E	E	E	E	E	E	80	100	50	90	100	84
The presence of cervical adenopathy	E	E	O	E	E	E	100	100	100	95	100	99
The presence of a skin rash (LTC)	E	E	O	O	E	E	80	100	50	80	100	82
The results of cardiac auscultation and abdominal palpation, if heavy or severe pharyngeal exudate or prominant cervical nodes—LTC & young adults	E	E	O	X	E	E	80	90	80	80	100	86
Temperature reading	O	X	E	E	O	none	20	90	50	100	100	72
Pharyngeal culture, dry pac or routine	E	E	E	O	E-O	E	100	100	100	100	100	100
CBC and mono test if enlarged spleen diffuse adenopathy or membranous exudate	E	E	E	X	O	E	100	100	100	100	100	100

14

Criterion												
A definite statement as to whether bacterial or viral, or viral etiology if infections	E	E	E	E	E	E	100	100	100	100	100	80
Appropriate treatment to eradicate beta hemolytic streptococcus when present	E	E	E	E	E	E	100	100	100	100	100	100
No use of tetracycline or sulfa if streptococcal infection	O	X	X	E	O	none	100	100	100	90	100	98
No use of penicillin without a culture	O	X	O	E	O	O	90	90	50	90	90	82
No use of ampicillin if infectious mononucleosis is suspected (LTA)	O	—	—	O	O	O	90	100	50	80	100	84
An explanation of the vital concern for streptococcal infection and the need for a culture to guide the therapy	O	E	X	E	E	none	100	100	100	100	100	100
Penicillin, bicillin or erythromycin for 10 days when streptococcal	E	E	E	E	E	E	100	100	100	100	100	100
An explanation of the need to complete a full course of therapy even if feeling well but not improving	E	E	E	X	E	E	100	100	100	100	100	100
An explanation of the drug dosage and duration of therapy	E	E	E	E	E	E	90	100	100	90	100	96
If strep infection, advise repeat culture 2–4 days after drug therapy	O	X	X	O	O	O	100	80	80	100	100	92
Treat family contacts with streptococcal infection if they become symptomatic or are culture positive	E	X	X	E	E	E	100	100	100	90	100	98

*No value assigned

Key: E = essential
      O = optimal
      X = exclude
      LTA = limited to adults
      LTC = limited to children

tunately, participating in the panel affected their reasoning.

Results of weightings of criteria developed for other diseases and problem areas demonstrated that, for the most part, individual judgments of item importance were lower than judgments made in the group setting. This was especially true for the disease hypertension. The chairman of this panel was diligent and hardworking, but a bit of an overbearing perfectionist in his leadership role. The result was a high level of agreement among panel members in the group setting on items that the chairman considered Essential. However, the individual importance weights assigned in private were very low. Even after one weeks' time, it seems that four out of five of the hypertension raters were still reacting negatively to the dominant behavior of the chairperson. (Hypertension was not included in the summary tabulation because there were 118 criterion items developed.)

Process Issues and Problems Noted in Criteria Development

Payne (1967) warns that the process of criteria development may be largely a function of each panel member's educational, experiential, personal, and socio-demographic characteristics. He questions the concept of "expert opinion" in the development of absolute standards of care. Wagner et al. (1976) found significant differences of opinion among physicians who differed in specialty, training, and experience. He noted that "consensus criteria" can be expected in areas "least likely to be associated with controversy—History, Physical Exam, and Follow-up Observation."

The CACS criteria were heavily weighted toward History and Physical Exam and it is possible that the groups slightly favored these components of care to avoid lengthy debate or disagreement which would have made them uncomfortable. However, Peterson et al. (1956), when constructing indexes of "overall capacity for goodness in medical care," asked physician judges to weight components of care. Thirty (30) and thirty-four (34) points, out of a possible 107, were allocated to Clinical History and Physical Exam, respectively. Indexes were then constructed using a factorial method and the resulting values were practically identical with the judgment type of quantitative index used in their analysis. The factor analyses confirmed the overall relative importance of History and Physical Exam.

Considerable effort was expended by both staff and panel members in developing initial lists of criteria for all nine topics. One indicator of the difficulties involved in this type of decision making is the large number of criteria which emerged at the beginning of the process.

Originally the panels were asked to choose no more than 10 criteria for each topic. The actual lists compiled after the first meetings ranged from 40 items for Pharyngitis to 118 for Hypertension. By observing the group dynamics of the early sessions, staff attempted to improve process efficiency in various ways.

A decision was made to designate future chairpersons based on leadership skills observed in meetings of the parent Technical Committee. (Chairman will be used hereafter since only two women were nominated to serve on the Technical Committee and the panels.) It was assumed that a strong chairman would complement a CACS staff member and that they could function as coleaders. Staff worked with panel chairmen very closely to maintain a high level of commitment to the project. The results of this strategy were mixed. In some panels, the chairman ran away with the group, making unilateral decisions and ignoring the resources of group members; in others, he remained passive and unwilling to take any risks. There were few who adopted the appropriate leadership style of asking their colleagues for information and assistance in making decisions on these very complex problems (Vroom and Yetton 1973). It was fortunate that the individually assigned weights of all criterion items in Phase III could be used as empirical indicators of Essentiality.

Because the use of predetermined criteria is such a widespread strategy, a more rigorous investigation of the methods of criteria development is needed in the field. A commonly used technique is the "modified Delphi" which seems to have as many modifications as the number of research teams using it. The originators of the Delphi method state that it should never be used unless the decision makers have a minimum of 45 days to devote to the process. Several descriptions of this technique are available (Dalkey 1967; and Helmer 1967), and it is important to remember that it was originally designed as a forecasting instrument.

Delbecq, Van de Ven and Gustafson (1975) developed the Nominal Group Technique (NGT) for group decision making in health and human services. The NGT is a six-step process which can be conducted easily in any surroundings:

1. Group members work independently, generating ideas and writing them down in brief statement form.
2. Individuals present their ideas to the entire group while one person keeps a record of all contributions.
3. The material is discussed and clarified.
4. A preliminary vote is taken on the importance of each item;

approximately five are selected and assigned priorities.
5. Results of the preliminary vote are discussed.
6. A final vote is taken and items are again given a relative
   importance ranking on a scale of 0 to 10.

The technique used for criteria development in the Connecticut
Ambulatory Care Study was similar, although certainly not identical,
to the NGT.

In addition to assigning Optimal and Essential criteria for each
topic, panels were also asked by the Technical Committee to develop
screening criteria for each disease or problem area. The boundaries
established were often unclear and had to be restated by the CACS
physician. (See Figure 2.2). He closely supervised the development
of the abstractor instructions and the abstract form. It was in this
process of development and field testing of the instruments used
for data collection that the physician and medical records staff worked
together to clarify many of the vague parameters that had been
suggested by the panels. An example of instructions and an accompanying abstract form for the disease Pharyngitis appears in
Appendix B.

CRITERIA VALIDATION

In order to determine whether the criteria of care selected by the
panels could be legitimately generalized to the physician population
in Connecticut, a Criteria Checklist was compiled for use as an
instrument of the study. It included some of the criteria suggested
by panel members in their individual interviews as well as standards
culled from other sources, such as the American Academy of Pediatrics
and the American Society of Internal Medicine. All criteria developed
by the CACS panels for selected topics were buried in this lengthy
list in such a way that it was impossible for the sample physicians
to identify them. The Checklist was divided into sections according
to major specialty. General practitioners were asked to choose Essential
criteria for all nine topics, pediatricians for five, and internists for
five. Although sample physicians were given the opportunity to add
items to the lists of criteria generated by the CACS panels or to
include criteria from other sources or from their own experience,
they rarely did so.

This instrument was administered to 100 of the private practitioners
participating in the study *after* data collection had been completed
in their respective offices. Originally hospital physicians had also

been included in this phase of the survey, but response rate among these was so low that the attempt was discontinued. Tables B.1 through B.9 (in Appendix B) demonstrate the extent of agreement on criteria between sample physicians and panel members on items that were designated Essential. The similarity in rating items can be seen in the Pharyngitis Criteria (Table 2.1 and B.5). In general, internists in the private practice sample were more likely to agree with the panel choices than pediatricians or general practitioners. The purpose of this example is to show that physicians from hospital and private practice and academic medicine share beliefs about what should be done. Their behavioral intentions are very similar.

Checklist Findings

Judging by the responses to the Criteria Checklist, there is a very high level of consensus between private practitioners and panel physicians with regard to the Essentiality of criteria. On the whole, items chosen by the internists and pediatricians are closer to the panel designations of Essential criteria than are those selected by the general practitioners. The analyses of performance measures presented in Chapter 7, indicate a large discrepancy between theory and practice. In other words, private practitioners theoretically subscribe to certain standards of care which they do not implement in actual practice.

Both the panel deliberations and the findings cited above seem to indicate that there is a strong tendency for practitioners to stipulate "textbook medicine," or an approximation, as criteria for evaluation. This fact should be taken into account by those responsible for the construction of criteria in future assessment programs. Once criteria have been established as normative, the resulting low congruence might turn out to be counterproductive to behavioral change in areas where deficiencies are noted. That is, busy practitioners could easily criticize the lofty criteria as unrealistic, given the constraints of time and resources, and thus dismiss the findings of the evaluation. The implications of this phenomenon should be given careful attention. It warrants additional research on the development of optimal methods for professional behavior modification. One cardinal rule of program evaluation should be kept in mind: consider the goals of the measurement when fashioning the measuring stick.

3

Selection of Reliably Weighted Criteria and Comparison of Alternative Scoring Mechanisms

In the beginning of the study, panel members were asked to assign weights (ranging from 0 to 100) to designate the importance of criterion items. We anticipated that the use of weighted criteria would improve the process of scoring physician performance as has been reported in previous research (Payne and Lyons 1972, and McClain 1970). An even more clinically sensitive scoring mechanism was developed by physician consultants. The element of clinical judgment in this more subjective system was expected to improve substantially the process of assigning performance scores.

As mentioned in Chapter 2, variability was noted among panel members when they assigned weights to the criterion items. On the other hand, both physicians who developed the clinically sensitive scoring system were, in the end, in almost perfect agreement in judging performance on subsamples of cases. The disparity among panel raters had to be resolved before appropriate comparisons among scoring mechanisms could be made.

ANALYSIS OF RATER AGREEMENT

Table 3.1 shows the number of items that were developed for all diseases and problem areas (except Pediatric Abdominal Pain) as well as the number of original raters or panel members who assigned weights to all criterion items. For example, the Well-Child (Infant) Exam panel chose 26 criterion items in the second stage of criteria development. Six physicians had assigned weights ranging from zero (0) to one hundred (100) to each of these twenty-six (26) items in the third stage of the decision process. Full-scale Reliabilities for these weights

TABLE 3.1
Summary Information on Raters and Rater Reliabilities
by Diseases/Problem Areas

Diseases/Problem Areas	Number of Original Raters	Full-Scale Reliability	Number of Retained Raters	Retained Rater Reliability
Adult Abdominal Pain	6	.85	3	.91
Chest Pain	5	.65	4	.80
Hypertension	4	.77	2	.84
Urinary Tract Infection	6	.83	4	.90
Pharyngitis	5	.81	3	.86
Otitis Media	6	.64	3	.88
Well-Child Examination (Infant)	6	.81	3	.91
Well-Child Examination (Preschool)	6	.83	4	.88

are also shown in Table 3.1; the full-scale reliability for the original raters in Well-Child (Infant) Exam was .81. (Full-scale refers to the reliability of the ratings when all possible raters of items are included.) The reliability index for this problem area, as well as others presented here, is based on the intercorrelations of the weightings of the original raters.

After examining these intercorrelations and analyzing differences in the mean weights assigned by the different raters, a subset of raters was chosen for all but Pediatric Abdominal Pain. (All of the original ratings were retained for this problem area because only three panel members submitted their weighting sheets.) The number of raters retained for each topic is also presented in Table 3.1. The reliability index calculated for each subset of raters appears in the last column of this table; these reliabilities are all satisfactory as compared with the full-scale reliabilities; the indexes for Chest Pain and Hypertension are much improved.

This strategy of rater analysis allowed us to clean up the ratings (or raters) so that only those who agreed systematically on the importance of items were retained. The importance of each item was determined by taking the average weight assigned to it by the retained group of raters. The standard deviations of the weightings for each item were considered in this cleaning-up process.

ITEM ANALYSIS

Just as the raters were examined for consistency of agreement, the items within each topic were analyzed in a similar manner. The

mean (M) rating per item was computed, based on the subset of
retained raters within each topic, as were the variance and standard
deviation (SD) (see Table 3.2). The standard deviation was taken
as the critical index of dispersion (i.e., variability of the weightings
for each item).

Because the purpose of these analyses was to provide a set of
reliable weights in preparation for comparing the three different scoring
systems, we used only the criterion items which were weighted .60
or more and on which there was high agreement as to their importance.
An experienced pediatrician and a fourth-year medical student supervised this selection process, intervening when it was necessary to
prevent the deletion of clinically relevant items. Low ranking unreliably
weighted criteria were excluded *for these comparisons only* to reduce
noise in the data.

Next, items were rank ordered according to SD, from lowest to

TABLE 3.2
Well-Child Examination (Infant) Criteria
Ordered by Item SD

	Rank of Item by SD	Criterion Item Number	Mean	SD	M/SD
	1	1	98	3	32.67
	1	5	88	3	29.33
	1	10	98	3	32.67
	1	11	98	3	32.67
	1	18	98	3	32.67
	1	19	98	3	32.67
	1	21	98	8	32.67
	9	8	87	6	14.50
	9	12	97	6	16.17
	9	15	97	6	16.17
	11	3	58	8	7.25
	12	2	85	9	9.44
	13.5	4	60	10	6.00
	13.5	20	90	10	9.00
	15	6	88	13	6.77
	16	7	87	14	6.21
M/SD Cutoff					
	17	25	72	19	3.79
	18	13	50	20	2.50
	19	26	73	21	3.48
	20	24	75	23	3.26
	22.5	16	72	26	2.77
	22.5	17	80	26	3.08
	22.5	22	80	26	3.08
	22.5	23	80	26	3.08
	25	14	28	28	1.00
	26	9	63	29	2.17

TABLE 3.3
Selection of Items Using M/SD Ratio

Diseases/Problem Areas	No. of Criterion Items	SD Cutoff	# Items Retained	# Items Dropped
Adult Abdominal Pain	30	19	12	18
Chest Pain	48	17	36	12
Hypertension	28	17	25	13
Urinary Tract Infection	62	14	39	23
Pharyngitis	36	17	28	8
Otitis Media	51	17	30	21
Well-Child Examination (Infant)	26	14	16	10
Well-Child Examination (Preschool)	24	15	10	14

NOTE: Where the M/SD ratio is ≥ 4 for the majority of items with SD equal to or less than the cutoff SD.

highest. The mean and standard deviation, as well as the mean/standard deviation ratio M/SD, for each item of the Well-Infant Examination are shown in Table 3.2. The ratio M/SD is a commonly used index of agreement for item weights. A large ratio might indicate two things: (1) the mean weight of the item is close to 100; and/or 2) the standard deviation of that item is small, indicating close agreement on its importance by all or most of the raters. A ratio of four was selected as the minimally acceptable ratio for retaining an item. The results of this strategy are displayed in Table 3.3.

One alternative considered was using breaks in the distribution of SDs to include items which congregated around certain SD values. This process was judged to have failed at producing sets of clinically meaningful criterion items. Other strategies which could have been used for finalizing these lists were judgment of physician experts or the use of tried and true criteria such as those developed for the Hawaii Studies (Payne and Lyons 1972).

SCORING MECHANISMS

Beginning with Lembcke in 1956, a number of studies have presented alternative ways of quantifying the adequacy of care provided by physicians to their patient population. In the Lembcke audit, care was considered adequate if 80 percent of the criteria were met for a selected case. His explicit criteria were developed from clinical texts and took into account contingencies in the case which might affect the outcome of care.

In a study sponsored by the American Society of Internal Medicine (Kroeger et al. 1965), ten physician judges reviewed abstracts of the internists' office records. A relatively subjective rating system was used, based on a scale of one ("excellent" care) to four ("very poor" care).

For the North Carolina Study (Peterson et al. 1956), a qualitative evaluation was made by trained physician observers who ranked performance on a scale from I (low performance) to V (high performance). A second rating, the quantitative evaluation, was made on the basis of explicit criteria developed by the author and weighted according to his judgment of particular importance. Possible scores ranged from 1 to 107. The criteria were divided into six categories: Clinical History, Physical Examination, use of Laboratory Aides, Therapy, Preventive Medicine, and Clinical Records. In this evaluation it was necessary for the observers to judge not only how well each task was performed but also whether or not a particular procedure was required in the given case. Results of both the qualitative and quantitative measures were highly correlated (.86).

Clute (1963) employed similar methods in his study of Canadian general practitioners. He had a qualitative rating scale (1–5) as well as an explicit criteria scale, with possible scores ranging from 1 to 80 (standards could only be assessed in 80 percent of the cases). Clute's two scales were intercorrelated at the level of .95. The three physician observers—a pediatrician, an internist, and a public health specialist—carefully verified the reliability of their observations by presenting them to one another for discussion in regularly scheduled meetings. This rigorous training might have contributed to the high correlation. Clute related performance to salient physician characteristics and geographic area.

Payne and Lyons (1972) presented a new way of quantifying care in the *Episode of Illness* and *Office Care Studies* which they conducted in Hawaii. In the process of developing the Physician Performance Index, the Hawaiian panels not only generated criteria of care for selected topics but also assigned weights to each criterion item. For example, pharyngeal culture was given a weight of three (3) while date of onset was only given a weight of one (1). A summary measure of physician performance was provided by summing across all criterion items. For certain kinds of analyses, a percent of total possible weighted items was also computed. Although criteria were divided into components of primary care, component weights were not attached.

With a summary score for physician performance, statements could have been made regarding level of care across a series of diseases. This method of scoring was carefully considered by the CACS because it would have provided a useful way of summarizing across selected topics as well as across components within each topic. For example, a general practitioner's score on all nine topics could have been used to develop a mean performance score for care delivered to his/her patients. A similar average performance measure could have been computed for internists on adult topics and pediatricians on pediatric topics. After a year of deliberation it was decided that constructing such a mechanism for the present study would have necessitated combining unlike tasks or activities. Combining the subtasks of History-Taking in a topic such as Hypertension (which is extremely complex) with History-Taking in Pharyngitis (which may include only a few criterion items) is like combining battleships and dinghies. We elected to portray performance in each topic and for each component of care separately (as delineated by factor analyses of the criterion items described in Chapter 7). Given this commitment we sought a scoring system appropriate for the task.

Scoring systems which were evaluated for use reflected the three schools of thought described above: *System One* merely indicated whether a criterion was or was not complied with; *System Two* worked with the assigned weights; and *System Three* was an attempt to formalize a subjective process of ranking performance, using explicit criteria developed. There were several reasons for developing more than one mechanism. In their description of the multi-trait/multi-method matrix, Campbell and Fiske (1959) recommended the use of more than one instrument or measurement strategy to ensure reliability and validity of the results. By this means, it should also be possible to determine the most cost-effective method of scoring. Initially, it was assumed that the more complex *System Three* would exhibit a greater sensitivity to nuances in performance than *Systems One* or *Two* and thereby tell us more about variations in performance.

Description of the Three Systems

System One is the simplest of all possible scoring systems based on data from the patient record. Under this system, all criterion items were viewed as being of equal importance. Whenever there was evidence that a particular criterion item was met (e.g., information was included in the patient record on a particular aspect of the History, Physical Exam, etc.), the physician received a score of one (1) for performance on that item. One criterion might be broken down into several items, each receiving a one (1) for met or a zero (0) for not met. In this way performance was assessed on each item regardless of performance on any other item.

Example of System One Scoring

Item	Possible Information	Score
Recording of patient's temperature	The actual temperature; normal, high, subnormal, or acceptable abbreviation	1
	Temperature not mentioned.	0

System Two is more complex than *System One* because it incorporates information on the relative importance of each criterion item. As described earlier in this chapter, relative importance was established by taking the average reliable weight given to each item by a panel of physician experts. As in *System One,* each item was scored independently, regardless of performance on other criteria.

Example of System Two Scoring

Item	Weight	Possible Information	Score
Recording of patient's temperature	57	The actual temperature; normal, high, subnormal, or acceptable abbreviation.	.57
		Temperature not mentioned.	.00
Examination of pharynx	100	Red throat, inflamed throat, normal or negative or abbreviation.	1.00
		Pharynx not mentioned.	.00

System Three originated with panel members who suggested that more characteristics of the individual patient be taken into account in assessing performance on the entire case. Since this complex system relied heavily on clinical judgment, all research assistants who were not medically trained were carefully supervised by a physician, a fourth-year medical student, and a Master's level registered nurse. It is *System Three* that uses fully the contingencies or branches (if . . . then statements) in the criteria. For example, "if beta hemolytic streptococcus is present, then eradicate with a 10-day course of penicillin, bicillin or erythromycin." *System Three* is more complex because each item is assessed according to all other information available on the particular case. In *Systems One* and *Two* the relative importance of each item remained the same across all patients. *System Three* takes into account the presence or absence of other information in the record and the quality of that information. Scores assigned in *System Three* ranged from minus three (−3) to plus three (+3). A −3 was the lowest score and a +3 the highest score that a physician could receive for a particular criterion item.

Example of System Three Scoring

Item	Possible Information	Score
Check for presence of diffuse adenopathy	No nodes, nodes normal, adenopathy, glands, etc. or abbreviation.	+3
	No mention of diffuse adenopathy *with* splenomegaly, cervical nodes, or tonsillar exudates.	−3
	No mention of diffuse adenopathy *without* indication of splenomegaly, cervical nodes, or tonsillar exudates.	0

Random Selection of Cases for *System Three* Scoring

Because *System Three* was implemented by medically trained staff and required a considerable amount of clinical judgment, it was too costly to use for all cases within all diseases and problem areas. In order to conserve physician manpower and project resources, a random sample of cases was selected for five of the nine topics. All cases of Well-Child Exam were used. Otitis Media and Hypertension were eliminated from *System Three* scoring in an attempt to further reduce the scope of the work. Otitis was excluded because of its similarity to Pharyngitis and Hypertension, because of size and complexity (i.e., number of items).

Although it would have been highly desireable to have the results of Hypertension available in *System Three* for future analyses, the complexity of the topic and the large number of items were prohibitive. The number of sample cases which were scored in *System Two* are as follows:

Type of Case	Total Number of Cases	Percent of Total Sample
Well-Child Exam (Infant)	359	100%
Well-Child Exam (Preschool)	613	100
Pediatric Abdominal Pain	265	25
Pharyngitis	240	25
Urinary Tract Infection	55	25
Chest Pain	82	25
Adult Abdominal Pain	130	25

Agreement Among Scoring Systems

A decision to use factor analysis to clarify the patterns of physician performance in the major analyses was made early in the study. Comparisons among scoring mechanisms would not have been meaningful had they been made in each criterion item! Further, these findings would have been very difficult to interpret (see Chapter 7). The first step in determining the extent of agreement was to factor analyze performance on the same cases in all three scoring systems. The method of factor analysis used is described in Chapter 7. Next, the rank order of the mean performance score for each of the factors in seven of the nine problem areas in *Systems One, Two,* and *Three* was noted. Physician mean performance scores on all the factors were grouped by practice setting, the characteristic which explained most of the variance in physician performance. The degree to which the rank order of mean performance factor scores were stable for factors across all three systems was used to reflect the extent of agreement among all three systems. The percentages in Table 3.4

TABLE 3.4
Average Agreement Among Scoring Systems One, Two, and Three with Cases
Grouped by Practice Setting

Topic	Average Percent of Agreement	
	Systems One and Two	Systems One, Two and Three
Well-Child Exam (Infant)	100.00%	100.00%
Well-Child Exam (Preschool)	100.00	100.00
Pharyngitis	100.00	91.67
Chest Pain	100.00	86.54
Urinary Tract Infection	100.00	84.92
Adult Abdominal Pain	100.00	78.57
Pediatric Abdominal Pain	100.00	71.43
Hypertension	100.00	—*
Otitis Media	100.00	—*

*Otitis and Hypertension were not chosen for System Three coding.

indicate the extent of agreement on rank order of mean performance on factors of *Systems One* and *Two* and in *Systems One, Two* and *Three*.

The criterion for agreement applied to these data was really too stringent but it was the only appropriate strategy for the data which were already in The Statistical Package for the Social Sciences, SPSS (Nie 1975). The rank orderings of performance in the topic factors were required to match perfectly for agreement to be considered present. Any slight deviation in rank across systems indicated (according to present criteria) 100 percent disagreement. This rigid method of determining agreement/disagreement across systems inflated the true amount of disagreement. Less stringent methods of comparison would have required using other computer languages which were prohibitively expensive for this single component of analyses.

There was 100 percent agreement between *Systems One* and *Two* in all diseases/problem areas. Some differences emerged when *System Three* was introduced. Except for Adult and Pediatric Abdominal Pain, where the extent of agreement drops slightly below the 80th percentile, variations are minor. In Well-Child Exams (Table 3.4) 100 percent overall agreement was demonstrated among all three systems in the assessment of physician performance. In Pharyngitis, a 91.67 percent rate of agreement existed across all three systems when performance was assessed according to practice setting.

In the other conditions the extent of agreement was lowered by the addition of *System Three*.

In Pediatric Abdominal Pain, there was 71.43 percent overall agreement among *Systems One, Two,* and *Three*. When physician performance was assessed by Setting in this topic, two of the seven factors did not show total consistency across systems. However, no statistically significant differences between levels of performance on either of these two factors were measured.

System One, The Preferred Scoring Mechanism

Conclusions drawn from alternative scoring mechanisms demonstrate that *System One*—a simple, straightforward determination of a criterion being complied with or not complied with—was adequate for the evaluation of care using explicit predetermined criteria. It was an easy decision to use *System One,* the least costly and the least complex, for the bulk of the analyses. However, it would be necessary to investigate further analyses in *System Three* before stating unequivocally that *System One* is superior for all explorations of physician performance regardless of their purpose. Looking at the findings in another way, one might say that subjective, weighted, or unweighted judgments of performance levels are all acceptable for scoring performance data. The additional benefits of adding weights to criterion items or of using physician judges have yet to be demonstrated quantitatively.

4

Physicians and Hospitals: Methods of Sample Selection and Recruitment of Participants

SAMPLE SELECTION

The distribution of primary care physicians by specialty in Connecticut is similar to that of New England as a whole. Compared with estimates for the United States, however, Connecticut has higher proportions of internists and pediatricians and a lower proportion of general practitioners (see Table 4.1). The distribution of primary care physicians in the state corresponds with population density. Previous research has demonstrated that approximately three-fourths of these physicians practice in the greater Hartford and greater New Haven areas. This fact was decisive in establishing parameters for the present inquiry. Because of the diversity of geographic and economic variables operative in other regions of the state, a study embracing all of Connecticut would have necessitated independent estimates for an additional three areas. Budgetary constraints precluded this possibility. The planning group believed that an in-depth analysis of practices in the two major areas would be more important for the purposes of program implementation than a superficial evaluation of patterns throughout the state.

Table 4.2 presents the distribution of primary care physicians in greater Hartford and greater New Haven by practice setting, specialty, age, and number of years in practice. These estimates were based on data obtained from the American Medical Association Physician Biographical Tape. Sixty-one percent of the primary care physicians in both areas are in private practice. Almost half of them are internists, one-third general practitioners, and one-fifth pediatricians. Parallels can be seen with regard to age and years in practice. There are fewer

TABLE 4.1
Number and Percentage of Physicians by Specialty
Connecticut, New England, United States 1972

Specialty	Connecticut			New England			United States		
	No.	% All*	% PC**	No.	% All*	% PC**	No.	% All*	% PC**
General/Family Practice	636	10.1	31.6	2,787	11.6	34.9	52,345	16.2	46.5
Internal Medicine	992	15.8	49.2	3,828	16.0	47.9	42,339	13.1	37.6
Pediatrics	387	6.2	19.2	1,380	5.8	17.3	17,951	5.6	15.9
Total Primary Care	2,015	32.0***	100.0	7,995	33.3	100.0	112,635	34.9	100.0
General Surgery	534	8.5		2,257	9.4		28,365	8.8	
Obstetrics/Gynecology	360	5.7		1,162	4.8		18,829	5.8	
Psychiatric	545	8.7		1,933	8.1		20,223	6.3	
Other	2,838	45.1		10,635	44.3		142,784	44.2	
All Nonfederal M.D.'s	6,292	100.0		23,982	100.0		322,836	100.0	

SOURCE: National Center for Health Statistics. *Health Resources Statistics, 1974.* United States Department of Health, Education, and Welfare, DHEW Pub (HRA) 75-1509, 1974, pp. 180–183.

* Percentage of all physicians.

** Percentage of primary care physicians.

*** Connecticut State Department of Health data indicate 40 percent of all physicians are primary care physicians. (Source: Hirakis, S. S. and Armondino, N. L. "Distribution of Physicians in Connecticut." *Connecticut Health Bulletin*, 86, 5, 1972, pp. 1–10.) The difference from national data is probably due to differences in data source and methodology. The above figures are assumed to provide meaningful relative comparisons of Connecticut with other states but should not be used as an absolute indication of Connecticut percentages.

TABLE 4.2
Distribution of Primary Care Physicians by Various Characteristics
(Greater Hartford and New Haven, 1972)

Characteristics	No.	Percentage
Practice Setting		
Private Practice		
Solo	473	50%
Partnership arrangement	80	8
Non-group	26	3
(Total Private)	579	61
Hospital Practice	124	13
Multi-Specialty Group Practice	48	5
Practice Setting Not Ascertained*	200	21
TOTAL	951	100
Major Specialty		
General/Family Practice	299	31
Internal Medicine	461	49
Pediatrics	191	20
TOTAL	951	100
Age of Physicians		
25 and under	0	—
26–35	154	16
36–45	242	25
46–55	238	25
56–65	167	18
66–75	106	11
76+	44	5
TOTAL	951	100
Number of Years in Practice		
Under 10	37	7
10–19	165	31
20–29	131	25
30–39	122	23
40+	77	14
TOTAL	532**	100

NOTE: Data for this tabulation were obtained from the AMA Physician Biographical Tape.
*Setting not available for these physicians on AMA Physician Biographical Tape.
**An additional 56 primary care physicians were identified through the Connecticut State Licensure files, but years in practice were not ascertained.

physicians under the age of 45, and only 7 percent of all primary care physicians have been in practice ten years or less. More than half are middle-aged or older, and 37 percent have been physicians for at least 30 years. The distributions for Hartford and New Haven were quite similar, with the exception of the higher percentage of physicians in private general practice in Hartford.

Sampling Procedures

In using the Physician Biographical Tape for preliminary analyses, probable errors of various sorts were noted, such as the coding of ophthalmologists as primary care physicians. It was decided to update and verify the AMA data with hard-copy files in the office of the Connecticut State Licensing Bureau. This process took several man-months, but the result was a very accurate listing suitable for sampling purposes. Data on hospital characteristics such as teaching affiliation, number of service contacts, and size of staff were readily available from Connecticut Hospital Association files (see Table 4.6).

The study objectives dictated that performance estimates of a certain order of specificity be constructed for physicians in each specialty group for both hospital and private practice. It was also considered important in sample selection to control on a few other readily discernible characteristics (years in practice and geographic area) to ensure appropriate representation. Accordingly, it was decided that a stratified random sample of private practices would yield the best estimates given the resources available. Specialty (three strata), years in practice (six strata), and geographic location (two strata) were the variables chosen for the stratification.

There had been no previous research of this type conducted at the time of the study design, and therefore rough guesses of expected findings had to be used to determine appropriate sample sizes. Estimates were made of the expected compliance with criteria, volume of cases with the presenting problems selected for evaluation, and refusal rate, by specialty. Based on these estimates, it was decided

Table 4.3
Distribution of Sampled Practices by
Specialty, Years in Practice, and Geographic Area

YEARS IN PRACTICE	GENERAL PRACTITIONERS			INTERNISTS			PEDIATRICIANS			ALL SPECIALTIES		
	Hart-ford	New Haven	Both	Hart-ford	New Haven	Both	Hart-ford	New Haven	Both	Hart-ford	New Haven	Both
<10	1	1	2	4	2	6	2	1	3	7	4	11
10–19	6	8	14	15	13	28	6	8	14	27	29	56
20–29	8	9	17	8	8	16	5	5	10	21	22	43
30–39	12	14	26	8	5	13	2	2	4	22	21	43
40+	7	11	18	4	2	6	1	2	3	12	15	27
Not Initially Ascer-tained*	2	3	5	4	3	7	4	2	6	10	8	18
All Years**	36	46	82	43	33	76	20	20	40	99	99	198

*Supplementary sample of primary care physicians identified through Connecticut State Licensure files but not contained in AMA Biographical Tape. Years in practice for these physicians was not initially known.
**Number of private practices chosen are not exactly 200 due to process of internal sampling.

TABLE 4.4
Response Rates for Private Practice Sample by Specialty and Geographic Area
(Percentage Response)

GEOGRAPHIC AREA	SPECIALTY			
	General Practitioners	Pediatricians	Internists	All Physicians
Greater New Haven	73%	75%	58%	68%
Greater Hartford	59	78	68	68
Both Areas	68	76	63	68

that 200 practices split evenly between New Haven and Hartford would be sufficient. After all physicians were arranged according to the stratification procedures mentioned above, appropriate sampling intervals were chosen and applied using random starts. The distribution of practices initially selected is presented in Table 4.3.

Early field experience indicated that excessive resources would be expended in collecting data from all of the general practitioners in practice thirty or more years (see Table 4.3). It was therefore decided to modify the sampling plan in two ways: first, to subsample the general practitioners in two strata (30–39 years in practice, and 40 or more years) at a rate of one-half; and second, to replace those physicians who refused with another selection from the same stratum. In some strata replacement was not possible because there were no other physicians with those characteristics. The combination of procedures yielded a total sample of 162 private physicians contacted for participation. The complexity of the sampling plan necessitated the use of a series of weights, reflecting the probabilities of selection, for application to data on practices and patient care. Therefore, the estimates contained in later chapters must be used with caution, and the interpretation contained in the text followed closely.

The response rates for private practices, by specialty and geographic area, are given in Table 4.4. While the overall response rate of 68 percent was the same in both geographic areas, the internists in New Haven and the general practitioners in Hartford had lower response rates than other physician groups. Table 4.5 compares the characteristics of respondents and nonrespondents. The largest differences occurred between graduates of foreign medical schools and others, with the former more likely to decline the opportunity to participate in the study. The differences by other characteristics were not found to be significant.

The Hospital Sample

The original study design called for the inclusion of all eight hospitals providing ambulatory services in the two areas. However, early field work indicated serious underestimates of the manpower and time necessary for data collection in the clinics and emergency rooms. A decision was therefore made to subsample the hospitals after stratification on a number of characteristics. Table 4.6 presents the characteristics of the eight hospitals at the time of the study. Four strata were finally constructed, with the two largest hospitals selected with certainty, and one institution in each of the three remaining strata chosen, producing a total sample of five. Various subsampling routines were involved for patient samples in a few of the hospitals because of an unexpectedly high yield in some problem areas. Here again, the complexity of the design necessitated the application of

TABLE 4.5
Comparison of Participants and Non-Participants
in the Study, by Various Characteristics

Characteristics	Participants %	Nonparticipants %	X^2
Specialty			
GP	42	40	1.47
IM	35	44	
PED	23	16	
Country of Medical School			
U.S.	88	74	5.02*
Foreign	12	26	
Specialty and Country			
GP			
U.S.	84	83	.00
Foreign	16	17	
IM			
U.S.	90	69	4.70*
Foreign	10	31	
PED			
U.S.	93	64	4.84*
Foreign	7	36	
Board Certification			
Certified	58	72	2.95
Not certified	42	28	
Years in Practice			
<10	4	2	3.70
10–19	22	21	
20–29	31	42	
30–39	22	24	
40–49	19	10	
50+	3	2	

*Significant at the .05 level.

TABLE 4.6

Description of Eight Short-term General Hospitals With Largest Outpatient Services by Size of Staff, Teaching Affiliation, Location, Diversity of Outpatient Services and Volume of Ambulatory Visits

Hospital	Size of Staff*	Teaching Affiliation	Location	Diversity of Services**	Number of Service Contacts
A	3,255	Med School	N.H. Metropolitan	Very Diverse	High
B	400	Med School	H. Metropolitan	Not Diverse	High
C	2,491	Teaching	H. Metropolitan	Very Diverse	High
D	2,064	Teaching	H. Metropolitan	Diverse	High
E	1,298	Teaching	N.H. Metropolitan	Diverse	Med.
F	847	Teaching	H. Metropolitan	Diverse	Med.
G	580	Teaching	N.H. Nonmetropolitan	Not Diverse	Med.
H	1,110	Teaching	H. Nonmetropolitan	Not Diverse	Med.

*Number of full-time employees and FTE's.
**Number of outpatient clinics.

various weights to the institutions and patient samples.

The response rate among hospital providers was extremely high; in each institution all of the providers were required by their clinic chiefs or department heads to cooperate. Succeeding chapters will provide additional information on the hospital characteristics.

RECRUITMENT OF THE PARTICIPANTS

Private Practitioners

Our recruitment efforts concentrated on developing a strategy for obtaining voluntary participation from solo or small-group practitioners who were assumed to be the hardest to convince. It was in this phase of activity that the study realized the greatest benefits from the sponsorship of the Connecticut State Medical Society. After the signing of the contract in 1972, a complete description of the Connecticut Ambulatory Care Study was presented to two separate sessions of the CSMS House of Delegates. In this way, grass roots representatives were kept informed of the purpose of the study and its progress. In addition, the project was carefully described to local medical and specialty societies; the medical director made himself available to their executive bodies for periodic discussions in order to gain their cooperation. The selection of the Advisory Committee and the process of nominating physicians for the Technical Committee and the panels did much to improve the credibility of the study. In July of 1973 *Connecticut Medicine* (the journal and house organ of the CSMS) carried an article which described the Connecticut Ambulatory Care Study to the entire membership. During the same month a colorful brochure was distributed to all physicians licensed to practice in the state. The brochure announced the objectives of the study and identified the sponsoring organizations and their representatives who were serving as investigators; the names of senior staff who would be likely to contact potential participants were also included.

Correspondence with the private physicians was initiated by the president of the state society or executives of local societies. Physicians who appeared hesitant were then approached by a colleague who was already familiar with the study; one who had perhaps taken part in the preparatory phases of criteria development and was convinced of the soundness of the endeavor.

The next step usually involved sending out a letter showing the personal signature of the CACS medical director. If there was no response, the potential participant was contacted by phone. Once communication had been firmly established, a meeting was arranged between the physician and a senior staff member who presented a thorough description of the project and asked permission to evaluate the practice.

Hospitals

Members of the study advisory groups helped the staff to gain entry to all of the institutions. Hospital recruitment was done through a series of meetings. Staff members usually discussed the project with the Director of Ambulatory Services and then made a formal presentation to the medical staff, including chiefs of services whose units or clinics were likely to be providing care to sample patients (i.e., Medicine, Pediatrics, Urology). Some hospitals negotiated with staff members for several months before agreeing to participate. However, in the end, all were most cooperative; some provided manpower to the CACS for logging and checking procedures.

The process of gaining hospital participation often involved private practitioners who had been approached outside the hospital as part of the private practice sample. These physicians were treated as two separate subjects in the respective settings and were assigned different identifying numbers. No attempts were made to look at care given by the same physician in multiple practice settings.

5

Professional and Personal Characteristics of Physicians Providing Primary Ambulatory Care

This chapter describes the personal and professional characteristics of the providers and outlines differences that exist among specialty groups in both practice settings. Tabulations of the physician attributes are presented by practice setting and major specialty. Analyses were also done according to number of years in practice within setting and specialty, but these are not included because of small cell sizes. Results of chi-square (X^2) calculations are presented with the tabulations.

The distribution of physicians by practice setting among three specialties is presented in Table 5.1. (The proportions of generalists, pediatricians and internists in the population are displayed and described in Chapter 4.) The physicians are also grouped according to number of years in practice. In this study physicians were included in specialty groups based upon their own designations of major specialty. These attributions of specialty were used in all subsequent analyses. Forty-one percent of the private practice physicians classified themselves as general practitioners, 21 percent as pediatricians, and 38 percent as internists.

Significant differences emerged across practice setting by number of years in practice and specialty. Over half of the younger hospital physicians were still in training during the survey, which accounts for the magnitude of this difference. Significant differences in number of years in practice within the hospital setting emerged among all three specialty groups. Fifty-nine percent of the hospital practitioners described themselves as internists, in contrast to 38 percent of the private physicians.

TABLE 5.1
Percentage Distribution of All Physicians
Presented by Practice Setting, Major Specialty, and Number of Years in Practice

Number of Years in Practice	Private Practice				Hospital				Both Settings			
	GP	IM	PED	All	GP	IM	PED	All	GP	IM	PED	All
<10	7%	—	7%	4%	33%	57%	81%	62%	9%	19%	30%	18%
10-19	7	36	31	23	17	15	10	13	8	29	24	21
20-29	24	42	41	34	42	8	8	12	25	31	30	29
30+	62	21	22	38	8	18	2	12	57	21	16	32
Total Percent	100%	99%	101%	99%	100%	98%	101%	99%	99%	100%	100%	100%
Number of Sample Physicians	38	43	29	110	12	74	41	127	50	117	70	237

NOTE: X^2 Values

By setting: Private vs. Hospital $X^2 = 89.27*$

By specialty: GP (Private) vs. GP (Hospital) $X^2 = 12.09*$
IM (Private) vs. IM (Hospital) $X^2 = +$
PED (Private) vs. PED (Hospital) $X^2 = 37.62$

Within setting, by specialty:

    Private
GP vs. IM $X^2 = +$ GP vs. PED $X^2 = +$ IM vs. PED $X^2 = +$

    Hospital
GP vs. IM $X^2 = 10.96**$ GP vs. PED $X^2 = 11.33**$ IM vs. PED $X^2 = 8.22**$

*significant at 0.01 level
**significant at 0.05 level
+X^2 calculation invalid due to low expected frequencies.
Percentage might not total 100 because of rounding error.

41

PROFESSIONAL TRAINING AND EARLY CAREER DECISIONS

Connecticut has a very mature population of general practitioners; most of these physicians graduated from medical school before 1949. In our study sample, general practitioners were older than pediatricians and internists in both practice settings. This finding may be indicative of the trend of specialization which has characterized the medical profession for the last twenty years. Over 56 percent of the private practice physicians who graduated prior to 1950 are arranged in general practice, as compared to only 21 percent of those graduating since 1960.

Because of the recent attention given to foreign medical school graduates, we were interested in determining the relative effects of U.S. versus foreign training. Rhee (1976) has stated that foreign medical graduates provide a lower quality of medical care on the average than graduates from U.S. medical schools which tend to emphasize research and specialization. The percentage of physicians for each of the three specialties who graduated from U.S. and foreign medical schools appears in Table 5.2. In private practice, general practitioners had proportionately more foreign medical school graduates (19 percent) than did internists (10 percent) and pediatricians (7 percent). A higher proportion of hospital physicians were foreign trained; about one-third graduated from foreign medical schools. Significant differences in U.S. versus foreign training by practice setting occurred for internists and pediatricians.

Table 5.3 presents the total number of years of training received in the U.S. It is once again notable that the percentage of practitioners reporting foreign training is higher in hospitals than in private practice. Because of the proportion of interns and residents in our hospital sample, private practitioners are shown as having had more years of training in the U.S. than hospital practitioners.

The CACS Advisory Committee was particularly interested in the relationship between the type of internship and residency programs the physician participated in and the performance in providing ambulatory care. This relationship had been explored by Peterson et al. (1956), revealing only the slightest suggestion of a correlation. Physicians in nonaffiliated, approved internship and residency programs were compared with physicians in affiliated, approved internship and residency programs according to practice setting and specialty. Significant differences were observed between hospital and private practitioners according to specialty. As expected, more hospital practitioners had participated in affiliated, approved internship programs. Pediatri-

TABLE 5.2
Location of Medical School Presented by Setting and Specialty
(Percentage Distribution)

Location of Medical School	Private Practice				Hospital				Both Settings			
	GP	IM	PED	All	GP	IM	PED	All	GP	IM	PED	All
United States	81%	90%	93%	87%	67%	61%	62%	62%	80%	80%	83%	81%
Foreign Country	19	10	7	13	33	39	38	38	20	20	17	19
TOTAL PERCENT	100%	100%	100%	100%	100%	100%	100%	100%	100%	100%	100%	100%
Number of Sample Physicians	38	43	29	110	12	74	41	127	50	117	70	237

NOTE: X^2 Values

By specialty: GP (Private) vs. GP (Hospital) $X^2 = 1.03$
IM (Private) vs. IM (Hospital) $X^2 = 11.26*$
PED (Private) vs. PED (Hospital) $X^2 = 8.67*$

*significant at 0.01 level

43

TABLE 5.3
Total Number of Years of Training Received in the United States
Presented by Setting and Specialty
(Percentage Distribution)

Number of Years of U.S. Training	Private Practice				Hospital				Both Settings			
	GP	IM	PED	All	GP	IM	PED	All	GP	IM	PED	All
None	3%	—	—	1%	8%	7%	17%	10%	4%	2%	5%	4%
1	26	2	—	11	42	22	27	26	27	9	8	15
2	43	10	4	23	25	26	13	22	42	16	7	23
3	4	10	59	18	8	6	29	13	4	9	50	16
4	18	56	17	33	17	20	4	15	18	44	13	28
5	6	16	19	12	—	15	6	11	5	16	15	12
6	—	5	—	2	—	2	2	2	—	4	*	2
7	—	—	—	—	—	2	2	2	—	1	*	*
TOTAL PERCENT	100%	99%	99%	100%	100%	100%	100%	101%	100%	101%	98%	100%
Number of Sample Physicians	38	43	29	110	12	74	41	127	50	117	70	237

NOTE: * Less than 1 percent

X² Values

By setting: Private vs. Hospital X² = 26.60*

By specialty:
GP (Private) vs.   GP (Hospital) X² = 3.11
IM (Private) vs.   IM (Hospital) X² = +
PED (Private vs.   PED (Hospital) X² = 24.72*

Within setting, by specialty:

Private
GP vs. IM X² = +   GP vs. PED X² = +   IM vs. PED X² = +

Hospital
GP vs. IM X² = 4.08   GP vs. PED X² = 7.19   IM vs. PED X² = 21.23*

*significant at 0.01 level
+X² calculation invalid due to low expected frequencies.
Percentages might not total 100 because of rounding error.

cians and internists in both practice settings were more apt to have participated in affiliated programs than were general practitioners. Because there was little indication that this variable might account for differences in performance beyond that explained by practice setting or number of years in practice, it was not selected for the final analyses.

The type of hospital training obtained by a physician was directly associated with major specialty and practice setting. However, internists and general practitioners were much more likely to have had a rotating internship than pediatricians. Surprisingly, 11 percent of the private pediatricians had chosen an internship in medicine. Hospital pediatricians differed: 58 percent had selected pediatric internships. About one-third of the private general practitioners reported two or more years of internship training. In contrast, only 21 percent of the private internists and 13 percent of the private pediatricians had undergone two or more years of internship. Some of the generalists with two or more years of internship spent their first year interning in a foreign country.

Clute (1963) explains some of the thinking behind physicians' occupational choices. Some of the respondents in his study chose to be internists because they considered this to be real medicine; others chose surgery because of movie portrayals or a childhood idol. However, in Connecticut we found that private practitioners were most likely to have chosen a medical career for reasons of professional status; they also spoke of following in the footsteps of another physician whom they admired. Hospital pediatricians were more often influenced by role models than were internists and general practitioners. Overall, hospital practitioners were primarily motivated to choose medicine because of intellectual interests or out of a desire to help people.

Physicians who were influenced in their career decisions by role models frequently mentioned particular family members, older friends or college faculty. Hospital general practitioners were least likely to attribute their interest in medicine to professional role models. Over half of the generalists queried said that they had simply decided on their own that they wanted to become doctors.

Still pursuing the issue of career choice, we asked physicians why they chose the particular area of medicine in which they were practicing. Clute (1963) showed that a large number of general practitioners chose their specialty because of personal or family circumstances which forced them to leave training early. For the most part, difficulty in financing medical education was reported by generalists who had begun practice more than 30 years ago. Over one-third of the Connecticut general practitioners resembled their Canadian colleagues in this respect (Table 5.4). Sixteen percent stated that they became general practitioners through a process of elimination. We do not know what motivated them to select this response. Perhaps they tried other avenues and found them wanting. It seems more likely that these physicians had been passed over for the more desirable specialty internships (Kendall and Selvin 1957). Twenty-seven percent of the general practitioners in private practice and 40 percent of those in the hospital setting selected "variety of practice" as their reason for choosing their field; this may have been used as a catch-all category.

In contrast to the range of responses regarding choice of general practice, pediatricians chose their field because of the type of patients and problems they anticipated (Table 5.4).

Respondents were asked to describe or characterize their own practices as "general" or "specialized." All private practice general practitioners considered their practices to be "general," but their hospital colleagues were less apt to agree. The reason for this might be that general practitioners in an institutional setting, regardless of previous training, are frequently specialists in emergency medical care by virtue of their experience. Several private internists but very few pediatricians characterized their practices as general. Observations of pediatric offices confirmed that pediatricians have rather routine, homogeneous caseloads (as described in Appendix E). Hospital pediatricians were even less likely to describe their practices as general, whereas hospital internists occasionally did so.

BOARD CERTIFICATION AND FACULTY APPOINTMENTS

Of growing concern to both consumers and providers of medical care is the issue of board certification. Specialty board certification has existed in the fields of pediatrics and internal medicine for over 30 years. However, it was not until 1970 that a specialty board in the field of family practice came into existence. This explains some of the differences among the three specialty groups in the proportion of those board certified in private practice. As illustrated in Table 5.5, 93 percent of all general practitioners were not board certified. However, a large number of the private practice internists (59 percent) had met all of the requirements for board certification. An even higher proportion of the private practice pediatricians (84 percent) were board certified. Similarly, in the hospital setting, general practitioners were less apt to have met requirements for board certification than were

TABLE 5.4
Reason for Choice of Field
Presented by Setting and Specialty
(Percentage Distribution)

Reason for Choice of Field	Private Practice				Hospital				Both Settings			
	GP	IM	PED	All	GP	IM	PED	All	GP	IM	PED	All
Intellectual Challenge	—	26%	—	10%	10%	37%	—	22%	1%	29%	—	12%
Type of Patients and Problems	9	38	74	34	30	36	86	51	11	37	78	37
Personal-Family Availability, Financial Need	37	—	—	15	—	—	4	1	34	—	1	12
Role Model	—	4	8	3	10	—	10	4	1	3	9	4
Process of Elimination	16	16	6	14	10	13	—	8	15	15	4	12
Total Family Involvement-Relationship	7	—	2	3	—	—	—	—	6	—	2	3
Faculty	5	5	8	6	—	—	—	—	4	3	6	4
Variety of Practice	27	12	—	15	40	14	—	13	28	12	—	15
TOTAL PERCENT	101%	101%	98%	100%	100%	100%	100%	99%	100%	100%	100%	100%
Number of Sample Physicians	38	43	29	110	10	57	39	106	48	100	68	216

NOTE: Information of 5 percent of weighted physicians was not ascertained due to short form of questionnaire. Percentages might not total 100 because of rounding error.

47

Table 5.5
Certification in Primary Specialty
Presented by Setting and Specialty
(Percentage Distribution)

Certification	Private Practice				Hospital				Both Settings			
	GP	IM	PED	All	GP	IM	PED	All	GP	IM	PED	All
Yes	7%	59%	84%	43%	8%	23%	27%	22%	7%	47%	67%	38%
No	93	41	16	57	92	76	73	78	93	53	33	62
TOTAL PERCENT	100%	100%	100%	100%	100%	99%	100%	100%	100%	100%	100%	100%
Number of Sample Physicians	38	43	29	110	12	74	41	127	50	117	70	237

NOTE: X^2 Values

By setting: Private vs. Hospital X^2 = 12.00*

By specialty: GP (Private) vs. GP (Hospital) X^2 = .01

IM (Private) vs. IM (Hospital) X^2 = 14.96*

PED (Private) vs PED (Hospital) X^2 = 22.08*

Within setting, by specialty:

Private

GP vs. IM X^2 = 24.10*   GP vs. PED X^2 = 40.52*   IM vs. PED X^2 = 5.07

Hospital

GP vs. IM X^2 = 1.44   GP vs. PED X^2 = 1.91   IM vs. PED X^2 = .20

*significant at 0.01 level

Percentages might not total 100 because of rounding error.

48

internists and pediatricians. As expected, the majority of the senior physicians in pediatrics and internal medicine in the hospital setting were board certified.

These same physicians were more likely to hold faculty appointments (Table 5.6). Our data showed that older general practitioners who were not board certified were less likely to be given privileges by major teaching hospitals. Whereas 40 percent of the pediatricians and 20 percent of the internists in private practice reported having appointments, only 4 percent of the general practitioners held teaching positions. None of the hospital general practitioners were formally appointed, in contrast to 100 percent of the pediatricians in the same practice setting. Nearly half of the hospital practitioners participated in teaching, mostly through rounds and preceptorship arrangements.

TIME SPENT IN PATIENT CARE ACTIVITIES

The North Carolina Study (Peterson et al. 1956) contained no variation in qualitative ranking of physicians according to number of hours worked. However, we decided that it would be worthwhile to include such information in the present inquiry. Sample physicians were asked to estimate the number of hours they spent each week caring for patients. One-third of the private practitioners, regardless of specialty, spent between 46 and 55 hours per week in patient care activities (Table 5.7). One-fourth spent between 35 and 45 hours and another between 56 and 65. None of the private practice pediatricians reported spending more than 79 hours weekly, but 4.1 percent of the general practitioners and 4.6 percent of the internists said they spent a minimum of 80 hours with ambulatory patients. The mean number of hours for internists (55.2) differs from the mean of 50.7 hours for general practitioners and 51.4 hours for the pediatricians. Part of this difference can be accounted for by older general practitioners and pediatricians with very short work weeks. Hospital general practitioners spent even less time providing patient care than did their private practice colleagues. The same was true for hospital internists. Differences between hospital and private practice pediatricians were not clearly defined.

A much greater variation in the number of hospital inpatient and outpatient contacts was sustained in the average work week. Private practitioners' estimates of the number of inpatient contacts varied by physician specialty. As anticipated, private pediatricians reported no more than 50 inpatients in one week, while 34 percent of the internists and 22 percent of the general practitioners saw no fewer

TABLE 5.6
Faculty Appointments
Presented by Setting and Specialty
(Percentage Distribution)

Faculty Appointment	Private Practice				Hospital				Both Settings			
	GP	IM	PED	All	GP	IM	PED	All	GP	IM	PED	All
None	96%	79%	59%	82%	100%	52%	—	54%	96%	77%	53%	80%
One	4	20	40	18	—	48	100	46	4	23	46	20
TOTAL PERCENT	100%	99%	99%	100%	100%	100%	100%	100%	100%	100%	99%	100%
Number of Sample Physicians	38	43	29	110	8	16	11	35	46	59	40	145

NOTES: Information on 18% of weighted hospital physicians was not ascertained, either because short form of questionnaire was used or because question was not applicable (e.g., interns, residents, fellows).

X^2 Values

By specialty: IM (Private) vs. IM (Hospital) X^2 = 4.48*
PED (Private) vs. PED (Hospital) X^2 = 11.52*

*significant at 0.01 level

Percentages might not total 100 because of rounding error.

TABLE 5.7

Estimated Number of Hours Spent by Physicians in Direct Patient Care Per Week
Presented by Setting and Specialty
(Percentage Distribution)

Number of Hours	Private Practice				Hospital				Both Settings			
	GP	IM	PED	All	GP	IM	PED	All	GP	IM	PED	All
1-34	3%	—	7%	3%	—	16%	22%	16%	3%	4%	12%	6%
35-45	26	20	22	23	50	16	12	19	28	19	19	22
46-55	39	39	23	36	30	5	16	12	38	29	21	31
56-65	22	22	36	25	10	16	14	14	21	21	30	23
66-98	9	18	11	13	10	48	35	38	9	26	18	18
TOTAL PERCENT	99%	99%	99%	100%	100%	101%	99%	99%	99%	99%	100%	100%
Number of Sample Physicians	38	43	29	110	10	56	39	105	48	99	68	215

NOTES: Information on 5 percent of weighted physicians was not ascertained due to short form of questionnaire and inability to answer the question.
X^2 calculations were not done because of vanishing cells.
Percentages might not total 100 because of rounding error.

51

than 51 patients during the same time period. The mean number of inpatient contacts for pediatricians (13) was less than one-half of the mean for general practitioners (27) and less than one-third of the mean number of inpatient contacts for internists (46). The majority of the hospital internists and pediatricians reported a small number of inpatient contacts per week, whereas all hospital general practitioners reported between 60 and 300 inpatient contacts for the same period. This is probably due to the fact that internists and pediatricians who provide the majority of ambulatory care in the hospital setting do not have major responsibility for hospital inpatients. However, the hospital general practitioners who were considered institutional staff were usually assigned to the emergency room.

Physicians' impressions of the total number of patient contacts they had in private offices during a one-week period ranged from less than 50 to more than 300 patients. When checked with the Patient Log maintained for the study, they were found to be quite accurate. Internists rarely reported seeing more than 149 patients in a week, whereas many general practitioners and pediatricians estimated at least 150 patients weekly.

MEMBERSHIP IN PROFESSIONAL SOCIETIES

According to Peterson et al. (1956), membership in professional societies is looked upon as a favorable sign of the doctor's favorable interest in medicine. However, they found very little relation between activity in professional societies and the quality of patient care. The Connecticut study was conducted under the auspices of the state medical society which was naturally curious about this aspect of their members' professional lives.

An overwhelming majority of all physicians belonged to the Connecticut State Medical Society (CSMS). Some attributed their continued membership to the availability of malpractice insurance through CSMS. Pediatricians were less likely to join this organization. Whereas 93 percent of the general practitioners and 95 percent of the internists in private practice were members of the state society, only 79 percent of the pediatricians belonged. Fewer hospital practitioners belonged to the CSMS—only 75 percent of the general practitioners, 60 percent of the internists, and 38 percent of the pediatricians belonged.

Private practitioners were also more likely to join the American Medical Association (AMA) than were physicians in the hospital setting. Again significant differences were found according to specialty, with only about one-third of the pediatricians belonging, in contrast to roughly two-thirds of the internists and general practitioners. In the hospital setting no general practitioners participated in the AMA; about half of the internists and one-third of the pediatricians belonged. These findings are quite different from the results of the North Carolina Study in which there was a small proportion of physicians who did not belong to the AMA.

Membership in second level specialty societies was related to the number of years in practice. About one-third of the older internists in both settings belonged to the American College of Physicians (ACP). Few pediatricians joined this professional society. Membership in the American Academy of Pediatrics (AAP) was most common among private practitioners (81 percent), but widespread in both settings. Younger general practitioners in private practice and half of the hospital general practitioners in the sample belonged to the American Academy of Family Practice (AAFP). The older private physicians might not have belonged to this specialty society because of its relatively recent development. However, as Peterson points out, the Academy makes considerable demands on the practitioner's time.

Older internists in both practice settings were much more likely to belong to the American Society of Internal Medicine (ASIM). We cannot understand why neither the younger private nor hospital internists were joining this professional society. The mean number of years in practice for members in both practice settings was 25 years.

As expected, only one-third of all private practitioners belonged to society committees and very few hospital practitioners participated actively in their professional societies. Differences within setting by specialty were not significant. However, it was interesting to note that 9 percent of the private pediatricians were extremely active, reporting membership in at least four society committees.

RELATIONSHIPS WITH PROFESSIONAL COLLEAGUES

The Physician Characteristics Advisory Committee hypothesized that patient care would improve as a practitioner increased contact with professional colleagues. As one might expect, hospital practitioners used this informal system much more frequently than private practitioners because of the convenience of working in the same organization. All hospital general practitioners reported consulting with colleagues on a regular basis and pediatricians did so almost as frequently. Of course, all of these data are subject to the difficulties of recall and problems associated with self-report.

Peterson et al. (1956) investigated the use of consultants by general practitioners in North Carolina and discovered that they were selected because of "proximity," "allegiance" to certain institutions, and perceived competence by the referring physician. Clute (1963) reported a negative relation between a high referral rate and the quality of care given. In the Canadian study referral rate may have been interacting with number of years in practice, as the older Canadian practitioners were more apt to refer their patients to other physicians. This was not true for the Connecticut physicians surveyed. The highest percentage of referrals in general practice occurred among younger physicians who had been in practice for less than 20 years.

An estimate of the proportion of patients referred into and out of a physician's practice may indicate several things: the physician's evaluation of patient needs, of his own competence, or of the abilities of his colleagues. Pediatricians reported referring a smaller proportion of their patients for specialized care. This result corresponds with an earlier finding that pediatricians have fewer patients who are in need of hospitalization. The mean percent of patients referred by private pediatricians (8 percent) is lower than the mean for general practitioners (11 percent) and internists (11 percent). Hospital practitioners referred proportionately more of their patients to other specialists or to specialty clinics within the hospital.

One of the more common reasons for referral was the primary physician's judgment that the patient was in need of psychiatric help. Private practice internists referred most often on this basis, probably because they did not wish to spend time counseling patients. Internists also reported being most irritated by complaints which they considered to be trivial. Private practitioners were more apt to refer patients for psychiatric help because of behavior that they described as psychotic. More general practitioners referred patients for "psychosis" than did internists and pediatricians. This finding may only reflect a difference in perception of symptom severity; physicians who were less familiar oi comfortable with emotional disturbance might be apt to judge behavior more severely. More private patients were being referred for "psychosis" than were hospital patients. Hospital general practitioners, who referred most often in that setting, attributed 40 percent of their referrals for psychiatric care to neuroses observed in their patients.

PHYSICIANS' FEELINGS ABOUT THEIR PATIENTS AND PRACTICES

In the beginning of the study, during the early discussions of physician performance, the issue of patient noncompliance was frequently brought to our attention. Panel members pointed out that, however qualified the physician, little would be accomplished if the patient refused to cooperate. Noncompliance with the recommended treatment poses an obstacle to medical care which is difficult to overcome: the patient is viewed as not keeping up his end of the bargain. It seemed important to measure the extent of this problem among our sample physicians.

Seventeen percent of the private pediatricians stated that noncompliance was not a problem for them in the process of providing care. However, only 4 percent of the private general practitioners and 2 percent of the internists reported problem-free interaction with patients over following treatment regimens. Significant differences emerged for practice setting and specialty when hospital internists and pediatricians were compared with their colleagues in private practice. Hospital practitioners reported that they had more difficulty managing their patients. As one might expect, they also reported that they knew very few of their patients well enough to develop relationships with them. This lack of continuity in care with one particular provider could explain the different patterns of compliance. However, the concept of patient compliance is measured here according to data reported by the physicians themselves and therefore reflects their own perception of the patient's compliance with treatment regimens. Hospital practitioners are perhaps socialized into viewing their patients as difficult, while private physicians are taught that controlling the patient is a very important aspect of practice. Some physicians may be reluctant to admit to a high noncompliance rate.

As Parsons (1951) suggests, both participants in a physician-patient interaction have expectations concerning each other's behavior. Patients who ask for more than the physician believes is legitimate will be described as demanding. Patient demands may be requests for additional tests, explanations, prescriptions, or more time from the physician. In private practice, significantly fewer general practitioners found excessive demands to be a serious impediment to providing care than did internists and pediatricians. Twice as many hospital general practitioners were bothered by patient demands as general practitioners in private practice. It must be pointed out that these physicians were dealing primarily with emergency cases and worked in the emergency room or an adjunct emergency unit. Generally speaking, older physicians were found to be less tolerant of what they perceived to be patient demands; older hospital pediatricians were the exception.

Hospital practitioners also reported having more difficulty communicating with their patients. This finding can be partly attributed to language problems experienced with Spanish-speaking patients. It also reflects difficulties with compliance and excessive patient demands. In hospital practice, internists tended to rank communication as more of a problem than did the other specialties. Only 8 percent of these internists believed that communication was not a problem for them, as compared with 17 percent of the general practitioners and 15 percent of the pediatricians. Estimates of this difficulty increased with number of years in practice. Among private practitioners, more internists rated communication as a moderate or severe problem than did general practitioners or pediatricians. Significant differences emerged within specialty across practice setting for general practitioners, internists and pediatricians.

Broken appointments were a source of frustration for many primary care physicians. In private practice, cancellations or no-shows were disruptive to the schedule, necessitating a reallocation of physician and staff time. Also, the private practitioner's income was directly affected by this patient behavior. Some were not willing to tolerate this type of irresponsibility and refused to continue seeing the patient until they had been reimbursed for these scheduled visits. Broken appointments were less of a problem for private practice internists: 39 percent reported that such behavior was not disruptive. In contrast, 70 percent of the private general practitioners and 77 percent of the pediatricians reported that they were moderately disturbed by broken appointments. Older private practitioners appeared to be less disturbed by broken appointments, despite the fact that many had dwindling practices. Hospital internists and pediatricians were very disturbed by no-shows. In fact, a few of the clinic chiefs had reverted to a first-come/first-serve appointment system because of a one-third "no show" rate.

The organizational literature contains three major viewpoints regarding the relationship between satisfaction and performance (Schwab and Cummings 1973): (1) satisfaction leads to performance; (2) the relationship between satisfaction and performance is moderated by intervening variables such as the perceived probability of achieving particular rewards and the value of these rewards; (3) performance leads to satisfaction. Herzberg's two-factor theory of satisfaction and motivation (1966) identifies certain motivators which are believed to spur employees to good performance: achievement, responsibility, recognition, advancement, and personal growth through increased competence. He also describes extrinsic motivators which enhance working conditions but have no direct effect on the quantity or quality of the employee's performance. Herzberg calls these variables "hygiene factors;" examples are pay plans, working conditions, supervisory practices, and company policies. Since the publication of this major work, social psychologists have continued to investigate the relationship between the intrinsic motivators and the quantity and quality of production.

In a description of the motivational basis of organizational behavior, Katz (1970) distinguishes between two types of gratification. The first is gratification obtained from performing a specific role. An individual experiencing this kind of intrinsic satisfaction finds the work so interesting that heavy financial inducement would be required to get him/her to change jobs. We suggest that this particular motivational pattern is a self-sustaining system. Such individuals are filling a role in the organization that encourages the use of personal skills and talents. They are aware that they are performing competently and the experienced competence is intrinsically rewarding. The second motivational pattern described by Katz is related to the first. The individual partially or fully identifies with the goals of the organization; through this process, such goals become internalized. For example, a physician who primarily enjoys being "a good physician" could be equally happy practicing medicine in any setting.

Because it was assumed that physicians would experience a rather high level of intrinsic satisfaction in their jobs, they were asked which aspect of medical practice they enjoyed the most. Initially we used an open-ended question to inquire about the sources of physician job satisfaction. Private pediatricians clearly preferred patient contact or relationships with patients over other aspects of their clinical practice (Table 5.8). Responses of private general practitioners were varied. Most reported that they preferred patient contact but were unable to be more specific. Hospital pediatricians and internists also opted for the patient-related categories. Physicians often included teaching activities in the "other" category.

Because of the difficulty in coding a wide range of responses to this question, physicians were given a limited number of options from which to select the most gratifying aspects of medical practice (Table 5.8). Given the opportunity to choose between making diagnoses, teaching and training, deciding on an appropriate treatment regimen, and dealing with patients, pediatricians in private practice clearly diverged from the other two specialty groups. About two-thirds of the general practitioners and 57 percent of the internists revealed that assembling the facts and arriving at a diagnosis was the most gratifying aspect of medicine for them; only 18 percent of the pediatricians reported to be similarly gratified by diagnostic work.

TABLE 5.8

Most Gratifying Aspect of Medical Practice Presented by Setting and Specialty
(Percentage Distribution)

Responses	Private Practice				Hospital				Both Settings			
	GP	IM	PED	All	GP	IM	PED	All	GP	IM	PED	All
Cannot Choose	3%	9%	12%	7%	—	14%	8%	10%	3%	10%	11%	8%
Making Diagnoses	65	57	18	52	75	47	35	47	66	53	23	51
Teaching and Training	2	9	3	5	17	4	19	8	2	7	8	5
Determining Treatment	—	11	—	4	8	24	12	20	2	15	4	8
Dealing with Patients	29	14	67	31	8	11	27	15	27	13	54	27
TOTAL PERCENT	99%	100%	100%	99%	100%	100%	99%	100%	100%	98%	100%	99%
Number of Sample Physicians	38	43	29	110	12	73	41	126	50	116	70	236

NOTE: Information on .1% of weighted physicians was not ascertained.

X^2 Values

By specialty: GP (Private) vs. GP (Hospital) $X^2 = 8.83$***
    IM (Private) vs. IM (Hospital) $X^2 = 5.31$
    PED (Private) vs. PED (Hospital) $X^2 = 15.29$

Within setting, by specialty:

Private

GP vs. IM $X^2 = 8.42$**   GP vs. PED $X^2 = 15.34$*   IM vs. PED $X^2 = 24.23$*

Hospital

GP vs. IM $X^2 = 4.05$ GP vs. PED $X^2 = 8.31$***   IM vs. PED $X^2 = 13.86$**

*significant at 0.01 level
**significant at 0.05 level
***significant at 0.10 level
Percentages might not total 100 because of rounding error.

As one might expect, two-thirds of the pediatricians (67 percent) declared that dealing with the patient and the patient's family provided the most gratification. Patient contact was preferred by about one-third of the private general practitioners: 29 percent as compared to 14 percent for internists. Since diseases which offer little intellectual stimulation such as well-child care and routine acute illnesses predominate in pediatric practice, it was not surprising that pediatricians achieved gratification from patient contact. However, it was surprising to find that such a large proportion of private general practitioners, who were responsible for continuous family medical care, preferred diagnostic activity to patient contact. Hospital general practitioners and internists also found diagnostic aspects of medicine to be most gratifying.

Many of the practitioners who had teaching appointments reported that the teaching and training of young physicians was the most gratifying aspect of their practice. However, a distinct preference for teaching activities was reported only by hospital pediatricians. This could be accounted for by the finding that hospital pediatricians had faculty appointments more often than did hospital internists or generalists.

Twice as many physicians in private practice as in the hospital setting indicated a preference for patient contact. They also reported a more thorough knowledge of their patients (Table 5.9). Half of all private practitioners maintained that they knew at least 76 percent of their patients well; only one-fifth of their hospital colleagues could make a similar claim.

During the development of the Physician Interview Schedule and its pretest, committee members often related that actual practice is the best teacher. When sample physicians were asked to consider their own skills and identify which of these had developed the most since the end of medical training, the majority of private practitioners referred to their increasing ability to encourage and support the patient. Eighty percent of the pediatricians believed that they had developed most in this area as compared with 62 percent of the general practitioners and 64 percent of the internists (Table 5.10). Hospital practitioners as a whole reported that they considered the improvement of their diagnostic skills to be most important. However, many hospital internists and pediatricians also mentioned that their interpersonal skills had improved since the end of their medical training.

Like Peterson et al. (1956), we were concerned with quality of care in different components or task areas such as History and Physical Exam. They had stressed the importance of history-taking in providing

TABLE 5.9
Percent of Patient Population that Physicians Report to Know Well
Presented by Setting and Specialty
(Percentage Distribution)

Percent of Patients Known Well	Private Practice				Hospital				Both Settings			
	GP	IM	PED	All	GP	IM	PED	All	GP	IM	PED	All
1–25%	3%	2%	12%	4%	100%	45%	67%	59%	8%	13%	29%	15%
26–50	12	17	25	16	—	12	12	11	12	16	21	16
51–75	36	27	14	28	—	8	10	8	34	22	13	24
76+	49	54	49	51	—	34	10	22	46	49	37	45
TOTAL PERCENT	100%	100%	100%	99%	100%	99%	99%	100%	100%	100%	100%	100%
Number of Sample Physicians	37	43	28	108	7	50	39	96	44	93	67	204

NOTES: Information on 8 percent of weighted physicians was not ascertained due to short form of questionnaire and inability to answer the question.

X² Values

By specialty: GP (Private) vs. GP (Hospital) $X^2 = 36.84$*   IM vs. PED $X^2 = 4.78$
              IM (Private) vs. IM (Hospital) $X^2 = 24.51$*
              PED (Private) vs. PED (Hospital) $X^2 = 3.24$

Within setting, by specialty:
        Private
        GP vs. IM $X^2 = 1.03$ GP vs. PED $X^2 = 6.32$***   IM vs. PED $X^2 = 7.41$***
        Hospital
        GP vs. IM $X^2 = +$ GP vs. PED $X^2 = +$

*significant at 0.01 level
***significant at 0.10 level
+X² calculation invalid due to low expected frequencies.
Percentages might not total 100 because of rounding error.

TABLE 5.10

Skill which Physicians Feel Has Been Most Developed Since Medical Training (i.e., in Actual Practice)
Presented by Setting and Specialty
(Percentage Distribution)

Skills	Private Practice				Hospital				Both Settings			
	GP	IM	PED	All	GP	IM	PED	All	GP	IM	PED	ALL
Cannot Choose	2%	4%	—	2%	10%	8%	6%	8%	2%	5%	2%	3%
Diagnostic Skills	29	27	9	24	60	49	41	48	32	33	18	29
Ability to be Supportive of Patients	62	64	80	66	20	27	37	29	59	53	67	58
Technical Skills	7	5	11	7	10	16	16	15	7	8	13	9
TOTAL PERCENT	100%	100%	100%	99%	100%	100%	100%	100%	100%	99%	100%	99%
Number of Sample Physicians	36	43	29	108	12	56	39	107	48	99	68	215

NOTES: Information on 5 percent of weighted physicians was not ascertained due to short form of questionnaire and inability to answer the question.

X^2 Values

By setting: Private vs. Hospital $X^2 = 31.08$*

By specialty: GP (Private) vs. GP (Hospital) $X^2 = 6.98$

IM (Private) vs. IM (Hospital) $X^2 = 13.96$*

*significant at 0.01 level

Other X^2 calculations were not done because of vanishing cells.

Percentages might not total 100 because of rounding error.

TABLE 5.11

Element in Patient Care which Physicians Consider to be Most Important
Presented by Setting and Specialty
(Percentage Distribution)

Most Important Element	Private Practice				Hospital				Both Settings			
	GP	IM	PED	All	GP	IM	PED	All	GP	IM	PED	All
Getting Patient to Follow Instructions	—	—	—	—	10%	1%	6%	4%	1%	*	2%	1%
Preventing Future Problems	12	4	14	10	20	6	4	7	13	5	11	9
Alleviating Symptoms	9	9	20	11	20	16	20	18	10	11	20	13
Providing Emotional Support	2	—	11	3	—	—	2	1	2	—	8	3
Providing Appropriate Explanations	7	9	15	9	—	12	20	13	6	10	17	10
Eliciting Symptoms and Complaints	69	78	39	66	50	64	47	57	67	74	42	64
TOTAL PERCENT	99%	100%	99%	99%	100%	99%	99%	100%	99%	100%	100%	100%
Number of Sample Physicians	38	42	29	109	10	55	39	104	48	97	68	213

NOTES: Information on 5 percent of weighted physicians was not ascertained due to short form of questionnaire and inability to answer the question.

* Less than 1 percent.

X^2 Values

By setting: Private vs. Hospital X^2 = 15.66*

Within setting, by specialty:

Private
GP vs. IM X^2 = 2.79   GP vs. PED X^2 = 7.41   IM vs. PED X^2 = 13.05**

Hospital
GP vs. IM X^2 = 6.41   GP vs. PED X^2 = 5.17   IM vs. PED X^2 = 5.45

*significant at 0.01 level
**significant at 0.05 level
Percentages might not total 100 because of rounding errors.

TABLE 5.12
Estimated Percent of Time Spent Weekly in Counseling Patients
Presented by Setting and Specialty
(Percentage Distribution)

Percent of Time Spent Counseling	Private Practice				Hospital				Both Settings			
	GP	IM	PED	All	GP	IM	PED	All	GP	IM	PED	All
1–10%	33%	17%	10%	22%	42%	57%	20%	44%	34%	29%	13%	27%
11–20	25	36	12	27	25	21	29	24	25	30	17	26
21–30	28	33	24	29	25	11	31	19	28	25	26	26
31–40	10	7	38	15	8	8	12	9	9	9	29	14
41–75	4	7	17	8	—	4	8	4	3	6	14	7
TOTAL PERCENT	100%	100%	101%	101%	100%	101%	100%	100%	99%	99%	99%	100%
Number of Sample Physicians	34	43	28	105	12	70	40	122	46	113	68	227

NOTES: Information on 4 percent of weighted physicians was not ascertained due to short form of questionnaire and inability to answer the question.

X^2 Values

By setting: Private vs. Hospital $X^2 = 13.92$*

By specialty: GP (Private) vs.   GP (Hospital) $X^2 = 2.87$
     IM (Private) vs.   IM (Hospital) $X^2 = 19.64$*
     PED (Private) vs. PED (Hospital) $X^2 = 9.51$**

Within setting, by specialty:

Private
GP vs. IM $X^2 = 3.42$ GP vs. PED $X^2 = 12.97$**   IM vs. PED $X^2 = 14.72$*

Hospital
GP vs. IM $X^2 = 2.53$ GP vs. PED $X^2 = 3.04$ IM vs. PED $X^2 = 15.47$*

*significant at 0.01 level
**significant at 0.05 level
Percentages might not total 100 because of rounding error.

the factual knowledge necessary for good care. In identifying the most important elements in providing care for patients (Table 5.11), our sample physicians demonstrated their approaches to medicine. Most private practitioners selected eliciting symptoms and complaints as the most important element in medical care; general practitioners and internists chose this response significantly more often than pediatricians, who were also concerned with alleviating symptoms. Pediatricians, substantiating the emphasis they placed on a relationship with the patient, selected alleviating symptoms and providing appropriate explanation twice as often as their private practice colleagues. It is also interesting to note that, while 12 percent of the private general practitioners and 14 percent of the pediatricians said that preventing future problems was the most important element in patient care, only 4 percent of the internists concurred. Of course, pediatricians spend more time providing preventive care, the most frequent reason for patient visits being the Well-Child exam. Over half of the hospital practitioners chose eliciting of symptoms and complaints as the most important aspect of care. All hospital physicians were also interested in alleviating symptoms. Only general practitioners in the hospital setting expressed notable concern for preventing future problems.

Table 5.12 shows that private practice pediatricians, the same group that enjoyed patient contact, also reported spending more time in counseling patients and their families. Thirty-eight percent reported spending about one-third of their office hours in providing guidance to their patients. General practitioners did not devote as much of their time to counseling as we had expected. Hospital practitioners reported even less time spent in counseling patients.

SATISFACTION WITH CASELOAD, ORGANIZATION OF PRACTICE, AND CAREER

Because of the extensive coverage that has been given in management literature to the relationship between satisfaction and performance, physicians were asked how satisfied they were with the structural aspects of their practice such as patient volume, types of cases seen, and the way in which their practices were organized. One difficulty with interpreting the series of satisfaction items is that the respondents were probably not provided with an adequate range of choices. Somewhat satisfied and moderately satisfied might be taken to mean the same thing. The absence of a satisfied category could have added misleading weight to the response of moderately satisfied. Extremely satisfied was the only option for expressing more than lukewarm satisfaction. Thus the physicians' true feelings may have been exaggerated in either direction.

Private general practitioners and pediatricians, who tended to have larger practices, were more apt to describe themselves as being extremely satisfied with patient volume than were internists. In general, private practitioners expressed greater satisfaction than their hospital colleagues, most of whom opted for the moderate category. Low satisfaction was most evident among hospital pediatricians, whose patient loads were very large. When these results were compared with reported satisfaction with the kinds of cases treated, it appeared that hospital physicians were more disturbed by patient volume than by the types of cases seen. However, they were still less satisfied with the types of cases handled than were the private physicians. A detailed description of the clinical caseloads in private and hospital practices appears in Appendix E.

Physicians were least satisfied with the way their practices were organized (Table 5.13). We cannot be sure exactly what the term organization conveyed to the physicians, but it was assumed that the concept would certainly connote the administrative and management aspects of medical practice. In the private offices, older general practitioners were somewhat less satisfied than their colleagues; several even admitted to being dissatisfied with their practices. About two-thirds of the private internists and pediatricians reported extreme satisfaction with the way their practices were organized, as compared with 44 percent of the general practitioners. There were two enormous differences in satisfaction by practice setting. Hospital internists (10 percent) and pediatricians (24 percent) were quite frank about their dissatisfaction with the organization of their practices. Slightly over one-fifth were extremely satisfied. Management problems encountered in these practices were explored and are described in Chapter 6.

The extent of physicians' satisfaction with the types of patients seen is shown in Table 5.14. Forty-two percent of the private physicians reported extreme satisfaction with their careers as compared with over one-fourth of the hospital physicians. Older pediatricians (20+ years) were more satisfied with their patients than their cohorts in general practice or medicine. These findings were significant at the .05 level.

If these aspects of job satisfaction are related to performance, then based on these findings alone, private physicians should be expected to provide better care. But as Schwab and Cummings (1973) report, the relationship is more complex. They suggest that both satisfaction and performance can be used as criteria of organizational effectiveness. Their extensive search of empirical studies in this area prior to 1973 indicated that the relationship between satisfaction and performance need be neither direct nor particularly strong. Triandis

TABLE 5.13
Extent of Physician Satisfaction with the Organization of Their Practices
Presented by Setting and Specialty
(Percentage Distribution)

Extent of Satisfaction	Private Practice				Hospital				Both Settings			
	GP	IM	PED	All	GP	IM	PED	All	GP	IM	PED	All
Not Satisfied	3%	—	—	1%	—	10%	24%	13%	2%	3%	7%	4%
Somewhat Satisfied	11	12	5	10	8	29	22	24	11	17	10	14
Moderately Satisfied	43	29	28	35	50	37	33	38	43	32	30	35
Extremely Satisfied	44	59	67	54	42	23	22	25	43	47	53	47
TOTAL PERCENT	101%	100%	100%	100%	100%	99%	101%	100%	99%	99%	100%	100%
Number of Sample Physicians	38	43	29	110	12	70	40	122	50	113	69	232

NOTE: Information on 1 percent of weighted physicians was not ascertained due to inability to answer the question.

X^2 Values

By setting: Private vs. Hospital $X^2 = 30.62$*

By specialty:
GP (Private) vs.   GP (Hospital) $X^2 = .55$
IM (Private) vs.   IM (Hospital) $X^2 = 17.58$*
PED (Private) vs. PED (Hospital) $X^2 = 18.72$*

Within setting, by specialty:

Private
GP vs. IM $X^2 = 3.29$ GP vs. PED $X^2 = 4.21$ IM vs. PED $X^2 = 1.11$

Hospital
GP vs. IM $X^2 = 4.79$ GP vs. PED $X^2 = 5.98$ IM vs. PED $X^2 = 3.87$

*significant at 0.01 level

Percentages might not total 100 because of rounding error.

TABLE 5.14
Extent of Satisfaction with Type of Clinical Cases Seen
Presented by Setting and Specialty
(Percentage Distribution)

Extent of Satisfaction	Private Practice				Hospital				Both Settings			
	GP	IM	PED	All	GP	IM	PED	All	GP	IM	PED	All
Not Satisfied	2%	—	—	1%	—	1%	4%	2%	2%	1%	1%	1%
Somewhat Satisfied	9	2	8	6	8	23	2	15	9	8	6	8
Moderately Satisfied	42	52	46	47	75	47	59	54	45	50	50	48
Extremely Satisfied	46	46	45	45	17	29	35	29	43	40	42	42
TOTAL PERCENT	99%	100%	99%	99%	100%	100%	100%	100%	99%	99%	99%	99%
Number of Sample Physicians	38	43	29	110	12	71	40	123	50	114	69	233

NOTES: Information on .5 percent of weighted physicians was not ascertained due to inability to answer the question.
X^2 calculations were not done because of vanishing cells.
Percentages might not total 100 because of rounding error.

(1959) posits that job performance and job satisfaction increase or decrease as a result of organizational pressure on the employee. Both satisfaction and performance are described by Triandis as being curvilinearly related to organizational pressure to perform. March and Simon (1973) stress two motivational determinants of performance: (1) the expected value of the reward, and (2) the aspiration level of the employee. Unfortunately, we do not have data from Connecticut physicians on their feelings about rewards received for the work they do; they were not questioned about their professional ambitions.

Another viewpoint, that performance leads to satisfaction, indicates that the performance-satisfaction relationship is circular. Good performance leads to valued rewards which, in turn, lead to satisfaction (Lawler and Porter 1967). Hackman and Lawler (1970) added important dimensions to the Lawler-Porter model by suggesting that feedback, variety of work tasks, autonomy, and feelings of personal growth through competent performance are all important aspects of work for individuals who are intrinsically motivated. They emphasized the significance of the interaction between characteristics of the work and needs of the individual employee. For example, a person who requires a high degree of task variety will not perform well on an assembly line job; individuals who prefer to work on tasks which are clearly identified and separable perform best in a highly structured environment. Hackman and Oldham (1976) point out that the salient aspects of a job vary according to individual preference and orientation.

TROUBLESOME ASPECTS OF MEDICAL PRACTICE

Physicians were asked to share which aspects of medical practice they found to be most disruptive. The problems identified were both organizational and patient-related. Internists were somewhat more disturbed by trivial patient complaints than other primary physicians. This may be related to the internist's focus on making diagnoses and eliciting symptoms and complaints. Forty-six percent of the private pediatricians reported that the worried-well disturbed them moderately and another 41 percent admitted that they were greatly disturbed by such patient/parent behavior (Table 5.15). These findings are not hard to understand in view of the predominance of well-child care and minor ailments that are routinely handled by these physicians. The great majority of hospital practitioners (92 percent of the general practitioners, 91 percent of the internists, and 76 percent of the pediatricians) also reported that the worried-well disturbed them either moderately or greatly.

TABLE 5.15
Extent to Which "Trivial" Patient Complaints Disturb Physicians
Presented by Setting and Specialty
(Percentage Distribution)

Extent of Disturbance	Private Practice				Hospital				Both Settings			
	GP	IM	PED	All	GP	IM	PED	All	GP	IM	PED	All
Does Not Disturb	14%	15%	13%	14%	8%	9%	23%	13%	14%	13%	16%	14%
Moderately Disturbed	50	35	46	44	50	42	36	42	50	37	43	43
Greatly Disturbed	35	50	41	42	42	49	40	45	36	50	41	43
TOTAL PERCENT	99%	100%	100%	100%	100%	100%	99%	100%	100%	100%	100%	100%
Number of Sample Physicians	37	43	29	109	12	73	41	126	49	116	70	235

Percentages might not total 100 because of rounding error.

Table 5.16
Extent to which Supervising Others Disturbs Physicians
Presented by Setting and Specialty
(Percentage Distribution)

Extent of Disturbance	Private Practice				Hospital				Both Settings			
	GP	IM	PED	All	GP	IM	PED	All	GP	IM	PED	All
Does Not Disturb	52%	42%	57%	49%	50%	43%	62%	53%	52%	41%	62%	49%
Moderately Disturbs	14	49	24	30	17	45	33	35	14	49	22	32
Greatly Disturbs	17	7	20	13	33	13	6	12	18	9	16	13
Not Applicable[1]	17	2	—	8	—	—	—	—	16	2	—	6
TOTAL PERCENT	100%	100%	101%	100%	100%	101%	101%	100%	100%	101%	100%	100%
Number of Sample Physicians	37	43	29	109	12	73	41	126	49	116	70	235

NOTE: Information on 1.2 percent of weighted physicians was not ascertained due to inability to answer the question.

[1]This question was not applicable to physicians in one-person practices.

X^2 Values

By setting: Private vs. Hospital $X^2 = 10.75$***

By specialty:

GP (Private) vs.   GP (Hospital) $X^2 = 3.21$

IM (Private) vs.   IM (Hospital) $X^2 = 2.47$

PED (Private) vs. PED (Hospital) $X^2 = 3.36$

Within setting, by specialty:

Private

GP vs. IM $X^2 = 14.57$*   GP vs. PED $X^2 = 5.96$ IM vs. PED $X^2 = 6.55$***

Hospital

GP vs. IM $X^2 = 4.72$***   GP vs. PED $X^2 = 6.66$**   IM vs. PED $X^2 = 4.06$

*significant at 0.01 level

**significant at 0.05 level

***significant at 0.10 level

Percentages might not total 100 because of rounding error.

Most physicians must interact not only with patients but with their staff who perform a variety of tasks instrumental to the provision of medical care. The function of administrator is one more role to be added to the physician's repertoire, either during medical training or shortly thereafter. When sample physicians were asked how they felt about supervising others, many did not appear to feel comfortable with this aspect of their work. Half of the internists in both settings reported that their supervisory responsibilities disturbed them moderately. Private pediatricians expressed the highest level of comfort in this area: 57 percent stated that supervision was not stressful for them. However, responses for this group ranged widely according to age and number of years in practice. The younger pediatricians reported a higher level of disturbance than their older colleagues. This might have been due to the fact that they must frequently supervise staff members who are older than themselves and more experienced in dealing with patients.

Overall, we believe that pediatricians, who are somewhat more oriented toward relationships, are likely to feel more comfortable supervising other people (Table 5.16). The internist, on the other hand, who appears to be more interpersonally controlled, is perhaps less sensitive to the interpersonal dynamics in the private practice setting. Another interesting statistic was that one-third of the hospital general practitioners also reported being greatly disturbed by supervisory responsibilities. This finding might be due to their low status in the hospital hierarchy which could influence their subordinates' perceptions and, consequently, their behavior toward them.

Physician record-keeping behavior was a particularly relevant aspect of medical practice considered in this study. Several Technical Committee members expressed their distrust of social science research in this field. They feared that results fed back to the physicians would encourage greater emphasis on record-keeping, to the detriment of direct patient care. As illustrated in Table 5.17, a very large proportion of physicians indicated that record-keeping was a serious problem for them; in fact, it was the most disturbing of all problems reported. Private practice pediatricians were more likely to report that it was not a problem. Thirty-five percent of the private general practitioners, 43 percent of the internists and 34 percent of the pediatricians reported record-keeping to be a severe problem. Hospital practitioners, whose records were more complete than those of their colleagues in private offices, reported a higher degree of disturbance with regard to record-keeping activity. Eighty-three percent of the hospital practitioners reported being disturbed at least moderately by record-keeping

TABLE 5.17
Extent to which Record-Keeping is Viewed as a Problem by Physicians
Presented by Setting and Specialty
(Percentage Distribution)

Extent of Problem	Private Practice				Hospital				Both Settings			
	GP	IM	PED	All	GP	IM	PED	All	GP	IM	PED	All
Not a Problem	22%	19%	36%	24%	8%	15%	23%	16%	21%	18%	32%	22%
A Moderate Problem	43	38	30	38	50	41	29	39	44	40	29	38
A Severe Problem	35	43	34	38	41	43	48	44	35	43	38	40
TOTAL PERCENT	100%	100%	100%	100%	99%	99%	100%	99%	100%	99%	99%	100%
Number of Sample Physicians	38	43	29	110	12	74	41	127	50	117	70	237

NOTES: X^2 Values
By setting:
Private vs. Hospital $X^2 = 2.44$
Within setting, by specialty:
Private
GP vs. IM $X^2 = .54$ GP vs. PED $X^2 = 1.90$ IM vs. PED $X^2 = 2.61$
Hospital
GP vs. IM $X^2 = .57$ GP vs. PED $X^2 = 2.39$ IM vs. PED $X^2 = 2.12$

Percentages might not total 100 because of rounding error.

as compared with 76 percent of private practitioners.

The degree to which providing explanations and instructions disturbed physicians is indicated in Table 5.18. It might be assumed that providing explanations to patients is an integral part of the medical care process, but Advisory Committee members were not certain that these tasks would always be done as a matter of course. The table shows that 42 percent of both private general practitioners and private internists reported that providing explanations and instructions to the patient was moderately troublesome. Eleven percent and 10 percent respectively reported feeling greatly disturbed by having to perform these tasks. As one might expect, three-fourths of the private pediatricians were not disturbed about the need to provide instructions and explanations. Hospital pediatricians reported a similarly low level of disturbance. We believe that pediatricians were more comfortable with instructional tasks because of their decided orientation toward relationships.

The degree to which medical practice interferes with a physician's life outside of the job setting was dramatized by Clute's description of the division of a physician's time between work, family, and leisure activities (1963). In the present study (Table 5.19), general practitioners (79 percent) and internists (74 percent) in private practice reported a higher degree of overall interference with their home lives than did pediatricians (57 percent). However, internists and pediatricians were more likely to report that their careers interfered greatly. In the hospital setting, more pediatricians and internists reported that their jobs greatly interfered with their home lives; many of these physicians were still in training and were more likely to be subject to night and weekend duty.

During working hours, in addition to an average number of 26 patient visits per day, primary care physicians had to be available to deal with phone calls. Some of the private pediatricians told us that they practiced nearly as much medicine over the phone as they did in person. Table 5.20 presents the degree to which telephone calls disturb the physician during working hours. Such interruptions appeared to create as much disturbance for private practice physicians as did record-keeping. Hospital practitioners also reported an unexpectedly high level of disturbance by phone calls and pages. As a rule, younger physicians were more distracted by telephone interference than their older colleagues. Only about one-fourth of hospital practitioners of all specialties reported being greatly disturbed.

Pediatricians in both practice settings reported that they were unsettled by having to discuss deaths with their patients or patients'

TABLE 5.18
Extent to which Providing Explanations and Instructions to Patients Disturbs Physicians Presented by Setting and Specialty
(Percentage Distribution)

Extent of Disturbance	Private Practice				Hospital				Both Settings			
	GP	IM	PED	All	GP	IM	PED	All	GP	IM	PED	All
Does Not Disturb	47%	48%	72%	52%	17%	53%	75%	55%	44%	50%	73%	53%
Moderately Disturbs	42	42	28	39	67	35	21	35	44	40	26	38
Greatly Disturbs	11	10	—	8	17	12	4	10	12	11	1	9
TOTAL PERCENT	100%	100%	100%	99%	101%	100%	100%	100%	100%	101%	100%	100%
Number of Sample Physicians	38	43	29	110	12	73	41	126	50	116	70	236

NOTES: Information on .3 percent of weighted physicians was not ascertained due to inability to answer the question.

X^2 Values

By setting: Private vs. Hospital $X^2 = .61$

Within setting, by specialty

Private

GP vs. IM $X^2 = .02$ GP vs. PED $X^2 = 5.86$***   IM vs. PED $X^2 = 5.56$***

Hospital

GP vs. IM $X^2 = 5.62$***   GP vs. PED $X^2 = 13.49$*   IM vs. PED $X^2 = 5.64$***

*significant at 0.01 level
***significant at 0.10 level
Percentages might not total 100 because of rounding error.

TABLE 5.19

Extent to which Practice Interferes with Physicians' Home Life
Presented by Setting and Specialty
(Percentage Distribution)

Extent of Interference	Private Practice				Hospital				Both Settings			
	GP	IM	PED	All	GP	IM	PED	All	GP	IM	PED	All
Does Not Interfere	21%	26%	43%	27%	27%	18%	17%	19%	21%	23%	35%	25%
Interferes Moderately	51	37	23	40	45	32	40	36	51	35	28	39
Interferes Greatly	28	37	34	33	27	50	42	45	28	41	37	36
TOTAL PERCENT	100%	100%	100%	100%	99%	100%	99%	100%	100%	99%	100%	100%
Number of Sample Physicians	38	43	29	110	11	73	41	125	49	116	70	235

NOTE: Information on .4 percent of weighted physicians was not ascertained due to inability to answer the question.

X² Values
  By setting: Private vs. Hospital X² = 4.03
  Within setting, by specialty:
    Private
      GP vs. IM X² = 1.62   GP vs. PED X² = 6.12**   IM vs. PED X² = 2.64
    Hospital
      GP vs. IM X² = 1.97   GP vs. PED X² = 1.01   IM vs. PED X² = .85

**significant at 0.05 level
Percentages might not total 100 because of rounding error.

TABLE 5.20
Extent to which Phone Calls Disturb the Physicians Presented by Setting and Specialty
(Percentage Distribution)

Extent of Disturbance	Private Practice				Hospital				Both Settings			
	GP	IM	PED	All	GP	IM	PED	All	GP	IM	PED	All
Do Not Disturb	13%	12%	14%	13%	33%	24%	37%	29%	15%	16%	21%	17%
Disturb Moderately	50	33	56	45	42	48	37	44	50	39	50	45
Greatly Disturb	37	55	30	42	25	29	27	28	36	46	29	38
TOTAL PERCENT	100%	100%	100%	100%	100%	101%	101%	101%	101%	101%	100%	100%
Number of Sample Physicians	38	43	29	110	12	73	41	126	50	116	70	236

NOTES: Information on .3 percent of weighted physicians was not ascertained due to inability to answer the question.

X^2 Values

By setting: Private vs. Hospital X^2 = 10.32*

By specialty:
GP (Private) vs. GP (Hospital) X^2 = 2.56
IM (Private) vs. IM (Hospital) X^2 = 8.18***
PED (Private) vs. PED (Hospital) X^2 = 4.70****

Within setting, by specialty:

Private
GP vs. IM X^2 = 2.84   GP vs. PED X^2 = .36   IM vs. PED X^2 = 4.63***

Hospital
GP vs. IM X^2 = .47   GP vs. PED X^2 = .12   IM vs. PED X^2 = 2.31

*significant at 0.01 level
**significant at 0.05 level
***significant at 0.10 level
Percentages might not total 100 because of rounding error.

families. Several volunteered to explain that this was because patient deaths were relatively rare occurrences. General practitioners and internists in both settings reported a more moderate degree of disturbance at having to discuss the patient's imminent death with him or her. When these findings were analyzed according to number of years in practice, we noted that the older physicians were less disturbed at the prospect of discussing death with terminal patients. Older pediatricians in both settings were the exception.

RESPONDENTS' DESCRIPTIONS OF PROBLEMS CONFRONTING MEDICINE

Once physicians had described their orientation toward medical practice, they were asked to comment on the current problems facing their profession in the United States. From a list of nine problems which had been mentioned frequently during the pretest period, practitioners were asked to choose the one which concerned them most. A different orientation among the three specialty groups in private practice emerged in response to this question. The high cost of medical care was chosen as the number one problem by 61 percent of the pediatricians, as compared with 23 percent of the general practitioners and 46 percent of the internists. Pediatricians had much lower net incomes than their private practice colleagues and might have been worried about decreased utilization of their services for preventive care. A greater proportion of the general practitioners and internists in private practice were concerned with paper work and legal liabilities than were private pediatricians. It was interesting to find that none of the sample private physicians considered evaluation of care to be a priority issue, and that only 3 percent of the general practitioners described record-keeping as an important problem that had to be faced rather than a nuisance to be avoided.

Hospital practitioners expressed different concerns for the future of medicine. Forty-two percent of the general practitioners focused on cost of care and legal problems. Internists also reported a high level of concern for these issues, and 12 percent mentioned the use of paramedical personnel. Twenty percent of the hospital pediatricians joined internists and general practitioners in selecting legal problems as the most important issue to be faced. The cost of care (40 percent), emergency care (12 percent), and evaluation of care (10 percent) were also identified as priority items. Varying responses were related to practice setting as well as major specialty.

Physicians were also asked to select the second most important problem facing medicine. The private general practitioners and internists again focused on increasing amounts of paper work and the cost of care, while pediatricians expressed second level concerns for the inappropriate utilization of the emergency room. Evaluation or quality of medical care still emerged as an issue of relatively minor concern; only 6 percent of the general practitioners, 7 percent of the pediatricians, and 4 percent of the internists considered it important enough to mention.

PRIMARY SOURCES OF MEDICAL INFORMATION AND CONTINUING EDUCATION ACTIVITIES

Peterson et al. (1956) demonstrated that the very best doctors participated in more continuing education activities than the poorest. This was especially true of physicians doing between 40 and 60 hours of postgraduate study. Their operational definition of postgraduate study was broad and included hospital staff and medical society meetings, as well as a variety of refresher courses. These activities and the reading of professional journals were said to be the major sources of the general practitioners' medical-intellectual sustenance.

Findings in the Connecticut study differed. About two-thirds of all ambulatory physicians reported that their primary sources of information were professional colleagues and the medical literature. A higher proportion of private practitioners reported using only literature for keeping up with current information than did hospital practitioners. Twenty percent of the general practitioners in private practice relied solely on interaction with colleagues, as compared with 4 percent of the hospital general practitioners. Most physicians reported a combination of literature and professional colleagues as their primary sources of information.

Participation in continuing medical education (CME) is widespread. Virtually all private practitioners (99 percent) reported being involved in one or more kinds of continuing education activities; about three-fourths of these participated mostly by way of courses and rounds. Only the internists reported participation in evaluation activities; these experiences were generally the self-assessment programs offered by their primary specialty society (ASIM). A very small number of private general practitioners (3 percent) stated that they were not involved in any form of continuing education. General practitioners in the hospital setting were most active in pursuing CME (74 percent); senior internists and pediatricians were not quite so enthusiastic.

PERSONAL BACKGROUND OF THE PHYSICIAN

Although we were not as concerned with personal data as Clute
(1963) and Peterson et al. (1956), we did inquire about several attributes:
age, sex, income, area of the country in which the practitioner grew
up, and father's occupation.

The average general practitioner was getting on in years. Data on
the age of the private practice physician shows that a majority of
the general practitioners (52 percent) were 60 years or older as compared
with 16 percent of the pediatricians and 20 percent of the internists.
Conversely, only 17 percent of the general practitioners were under
50 years of age, while 58 percent of the pediatricians and 55 percent
of the internists were between 30 and 49 years of age. The mean
ages for general practitioners, pediatricians, and internists were 58,
50 and 40 respectively.

Of the total number of Connecticut physicians, three-fourths of
the private practitioners and half of the hospital practitioners grew
up in the northeastern United States. Slightly higher proportions of
hospital physicians grew up in other areas of the United States, and
many had spent their childhoods in foreign countries.

Sixty-four percent of the general practitioners had fathers who were
craftsmen (19 percent), clerical workers (24 percent), or managers
(21 percent). Nearly one-third of all physicians' fathers held managerial
positions and one-third were professionals, including 12 percent who
were themselves physicians. Data indicate that general practitioners
were least likely to have had professional fathers.

Physicians were asked to reveal their net incomes for the past
calendar year. Although this is a sensitive area, only a few participants
(2 percent) refused to respond. The majority of private practitioners
reported a net income of between $30,000 and $50,000 annually.
Average incomes were $30–39,000 for general practitioners and pedia-
tricians, and $50–59,000 for internists. Eighteen percent of all private
physicians reported an annual income of less than $30,000. Fifteen
percent of the general practitioners reported net incomes of over
$60,000 per annum; 7 percent declared their incomes to be $80,000
or more, which was true for none of the pediatricians or internists.
Hospital practitioners all reported making less than $60,000 a year.
Only 13 percent of all practitioners in the hospital setting reported
making $40,000 or more.

Because the distribution of men and women in the physician
population of Connecticut is so skewed, we did not use this attribute

in any of the analyses. The proportion of women in hospital practice
is less than 10 percent and has decreased slightly since 1966. In the
private practice sample, all of the general practitioners were men,
and only 3 percent of the pediatricians and 5 percent of the internists
were women.

MANAGERIAL STYLE OF THE PRIVATE PRACTITIONERS

As described in Appendix A, the Leadership Opinion Questionnaire
(LOQ)/Leader Behavior Descriptor Questionnaire (LBDQ) was used
as a collateral instrument to the Physician Characteristics Interview.
(Examples are included in Appendix C). The original LOQ and LBDQ
were designed by industrial social psychologists (Fleishman et al.
1955) to describe the leadership behavior of a foreman toward his
work group. After using factor analysis on questionnaire responses,
Fleishman reported that there were two major traits of leadership:
consideration and initiating structure. Consideration referred to behavior in which the leader demonstrated concern for others, a socio-
emotional aspect of leadership. Initiating structure referred to behavior
in which the leader organizes work and resembles task orientation
as described by Bales (1970). The two-factor structure, according
to Fleishman, accounted for 83 percent of the variance. It emerged
when the questionnaire was given many times to different subjects
in various organizations. We were not sure that a two-factor structure
resulted in the best description of the behavior of the physician
(supervisor) in relation to his office staff (subordinates); therefore,
two, three, four, five, six, and twelve-factor solutions were run for
both physician (LOQ) and staff (LBDQ) responses. We found the
two-factor solution to be unsuitable for our population because most
of the items for both consideration and initiating structure fell on
one factor (i.e., *Factor I*).

The four-factor solution appeared to be the most interpretable and
descriptive of physicians' behavior in relation to their subordinates.
Figure 5.1 presents the items for the four factors and their loadings
for superiors and subordinates. Items which either loaded below .20
on all factors or loaded between .20 and .50 on more than one factor
were eliminated from the list. The four-factor solution accounted for
50 percent of the variance.

It was relatively easy to interpret *Factors III* and *IV* (see Figure
5.1). *Factor III* (feedback factor) was a negative feedback factor.
It indicated that feedback provided by the physicians to staff on
their performance was generally negative; for example, instead of

FIGURE 5.1
Four-Factor Solution to Revised LOQ/LBDQ with Factor Loadings for Superiors
(N=90) and Subordinates (N=176)

Item #		Superior	Subordinate
Factor I:	Autocratic to Laissez-Faire or Structuring to Not Structuring the Work		
8	Asks that people under you/him follow to the letter standard routines and procedures.	.64	.44
9	Offers new approaches to problems.	.53	.59
11	Insists that you/he be informed on decisions made by staff under you/him.	.64	.62
15	Emphasizes meeting of deadlines.	.62	.52
16	Decides in detail what shall be done and how it shall be done by staff.	.67	.65
18	Sees to it that staff are working up to capacity	.62	.64
	Factor II. Autonomy for Other (Hi, Lo)		
2	Encourages others to try out new ideas.	−.53	−.52
19	Refuses to compromise a point.	.62	.43
25	Insists that everything be done your/his way.	.51	.53
26	Rejects suggestions for change.	.74	.76
28	Resists changes in ways of doing things.	.72	.73
	Factor III. Feedback (Negative, Neutral)		
4	Criticizes poor work.	.48	.59
5	Talks about how much should be done.	.67	.59
6	Encourages slow-working people to work harder.	.66	.63
14	'Needles' people under you/him for greater effort.	.48	.70
	Factor IV. Personal Help (Does, Does Not)		
20	Does personal favors for people.	.65	.83
23	Helps people on staff with their personal problems.	.68	.62
24	Stands up for those on staff under you/him, even though it makes you/him unpopular.	.55	.48

praising them for good work they were more likely to criticize them for poor work. *Factor IV* (personal factor) focused on helping behavior and showed that a physician's way of being supportive to staff was to do personal favors for them. This is a way of helping others that does not involve much risk-taking on the part of the supervisor and is not as effective as other means of providing support. *Factor I* (autocratic factor) included questionnaire items referring to the extent to which the job was structured or organized by the physician. *Factor I* could also be described as a group of items which reflected control or the absence of control by the supervisor (physician) over his/her staff. *Factor II* (autonomy factor) focuses on the superior's hindering or supporting staff's attempts to initiate or start new things. Depending on his score on this factor the physician could be described as providing a great deal of or very little autonomy for his staff.

The range of possible scores on these factors was zero (0) for lowest to four (4) for highest. A physician who received a score of 1.00 on the autonomy factor would rarely encourage staff to do things on their own. The mean score for all physicians on job structure and control factor (autocratic), was 1.86. The mean score for hindering innovation (autonomy) was 1.64. Mean scores for the feedback and personal helping factor, were 1.81 and 2.36 respectively. When scores were grouped by physician specialty no significant differences were found. Nevertheless, these scores were included in the final analyses. Our working hypotheses were the following:

1. Physicians who were high on autocratic, controlling behavior interfered with staff performance; the final result would be lower performance for that practice.
2. Physicians who were unlikely to allow their staff to function autonomously (i.e., low on autonomy) would receive lower performance scores.
3. Physicians who provided much negative feedback (i.e., higher on feedback) to their staff would receive lower performance scores.

We had no hypothesis in regard to personal helping behavior because it did not seem that it should be related to physician or staff performance.

In this chapter we have described many of the attributes of the primary care physicians who participated in the study. Next we will look at the organization of their practices for salient features which might be significantly related to physician performance.

6

Characteristics of the Organizations Providing
Primary Ambulatory Care

No single overriding theoretical framework guided staff or committee members in their selection of attributes of organizations which they believed to affect the quality or patterns of care. Several approaches to studying private practices such as the work of Peterson et al. (1956) and Clute (1963) were considered. As Yuchtman and Seashore (1967) point out, studying the conditions under which organizations are more or less effective is problematic at best. Independent variables such as productivity, job satisfaction, efficiency and effectiveness, have traditionally been used to explain why organizations have or have not realized their goals. The assumptions of the goal approach, once widely used, have been questioned by systems theorists (Katz and Kahn 1966, and Buckley 1968). Organizational theorists are currently more concerned with the relationship of the organization to its environment. Inherent in this approach were insurmountable conceptual difficulties which could not be resolved.

Instead we chose simply to look at the variety of material and human resources that could be used in various ways by providers of primary care. The so-called structural variables thought to affect care (i.e., time, personnel and equipment resources) were the chief concern of the Advisory Committee.

Peterson et al. (1956) investigated the resources of the physician's office, on the assumption that the doctor's working space and the equipment and personnel within it told something about how well medicine was being practiced. They described the following characteristics of the physical plant: the use of space for consultation rooms and patient waiting areas, the presence of laboratory and X-ray facilities, and the types of "auxiliary" personnel employed. However, these researchers did not seem convinced that such indicators were very important in predicting the quality of care provided; for them, the relationship between tools and practice was just another part of the pattern.

In contrast to this view, the Connecticut study considered characteristics of the organization to be of primary interest in predicting variation in physician performance. Accordingly, descriptive information on the private practice and the hospital clinic or emergency room was elicited by means of a lengthy and comprehensive interview schedule. Examples of selected items appear in Appendix D. Full compliance with this schedule was not always possible in the private practice setting. Sample physicians often hesitated to allow their senior staff persons to take an hour and a half of their work time to participate in the interview. In some offices we obtained incomplete data because respondents had to interrupt the interview to respond to patient needs or to assist the physician. A shorter schedule was developed for the solo practitioners who were understandably reluctant to devote more than an additional half hour to this part of the study. In this chapter, descriptive emphasis is placed on the office of the private practice physician. Comparative data are presented for attributes of hospital clinics and emergency rooms.

PHYSICAL PLANT RESOURCES: LOCATION, DESIGN, FACILITIES

The Design of the Physical Plant

Advisors on the Organizational Characteristics Committee were concerned about the relationship between the design of the physical plant in which practices were located and the level of care provided. It was expected that a facility which appeared to be well designed for medical purposes would enhance the delivery of health care services. The most common type of building selected by our physician sample for establishing a private practice was a former single-family or multi-family private home. Such a setting was preferred by over half of the general practitioners, especially those with small and medium practices. Internists and pediatricians were more often found in professional office buildings or buildings designed for small group practices.

The relationship between choice of building and number of years in practice was also explored. The pediatricians who had been in practice for less than ten years were all located in professional office buildings. We had expected that the older physicians who had been in practice for twenty years or more would have their offices in former private homes because there were more of these available at the time they began practicing medicine. However, three-fourths of these older practitioners were located in professional office buildings or buildings designed for small group practices.

The majority of hospital staff felt that their buildings were not well-designed for medical purposes. When asked about alterations which might improve the physical plant, three hospital respondents suggested that the building should be blown up. Sixty percent of the private practice staff felt that improvements were not required. The most frequent recommendation made in private practice was the addition of examination rooms and business office space. Hospital staff referred to awkward traffic patterns and overcrowded space, both within and outside the building, as major difficulties.

Laboratory and X-ray Equipment

Advisory Committee members assumed that there would be a relationship between the presence of laboratory facilities and compliance with standards for laboratory tests and procedures for selected diseases and problem areas. However, Clute warns us that the mere presence of facilities does not always make a difference: it is their use that counts. As expected, a strong relationship was observed between number of years in practice and the presence of laboratory facilities for physicians who had been in practice less than ten years. Younger practitioners were routinely equipping their offices with facilities necessary for simple laboratory tests and procedures. The offices of their older colleagues who had been in practice for thirty years or more were not as well-equipped.

Table 6.1 shows that, overall, internists had significantly more laboratory facilities than did general practitioners, but no significant differences were found between general practitioners and pediatricians or between internists and pediatricians. Differences among the specialty groups in the percentage of lab work done on the premises reflected the availability of facilities.

One-fourth of the private practice offices in our sample were equipped with X-ray facilities. When years in practice were considered, newer practices were more likely to have X-ray equipment. Table 6.1 shows that pediatricians were less apt to have X-ray machines than were general practitioners or internists. The category of practice identified as most likely to have X-ray facilities was the medium

TABLE 6.1
Laboratory and X-ray Equipment in Private Offices
By Size and Type of Practice
(Percentage with equipment)

Type of Equipment	General Practice				Internal Medicine				Pediatrics				All Practices			
	Small	Medium	Large	All	Small	Medium	Large	All	Small	Medium	Large	All	Small	Medium	Large	All
Laboratory	53%	67%	38%	50%	74%	76%	100%	79%	24%	92%	81%	72%	57%	77%	59%	65%
X-ray	10%	67%	16%	27%	45%	32%	—	33%	—	16%	—	6%	25%	40%	9%	25%
Number of Sample Practices	9	9	18	36	16	17	5	38	5	10	10	25	30	34	35	99

NOTE: Information on 1.1 percent of weighted practices was not ascertained.

X^2 Values (for Laboratory Equipment)

GP vs. IM X^2 = 7.07*

GP vs. PED X^2 = 3.28

IM vs. PED X^2 = .33

*Significant at 0.01 level

general practice. Significant differences by specialty category emerged between pediatricians and other specialists.

MANAGEMENT OF HUMAN (PERSONNEL) RESOURCES

Staffing Patterns

Peterson et al. (1956) suggested that physicians who delegate responsibilities and duties to ancillary personnel leave themselves more time to devote to actual patient care. Because we supported this contention and believed that the appropriate delegation of tasks would be positively related to good physician performance, we obtained information on staffing duties and responsibilities of office personnel. One hundred percent of our sample practices had full-time physicians (Table 6.2). Single practitioners made up 88 percent of the general practices and 67 percent of the pediatric practices we surveyed; 74 percent of the internists were also solo practitioners. Thirteen percent of all private practices had two physicians, and 17 percent of the pediatric practices had more than two. Data on the proportion of full-time to part-time physicians in the hospital settings could not be obtained in a survey of this nature because it was difficult for administrators to remember which of the physicians fell into each category. Apparently there were no staffing plans which provided this type of information at a glance.

Two-thirds of the private practitioners did not hire registered nurses; practices that hired one nurse often did so on a part-time basis. Licensed practical nurses (LPNs), who were rarely employed in the private offices, were more often retained on a part-time basis. As Table 6.2 shows, internists employed LPNs more frequently than did general practitioners. One-fifth of all practices hired aides or medical assistants, usually on a full-time basis. No pediatricians reported hiring laboratory or X-ray personnel and only one-tenth of the general practitioners and internists employed technicians. One-fourth of all practices did not have secretarial staff. One-half hired one secretary who was usually full-time. If they hired additional secretarial help, it was usually on a part-time basis. About 10 percent of the primary practices used clerks for secretarial back-up. One-fifth of these practices hired bookkeepers, mostly on a full-time basis. Physician's Assistants and Pediatric Nurse Practitioners were rarely used by primary care physicians in private practice. The use of Physician's Assistants in sample hospitals was not widespread. As might be expected, the hospital staffing plans exhibited a full range of personnel including categories

TABLE 6.2
Full-Time and Part-Time Personnel
by Category and Practice Setting
(Percentage Distribution)

TYPE OF PERSONNEL	PRIVATE PRACTICES				HOSPITALS
	All Practices	GP	IM	PED	
MDs					
Full-time	100%	100%	100%	100%	N/A
No. of Sample Practices	100	36	39	25	
No. of Sample Hospitals					5
RNs					
Full-time	17	15	20	27	78
Part-time	20	21	14	16	22
None Employed	63	64	68	57	—
TOTAL PERCENT	100	100	102	100	100
No. of Sample Practices	99	36	38	25	
No. of Sample Hospitals					5
LPNs					
Full-time	6	4	11	3	78
Part-time	8	3	13	8	22
None Employed	85	94	76	89	—
TOTAL PERCENT	99	101	100	100	100
No. of Sample Practices	98	35	39	24	
No. of Sample Hospitals					5
Aides					
Full-time	14	6	23	15	78
Part-time	6	9	5	5	22
None Employed	79	85	72	80	—
TOTAL PERCENT	99	100	100	100	100
No. of Sample Practices	98	34	39	25	
No. of Sample Hospitals					5
Technicians					
Full-time	7	4	14	—	67
Part-time	4	4	5	—	33
None employed	89	91	81	100	—
TOTAL PERCENT	100	99	100	100	100
No. of Sample Practices	99	35	39	25	
No. of Sample Hospitals					5
Secretaries					
Full-time	54	47	60	54	78
Part-time	18	18	14	24·	22
None Employed	28	34	26	22	—
TOTAL PERCENT	100	99	100	100	100

TABLE 6.2 (CONTINUED)

No. of Sample Practices	95	34	36	25	
No. of Sample Hospitals					5
Clerks					
Full-time	3	2	4	5	67
Part-time	8	4	14	8	33
None Employed	88	94	82	87	—
TOTAL PERCENT	99	100	100	100	100
No. of Sample Practices	99	35	39	25	
No. of Sample Hospitals					5
Bookkeepers					
Full-time	11	6	13	18	22
Part-time	8	6	8	15	78
None Employed	80	88	79	68	—
TOTAL PERCENT	99	100	100	101	100
No. of Sample Practices	99	35	39	25	
No. of Sample Hospitals					5
PAs, PNAs, PNPs					
Full-time	3	—	6	5	78
Part-time	1	—	—	3	—
None Employed	96	100	94	92	22
TOTAL PERCENT	100	100	100	100	100
No. of Sample Practices	99	35	39	25	
No. of Sample Hospitals					5

NOTES: Information was not ascertained on .9 percent of weighted practices for MDs and RNs; 2 percent for LPNs; 2.7 percent for Aides; 1.6 percent for Technicians and Clerks; 6.4 percent for Secretaries; 1.1 percent for Bookkeepers; and .8 percent for PAs, PNAs and PNPs.
Private practice is presented by specialty; hospital setting includes all services.
The calculation of X^2 values for this table were all invalid due to low expected frequencies.
Percentages might not total 100 because of rounding error.

that are not presented here such as Social Service, Dietary, Security, Maintenance, and a clearly differentiated category of Administrative Support Services.

Little research has been done on the office staff of solo or small group practitioners. They are generally passed over in favor of their employers, and their contributions to the organization of the practice is overlooked. Eighty-eight percent of the sampled primary physicians employed one or more secretaries who assisted in performing routine tasks, including a remarkable number of tests and procedures. The role of the secretary in private practice is broadened to encompass paramedical duties: obtaining the height and weight of the patients, performing ECGs, giving injections, and conducting simple laboratory tests. The secretary who performs medical tasks is sometimes described as a nurse although she does not have a degree to certify this extension of her role.

The Delegation of Tasks

As described above, relatively few private practitioners hired registered nurses, LPNs or assistants. The assumption of the Advisory Committee and staff was that practices with a broader spectrum of personnel would be more likely to comply with the essential criteria of care than would one-person practices. Similarly, practices with only secretarial assistance were expected to perform less well than practices with medically trained assistants and laboratory technicians. It was also anticipated that practices with more than one physician in the office would perform at a higher level than solo practices.

Moreover, we assumed that the presence of a variety of staff would enhance the appropriate delegation of tasks according to particular skill. For example, if a lab technician were present, all laboratory tests and procedures would be delegated to that technician. Instead

TABLE 6.3

Summary Tabulation of Delegation of Responsibility for Tests and Procedures in
Private Practice
By Type of Procedure
(Percentage Distribution)

Type of Test/Procedure	Percent Delegated	Done by Physician (Not Delegated)	Patient Referred Or Specimen Sent Out	Test Not Done	Total Percent	Number of Sample Practices
ECG	47%	8%	2%	42%	99%	88
Hemoglobin	44	9	6	41	100	87
Hematocrit	41	7	6	46	100	87
Sedimentation Rate	27	5	7	60	99	87
Urinalysis	74	13	1	12	100	87
Blood Pressure	38	36	—	25	99	92
Temperature	62	38	—	—	100	92
Height and Weight	77	23	—	—	100	92
Give Injections	47	53	—	—	100	92
Routine Immunizations	44	28	—	28	100	92

NOTES: For ECG's information on 9.1 percent of weighted practices was not ascertained.

For Hemoglobin, Hematocrit, Sedimentation Rate, and Urinalysis, information on 9.9 percent of weighted practices was not ascertained.

For Blood Pressure, Temperature, Height and Weight, Giving Injections, and Routine Immunization, information on 7.6 percent of weighted practices was not ascertained.

Percentages might not total 100 because of rounding error.

we noted that underdelegation occurred. Results show that, even when a variety of personnel were available, physicians were assuming primary responsibility for tasks which could have been delegated to their employees. In hospitals, tasks were more routinely assigned to staff with appropriate levels of training; the only exception was immunizations, which were done by physicians 44 percent of the time.

Private general practitioners seemed to do more of their own tests and procedures than did their colleagues in internal medicine. Pediatricians also assumed a large share of responsibility for tasks which could have been delegated to other personnel. Upon further investigation we found that physicians frequently provided back-up to other staff. Some physicians interviewed said that this was essential because their staff worked too slowly and got behind.

Table 6.3 summarizes the extent of task delegation in private practices for specific tests and procedures. It also includes the proportion of offices in which tasks were done by the physician, referred outside of the organization, or simply not done. During the field work many of the private practice clerical staff told us that they did not wish to assume additional responsibilities such as the performance of simple medical tasks. Most preferred the gatekeeper role: scheduling appointments and screening phone calls and other patient-physician contacts.

The Staff's Assessment of Management Problems

Previous research has identified divergent functions of the primary private practice. Like all other organizations, the practice must develop a number of competencies in transactions with different sectors of its environment (Lawrence and Lorsch 1969). At the very least, it is necessary for the private practice to function simultaneously as the sole provider for the majority of people seeking primary care (a complex production function), and as an organizational unit in the medical care delivery system. In order to acquire necessary resources from the environment, it must conduct transactions with suppliers (a purchasing function) and the labor market (a personnel function). Transactions with technology and equipment suppliers are required to obtain diagnostic tools such as laboratory, ECG, and X-ray equipment. Basic competence in finance and control is necessary in order to execute the appropriate collection procedures which will ensure funds for salaries and future expenditures.

As mentioned previously, many of the serious problems which

TABLE 6.4
Summary of Management Problems Cited as Most Serious by Private Office Staff
(Percentage Distribution)

Management Problem	Percent of Private Practices
Increasing Paperwork	43%
Steadily Rising Overhead	13
Slow Payment of Insurance Claims	10
Third Party Payment	10
Milfiled Financial and Medical Records	8
Low Collection Ratio	6
Poor Appointment Planning	5
Frequent Outside Emergencies	1
Billing Errors	1
Other Problems Described	3
TOTAL PERCENT	100
Number of Sample Practices for All Management Problems	93

emerge in private practices today are related less to clinical medicine
than to the areas of organization and management. In this chapter,
we have attempted to focus on the problems identified by private
practices as impediments to the delivery of good medical care. Table
6.4 presents a summary of the management problems cited as most
serious. Steadily increasing amounts of paper work, rising overhead,
and difficulties with third-party payers, such as slow payment on
insurance claims, are the foremost critical areas identified by private
practices. These data on administrative difficulties deserve special
attention. Management problems in private practice are issues which
can be dealt with more easily than issues associated with the clinical
skills of the practicing physician.

ORGANIZATION / PATIENT INTERACTION

Size of the Practice

In organizational research a number of studies have been done
using size of the organization as the dependent variable. Our advisory
group believed that an increase in the size and complexity of the
organization could contribute to increased problems in providing
service to clients or patients. In Table 6.5, size of private practice
is presented by specialty and number of years the physician had
been in practice. No attempt has been made to include data on hospital
size here because all of these organizations had patient volumes which
were too large to be useful for comparative purposes.

TABLE 6.5
Percentage Distribution of Private Practice
By Specialty, Size, and Number of Years in Practice

Number of Years in Practice	All Practices				General Practice				Internal Medicine				Pediatrics			
	All Sizes	Small	Medium	Large	All Sizes	Small	Medium	Large	All Sizes	Small	Medium	Large	All Sizes	Small	Medium	Large
All Years	100%	32%	34%	34%	42%	30%	25%	46%	38%	40%	44%	16%	20%	20%	36%	42%
<10 Yrs	5	—	9	5	8	—	15	8	—	—	—	—	8	—	22	—
10–19	23	17	26	25	8	—	—	17	38	36	46	16	27	—	19	49
20–29	34	27	37	38	22	—	22	37	44	51	40	35	42	24	51	44
30+	38	55	27	32	63	100	63	38	17	13	13	48	22	76	8	7
TOTAL PERCENT	100	99	99	100	101	100	100	100	99	100	99	99	99	100	100	100
No. of Sample Practices	100	30	36	34	36	9	9	18	39	16	17	6	25	5	10	10

X^2 Values:

GP—IM X^2 = 23.08*

GP—PED X^2 = 10.73**

IM—PED X^2 = 3.88

*Significant at 0.001 level

**Significant at .02 level

Percentages might not total 100 because of rounding error.

93

Looking at practice size presented by specialty, internists had the highest percentage of small practices (i.e., less than 60 patients per week) and pediatricians had the lowest. A greater proportion of medium practices (i.e., between 60 and 200 patients per week) also occurred in internal medicine. Internists had large practices (i.e., over 200 per week) significantly less often than pediatricians and general practitioners. Significant differences are shown among specialty groups in all sizes by number of years in practice. No significant differences were found between internists and pediatricians.

Access

Committee members who advised the CACS staff on the construction of the Organizational Characteristics Interview Schedule recommended

TABLE 6.6
Private Physicians Whose Home Phones are Listed by Type of Practice and Number
of Years in Practice
(Percentage Listed)

Years in Practice	All Practices	General Practice	Internal Medicine	Pediatrics
All Years	46%	46%	48%	38%
10 years	13	—	—	38
10–19 years	40	—	48	41
20–29 years	45	34	57	35
30+ years	53	61	28	43
Number of Sample Practices	100	36	39	25

that data be collected on access to the physicians in private practice. One indication of accessibility is the presence or absence of the physician's home phone number in the local telephone directory. Table 6.6 shows that less than half of all private practitioners had their home phones listed. Differences by major specialty on this indicator are not significant. Home phone listings were less prevalent among the younger physicians; this trend was especially noticeable within general practice. However, 38 percent of the pediatricians who had been in practice for less than ten years were available to their patients by home phone.

Perceptions of Patient Status

Peterson and his colleagues (1956) allude to the importance of patient convenience and comfort in the primary care delivery site. Out of concern for the clients' psychological as well as physical comfort, we wanted to know more about how patients were perceived by office staff, their first contact with the health care provider. In an article entitled "The Sick Role and the Role of the Physician Reconsidered," Parsons (1975) describes therapy as a reintegrative process. In order to be successful in solving the central organization problem—that of symmetry-asymmetry—which exists between sick people and therapeutic agents, physicians and staff must take into account the nature of the patients' adaptive problems. Szasz and Hollander (1956) advocate active participation of the patient in the treatment process. The condition of mutual participation requires a high degree of symmetry between the physician and the patient.

Perceived low status was considered by the study group to be one indicator of asymmetry or lack of cultural similarity between the providers and the patients. Table 6.7 shows the proportion of patients who were considered to be of low Socio-Economic Status (SES) by private office staff. General and pediatric practices reported more as being low SES. Significant differences in perception of low SES were recorded by the three major specialties. Other analyses indicated that more internists felt that the majority of their patients were middle-class (i.e., middle SES) than did general practitioners and pediatricians. However, differences across major specialty in this area were not significant. Both internists and pediatricians identified 21–30

TABLE 6.7

Percent of Patients Described as Low Socio-Economic Status (SES) by Private Office Staff of General Practitioners, Internists, and Pediatricians
(Percentage Distribution)

Percentage of Low SES Patients	All Physicians	GP	IM	PED
0–5	18%	19%	21%	11%
6–10	26	13	34	33
11–20	21	16	30	16
21–30	21	27	12	28
31+	13	24	3	11
TOTAL PERCENT	99	99	100	99
No. of Sample Practices	92	31	36	25

NOTES: Information on 8.7 percent of weighted practices was not ascertained.
Percentages might not total 100 because of rounding error.
X^2 Values:
GP vs. IM $X^2 = 12.21*$
GP vs. PED $X^2 = 4.39*$
IM vs. PED $X^2 = 5.62*$
*Significant at 0.025 level

percent of their patients as coming from an upper socio-economic grouping which they describe as upper-class. Internists also described a higher proportion of their patients as having professional occupations. These data were not obtained from the one-person offices.

Private office staff were also asked to describe what percent of their patients were black or Spanish-speaking. About half of the practices reported that less than 2 percent of their patients were black or Spanish-speaking. A small number of the private practices and less than half of the hospitals were in a position to communicate with their Spanish-speaking patients because they had bilingual staff (Table 6.8). We do not know whether Spanish-speaking staff were acquired unintentionally or by design. However several of the hospitals reported that they made special efforts to hire bilingual staff with a view to improving communications with their patients. Two of the hospitals employed trained interpreters. With the exception of Italian, other foreign languages spoken in the selected sites were not used extensively.

Characteristics of the patient population are described in Appendix E. When the results of these analyses were later compared with the descriptive findings on the patient population, staff perceptions were found to be more accurate than anticipated. A higher degree of stereotyping had been expected, especially in regard to low SES patients. These characteristics were included because we believed that perceived SES would be related to the kind of care provided.

Descriptions of patient status as reported by hospital staff are not presented because of reliability problems. However, our data indicate that one-third to one-half of the hospital patient population were described by staff as being black or Spanish-speaking. No empirical checks were made on the perceptions of hospital respondents.

Problems with the Worried-Well and Patients Needing More Specialized Care

Professionals involved in the delivery of primary care perceived that there was not always a good match between the needs of the patient population and the resources available in the practice. One-third of our sample private practices reported that fewer than 10 percent of their patients required more specialized care. Another third estimated that 10–15 percent of their patient population were in need of such care. The remainder believed that more than 15 percent of their patients had to be referred to other specialists. It was anticipated that older general practitioners would be the heaviest users of other

TABLE 6.8

Foreign Languages Spoken by Staff
By Size and Type of Organization
(Percentage Distribution)

| TYPE OF LANGUAGE | ALL PRACTICES | | | | PRIVATE PRACTICE | | | | | | | | | | | | HOSPITAL |
| | | | | | GENERAL PRACTICE | | | | INTERNAL MEDICINE | | | | PEDIATRICS | | | | |
	All Sizes	Small	Medium	Large	All Sizes	Small	Medium	Large	All Sizes	Small	Medium	Large	All Sizes	Small	Medium	Large	
Foreign, not specified	21%	16%	27%	19%	3%	—	11%	—	34%	26%	43%	32%	34%	24%	18%	55%	56%
Spanish	13	30	6	5	12	31	—	8	14	27	6	—	13	38	13	—	44
Italian	2	3	—	5	4	—	—	8	2	5	—	—	—	—	—	—	—
Others	2	—	3	2	2	—	—	4	—	—	—	—	5	—	13	—	—
More than one foreign language spoken	13	14	9	15	26	31	30	21	3	—	—	16	5	24	—	—	—
None Spoken	49	37	55	54	53	37	59	58	48	42	51	52	42	14	55	45	—
TOTAL PERCENT	100	100	100	100	100	99	100	99	101	100	100	100	99	100	99	100	100
No. of Sample Practices	98	29	36	33	35	8	9	18	39	16	17	6	24	5	10	9	
No. of Sample Hospitals																	5

NOTES: Information on 1.8 percent of weighted practices was not ascertained.
Private practice is presented by specialty.
Percentages might not total 100 because of rounding error.

TABLE 6.9

Percent of Patients Seen for "Trivial Disorders," as Described by Staff, By Type of Organization and Number of Years in Practice
(Percentage Distribution)

Percent of Patients Seen for Trivial Disorders	PRIVATE PRACTICE																									HOSPITAL
	ALL PRACTICES					GENERAL PRACTICES					INTERNAL MEDICINE					PEDIATRICS					
	All Years	<10 Yrs	10-19 Yrs	20-29 Yrs	30+ Yrs	All Years	<10 Yrs	10-19 Yrs	20-29 Yrs	30+ Yrs	All Years	<10 Yrs	10-19 Yrs	20-29 Yrs	30+ Yrs	All Years	<10 Yrs	10-19 Yrs	20-29 Yrs	30+ Yrs	
0-9	25%	33%	22%	27%	25%	23%	50%	25%	19%	20%	19%	—	7%	31%	16%	46%	—	65%	33%	81%	11%
10-15	30	33	16	36	32	34	—	25	28	42	23	—	19	35	—	36	100	—	48	19	22
16-25	27	33	26	22	30	31	50	50	37	24	28	—	17	20	66	14	—	35	13	—	57
26+	17	—	36	13	12	12	—	—	19	13	29	—	58	14	16	4	—	—	8	—	11
TOTAL PERCENT	99	99	100	98	99	100	100	100	103	100	100	—	101	100	98	100	100	100	102	100	101
No. of Sample Practices	86	4	21	32	29	33	2	4	8	19	33	0	12	15	6	20	2	5	9	4	
No. of Sample Hospitals																					5

NOTES: Information on 12.2 percent of weighted practices was not ascertained due to inability to answer the question.
Private Practice is presented by specialty.

X^2 Values:

GP—IM $X^2 = 3.20$

GP—PED $X^2 = 4.45$

IM—PED $X^2 = 8.89*$

*Significant at 0.05 level

Percentages might not total 100 because of rounding error.

98

specialists (Clute 1963), but this did not appear to be true for older practices in Connecticut.

Physician advisors to the study were very concerned about practices being bogged down by large numbers of patients seeking care for trivial disorders (Table 6.9). Over half of all practices reported that at least 15 percent of their patients were the worried-well, i.e., people who were not physically ill, but lonely or in need of counseling for emotional problems. Higher proportions of worried-well were reported by the offices of internists and general practitioners who had been in practice for twenty years or more. The lowest percentage of worried-well was reported by the older pediatric practices. Perhaps these practices were dwindling and the decreased patient volume permitted physicians and their staff to spend more time with each patient. Therefore, trivial complaints would not have been perceived as inappropriate demands.

Telephone Communications

A great deal of information and assistance can be provided to patients by way of telephone communication with private office or hospital staff. In fact, some of our sample pediatricians suggested that our observations of their patient care activities would be incomplete because we were not monitoring phone conversations. It seemed important to learn whether or not auxiliary personnel had been properly trained to assume this function of communicating with patients.

All hospital staff reported that they had received a formal set of instructions regarding telephone procedures, whereas only a little more than half of the private practice staff were similarly equipped. Procedures of this nature are more routinely followed in a larger organization but may be informally provided in private practices. Internists provided formal telephone instruction to their staff much more often than did general practitioners, but none of the other statistical comparisons proved to be significant.

Appointment Systems

Peterson et al. (1956) stressed the importance of appointment systems and maintained that they were positively correlated with good medical care. The great majority of private practitioners in our sample used such a system for scheduling patients. General practitioners were the only physicians who received their patients on a first-come/first-serve basis. Table 6.10 shows the number of minutes allotted to patients

TABLE 6.10

Physician Time Allotted to Patients for Office or Clinic Visits
By Size and Type of Organization
(Percentage Distribution)

Time Allotted to Patients	PRIVATE PRACTICE																HOSPITAL²
	ALL PRACTICES				GENERAL PRACTICE				INTERNAL MEDICINE				PEDIATRICS				
	All Sizes	Small	Medium	Large	All Sizes	Small	Medium	Large	All Sizes	Small	Medium	Large	All Sizes	Small	Medium	Large	
Not Applicable¹	9%	18%	4%	6%	21	43%	14%	10%	2%	—	—	—	10%	24%	—	—	75%
5–10 minutes	8	4	8	15	13	—	19	20	66	40%	5%	100%	60	14	76%	10%	24
11–15 minutes	59	39	69	68	52	46	49	57	17	31	78	—	15	38	15	73	—
16–25 minutes	11	19	9	3	2	—	—	5	14	29	12	—	15	24	9	—	—
26–30 minutes	13	20	10	8	11	10	19	8	—	—	5	—	15	—	—	17	—
TOTAL PERCENT	100	100	100	100	99	99	101	100	99	100	100	100	100	100	100	100	99
No. of Sample Practices	86	27	33	26	31	9	7	15	34	13	17	4	21	5	9	7	
No. of Sample Hospitals																	5

¹ Some of the general practitioners saw patients on a first-come/first-serve basis.
² Sample hospitals were differentially weighted.
NOTES: Information on 14.2 percent of weighted practices was not ascertained due to inability to answer the question.
Private practice is presented by specialty.
X^2 Values:
  GP—IM $X^2 = 14.20$*
  GP—PED $X^2 = 7.71$
  IM—PED $X^2 = 1.75$
*Significant at 0.01 level
  Percentages might not total 100 because of rounding error.

100

for the average office visit. Hospital data are presented only to show that more than three-fourths of all clinic visits were not formally scheduled appointments. Data for both practice settings are based on self-report and no attempt was made to clock the length of the patient-physician contact. However, informal observations made during data collection activities suggested that the length of appointment time as presented in this tabulation could have been overreported. Particularly in adult practices, many two-minute appointments were observed. Similar discrepancies were noted during the in-person observations conducted on a subsample of the respondents.

Internists reported spending the greatest amount of time with their patients: 96 percent of their appointments lasted more than ten minutes. General practitioners and pediatricians reported more five to ten minute appointments, and our informal observations substantiated this finding. When we categorized the data according to number of years in practice, the greatest variation appeared among private physicians who had been in practice for thirty years or more. Most of the variance can probably be accounted for by: (1) the older, big-volume practices in which practice size affects number of minutes allotted; and (2) the older, dwindling practices in which patients could be given longer appointments because the physician had more time available.

Many physicians in both hospital and private practice complained to project staff about patients who missed their appointments. Upon further investigation, we noted that there were two basic policies for handling no-shows: (1) either the appointment was rescheduled, with or without contacting the patient; or (2) the patient was given another appointment after calling to request it.

Approximately 15 percent of all practices billed patients if they consistently missed their appointments. More general practitioners refused to reschedule these patients than did internists or pediatricians. Internists were more apt to contact the patient to reschedule, while general practitioners and pediatricians tended to wait for the patient to call for another appointment. About 10 percent of the private practices answered that they had no routine procedure for handling no-shows. Half of the hospital clinics which did reschedule patients had policies dictating that it was the patient's responsibility to call. This was not surprising in view of the very high no-show rate in these clinics.

Flexibility in Scheduling

One of the most important aspects of primary ambulatory care is the extent to which a practice can accommodate the needs of

the individual patient. Although most presenting complaints do not
have to be attended to immediately, the patient will be much more
comfortable without long waits. In their fashion, hospitals have always
accommodated the walk-in or short-notice patient, usually without
regard to severity of the complaint. This policy often creates a back-up
at the entry point and in other parts of the system, with patients
having to wait for hours before they are seen. In private practice
the pattern is different. Over two-thirds of all private practices reported
that they could work in short-notice patients who presented for
emergency care. Pediatricians were most likely to accommodate
walk-ins, while the schedules of internists seemed least flexible in
this regard.

Departures from Standard Billing Practices

One of the early objectives of this study was to estimate the cost
of care provided to sampled patients and to make appropriate comparisons with quality of care or level of physician performance (see Chapter
1). For this reason it was important to know more about departures
from standard billing practices. Although the study design had to
be modified somewhat, Advisory Committee members suggested that
we pursue this area of investigation as an indicator of the organization's
concern for the financial status of the patient. In half of the private
practices, the patient's financial situation was the primary reason
for altering standard billing procedures. Professional courtesy was
mentioned as the reason for charging less in approximately 15 percent
of all practices. Differences according to size of practice indicated
that smaller pediatric and general practices demonstrated a greater
sensitivity to the patient's income than did the larger practices. When
these findings were categorized according to number of years in
practice, pediatricians who had been practicing medicine for at least
thirty years appeared to be more sensitive to the patient's finances
than were younger practitioners. General practitioners and pediatricians who had been in practice for less than ten years were more
likely to exhibit professional courtesy than were their older colleagues.
  Secondary reasons for departures from standard billing procedures
were unremarkable except for family visit discounts. General and
pediatric practices were more likely to offer reduced rates when several
members of a family were regular patients. Of course, these practices
were more geared toward family care.
  We also inquired about the collection ratio in both practice settings.
Older private practices were experiencing the most difficulty in this

respect; they reported that their collection ratios were falling. In contrast, a majority of the hospitals reported that their collection ratios were on the rise. In one hospital we were told that this information was in the computer, but that staff had no way of estimating the success of their organization's collection policies.

Use of Forms and Other Printed Materials

During the pretest period we were surprised to note the variety of medical record systems used by physicians, especially in private offices. We decided to investigate the extent to which printed forms and questionnaires were used to collect data on patient history or to instruct patients on routine procedures. Printed instruction forms were more prevalent than questionnaires, which were used in only one-third of all practices studied. Significant differences among major specialty groups emerged for the utilization of printed instructions; pediatricians used them most. No significant differences were found among specialty groups in the use of questionnaires to assist in history-taking. Of course, hospital clinics also reported much greater utilization of forms and questionnaires than did private practices.

We were also surprised but encouraged by the many different means of reminding patients of future appointments. The use of appointment cards was more widespread among pediatricians and internists than in general practices. Hospital clinics did not use appointment cards as frequently as did the private offices. About one-fifth of all private practices mailed reminders to their patients shortly before an appointment date; internists did this most frequently. Some practices contacted the patient by phone several days before a scheduled appointment.

Two-thirds of the private practices and over half of the hospital clinics made distinctions in time allotted to old and new patients. New patients were given longer appointments, ranging from 45 to 90 minutes, for comprehensive history and physical exams; repeat patients were allotted an average of 17 minutes for each office visit. No distinctions were made in first-come/first-serve practices. Internists appeared to be more careful about separating initial visits from the mainstream.

The communication system in private practices, namely telephone, is used to maintain contact with resources which are external to the practice but central to its function. The Organizational Characteristics Committee suggested that a list of frequently used numbers placed near the telephone would be a helpful procedure in any busy office. They also mentioned that one unlisted number in each private practice would provide a line that would be free from incoming calls and could be used to expedite contact with pharmacies, ambulance services, hospitals or consultants. Internists and pediatricians were more likely to have such unlisted numbers than were general practitioners. About one-third of all practices posted frequently used numbers near the telephone. Pharmacy numbers were more likely to be posted than were numbers of consultants or hospitals. This may simply reflect the relative difficulty of remembering the phone numbers of many pharmacies in various neighborhoods.

Forms have usually been designed within hospitals and private practices to improve the storage of information or to facilitate both in-house and external communications. The prominent feature of the management information system in health care organizations is the medical record. The relationship between the record-keeping system, which provides accurate and timely information to the physician or paraprofessional, and the quality of care has frequently been demonstrated. Two major kinds of forms were used for patient records in our private practice sample: (1) three by five (3×5) or five by eight (5×8) cards, which are used more frequently by the general practitioner; and (2) a combination of eight-and-one-half by eleven (8-1/2×11) forms supplemented by handwritten notes. Pediatricians, and especially internists, were more likely to use preprinted forms for record-keeping; this may be because they are directly encouraged to obtain them by their specialty societies. Both types of filing systems in private practice were maintained alphabetically by patient name. Hospitals most often used an identifying number which could be cross-referenced with an alphabetic listing of ambulatory patients.

Staff in both practice settings were asked whether they often had difficulty reading entries in medical records. Most private practice staff reported that they rarely had difficulty with the legibility of patient records. Hospitals, on the other hand, very honestly acknowledged that staff often had trouble deciphering handwritten reports and other notations. Very few of the private practices had any formal chart review procedure. One-third of the private practices across all three specialties reported that a review of the patient record was conducted to make sure that patient data were complete. In hospital clinics a variety of chart review procedures were used, ranging from concurrent review to merely attempting to update information contained in the records.

Patients' Complaints about Management

Frequent complaints from staff and patients are often symptoms of more serious administrative problems. When patients complain

TABLE 6.11
Summary Tabulation of Most Frequently Mentioned Patient Complaints as Described
by Staff, by Type of Complaint and by Size and Type of Organization
(Percentage Distribution)

| Type of Complaint | Private Practice | | | | Hospital |
	All Practices	Small Practice	Medium Practice	Large Practice	
Long Waiting Time	52%	37%	61%	56%	100%
Billing Errors	31	23	38	30	57
Parking Problems	35	41	27	38	75
Telephone Communication	28	21	35	27	11
Number of Sample Practices	94	28	34	32	
Number of Sample Hospitals					5

NOTES: Information on 6.7 percent of weighted practices was not ascertained.
Percentages total more than 100 because of multiple complaints.

about the organization they are usually attended to by staff whose first objective is to render health care. Many staff reported feelings of extreme frustration at having to deal with patient complaints which were unrelated to their presenting physical problems.

Table 6.11 is a summary of the most frequent patient complaints as described by staff. They reported that patients complained most about long waits to receive care, errors made in billing, the scarcity of parking places near the office or hospital, and difficulty in reaching the provider location by telephone. The medium-sized private practices appeared to have more difficulty with billing errors and patient waiting time than did the smaller and larger practices. These offices might have been at an awkward intermediate stage because their patient volume had outgrown the personnel resources available. Telephone communications also appeared to be more of a problem in these practices. As one might expect, the great majority of hospital patients complained about waiting for service and inadequate parking facilities. Although physicians, and especially private practitioners, may have contributed to patient difficulties by their personal decisions regarding the size and location of their practices, these complaints are essentially management problems. They could be dealt with most effectively by staff whose primary responsibility is administration and not the direct provision of patient care.

Table 6.12 suggests that patient complaints were probably attended to by whoever happened to be available in the private office, i.e., either the physician or a staff person. There seemed to be no system set up to deal with these management problems. In approximately

TABLE 6.12
Staff Attending to Patient Complaints
by Type of Staff and by Size and Type of Organization
(Percentage Distribution)

Type of Staff Member	Private Practice				Hospital
	All Practices	Small Practices	Medium Practices	Large Practices	
Physician and/or any Staff	40%	30%	40%	48%	—
Physician/Clinic Chief	24	33	25	15	56
Other Particular Member of • Staff	18	18	20	16	11
Office Manager/Administrator	5	—	10	2	33
Nurse	6	6	2	10	—
Medical Assistant	4	3	3	6	—
No One/NA	3	8	—	2	—
TOTAL PERCENT	100	98	100	99	100
No. of Sample Practices	99	29	36	34	
No. of Sample Hospitals					5

NOTES: Information on .9 percent of weighted practices was not ascertained due to short form of questionnaire and absence of staff in solo practices.
The calculation of X^2 Values for this table were all invalid due to low expected frequencies.

one-third of the offices, the physician himself had to listen to and/or attempt to deal with patient complaints. Routinely delegating such tasks to nurses or office managers would have constituted a more efficient use of everyone's time. Even in hospital clinics, where a greater differentiation of roles should have been evident, the physician clinic chief handled over half of all patient complaints.

Staff's Assessment of Organizational Problems

Although patient satisfaction may have repercussions on the level of care provided in the practice, satisfaction of the providers themselves is more apt to be closely related to the quality of that care. Summary Table 6.13 shows that more staff in medium-sized practices complained about overwork than did their colleagues in the smaller and larger practices. The same group felt that they were underpaid and that they deserved more fringe benefits for the energy expended in their jobs. Hospital staff also felt that they were underpaid, but expressed proportionately more concern about interpersonal problems with other staff members. This finding could be explained by the size and complexity of the hospital organization which provides more opportunities for conflict as well as collaboration. It is also possible that, since friction among staff is a particularly disruptive problem which

TABLE 6.13
Summary Tabulation of Most Frequently Mentioned Staff Complaints,
by Type of Complaint and by Size and Type of Organization
(Percentage Distribution)

TYPE OF COMPLAINT	Private Practice				Hospital
	All Practices	Small Practices	Medium Practices	Large Practices	
Overwork	17%	18%	25%	8%	11%
Too Little Pay	16	7	32	8	33
Insufficient Fringe Benefits	10	9	15	6	—
Friction Among Staff Members	—	—	—	—	78
Not Applicable[1]	8	14	8	2	—
No. of Sample Practices	97	29	35	34	
No. of Sample Hospitals					5

[1]This question was not applicable to offices where there was no staff.
NOTES: Information on 3 percent of weighted practices was not ascertained due to inability to answer the question.
Percentages total more than 100 because of multiple complaints.

is not easy to deal with, hospital administrators and clinic chiefs tend to exaggerate its occurrence.

Attempting to elicit more information on managerial staff's feelings of being overworked, we asked whether or not they were satisfied with their patient volume or caseload (Table 6.14). Over half of the private practice staff reported that they were satisfied with this aspect of their organizations. In contrast, only one-third of the hospital administrators or clinic chiefs reported satisfaction with patient volume. This finding is not surprising when one considers the uneven flow of work in hospital emergency rooms, and even in most of the clinics.

One dramatic finding indicated that 99 percent of the private office staff felt that no one cared about the difficulties they were experiencing on the job. Thus far, it is impossible to determine what contributes to such a high level of cynicism. Further investigation needs to be done in this area because of the significant effect that clerical and other paraprofessional staff can have on the quality of patient care delivered. The extent to which office managers or senior secretaries influence the performance of the private practitioner should never be underestimated.

In the hospital settings, administrators and clinic chiefs reported that they invested a considerable portion of their time and energy

TABLE 6.14
Satisfaction with Patient Volume, as Described by Staff,
by Type of Organization
(Percentage Distribution)

Satisfaction With Load	Private Practice				Hospital
	All Practices	GP	IM	PED	
Satisfied	60%	51%	64%	72%	33%
Dissatisfied	30	27	33	28	67
Not Applicable[1]	10	22	2	—	—
TOTAL PERCENT	100	100	99	100	100
No of Sample Practices	99	35	39	25	
No. of Sample Hospitals					5

[1] The "Not Applicable" category refers to physicians who were semi-retired.
NOTES: Information on 1 percent of weighted practices was not ascertained due to inability to
answer the question.
Private practice is presented by specialty.
Percentages might not total 100 because of rounding error.

in dealing with staff complaints. Even so, lower echelon staff with
whom we spoke informally during our data collection activities were
often not very cheerful or enthusiastic about their work. We were
left with the impression that they also felt alienated and ignored,
but they were more aggressive in expressing their feelings.

In this chapter we have described the organizational characteristics
of the private practices which participated in the Connecticut Ambulatory Care Study and provided comparative information on hospital
outpatient departments. Management problems which may tend to
inhibit the delivery of good patient care have also been identified.

In the following chapter we will identify the attributes of the physician
and the practice associated with technical performance.

7

Determinants of Technical Performance: Attributes Associated with Adherence to or Departure from Standards

As is evident from the preceding chapters, our field work generated a vast quantity of data on the characteristics of the physicians who participated in the study, the organization of their practices, and their patient population. Before presenting the results of analyses on these many variables, we will demonstrate the basic extent of congruence of physician performance with the predetermined criteria for the nine selected topics. Tabular material is displayed by practice setting and specialty, and the accompanying text elaborates on noteworthy variations in performance on certain criterion items. The difficulty of interpreting these initial results on an item-by-item basis is also explained.

The second section of this chapter describes the process of selecting a factor analytic technique to reduce the data and facilitate a meaningful interpretation of results. We indicate how the factors for each topic were established and the steps taken to ensure their validity and reliability. The use of analysis of variance and t-tests on the performance factors for the study topics is presented in the third section of the chapter.

The fourth section explains the process of selecting additional physician and organizational variables for the second level analyses. An interactive computer system (AUTOGRP) was used to partition variance in performance, and the results of the application of this technique are provided for one of the study topics. Summary tables display the results of second level analyses for salient organizational and physician characteristics and the percent of variance explained by each.

The chapter concludes with a section on the presentation of the findings to the Advisory Committee for the study and to the Connecticut State Medical Society. The reactions of committee members were varied, as were their interpretations of the results. They also offered suggestions for further action to be taken on the basis of the given data.

Congruence with Criterion Items for Selected Topics

The extent to which physicians complied with criteria that were developed by the panels for selected topics is demonstrated in Tables F.1 through F.9 in Appendix F. The percent of patients for whom criteria were met are presented by practice setting and major specialty. It is easy to see that, from the basic lists of Essential criteria enumerated, an even larger number of criterion items (i.e., sub-components of these criteria) had been included in the abstracting of patient records. When a statistical grouping of individual criteria, validated by physician consultants, was compared with the use of multiple items in scoring, there was no difference in the overall score received by a physician. Furthermore, no matter how the criterion items were weighted, the summary scores for physician groups remained the same.

In some of the tables, percentages for several criterion items are inflated due to the application of *System One* scoring; a weight of one (1) was assigned to the "not applicable" category so as not to detract from the overall score of the physician. These items are identified by footnote in the tables affected by this artifact.

The tabulation for Adult Abdominal Pain (Table F.1) indicates that care provided to 20 percent of all patients was congruent with a criterion requiring the physician to elicit information regarding the type of abdominal pain experienced. Compliance was higher among hospital physicians (42 percent) than it was for private practitioners (14 percent). The hospital general practitioners appeared to provide care which was most compliant with this criterion: they elicited information on type of pain from 58 percent of their patients. They are followed by hospital internists whose performance was congruent with this item in 32 percent of their sample cases. The major specialties involved in giving care to patients presenting with Adult Abdominal Pain were, of course, general practitioners (128 sample cases) and internists (230 sample cases).

It is noteworthy that on such items as "onset of pain" and "location of pain" the pattern of compliance was quite different. Care provided to patients in both settings by all physicians was congruent in one-half to two-thirds of the cases. Other criterion items in which performance compliance was relatively high are history of "previous pain," "blood pressure," examination for "abdominal tenderness," and the "working diagnosis." Overall, the table shows that care provided to a rather low percentage of patients treated in ambulatory settings was congruent with criteria developed by the panels of experts. Hospital practitioners adhered to criteria in a greater proportion of cases than did private practitioners. The items for Adult Abdominal Pain which are inflated due to the application of the scoring mechanism are "medication," "relationship to menses," and "pelvic exam."

Without going into an item-by-item interpretation it is difficult to provide a coherent summary description of these findings. One can only pick out certain areas of strengths and weaknesses in relation to criteria designed by the physician panels. Relatively few summary statements can be made from these commonly used displays with regard to components of care—History, Physical Exam, Laboratory, Medications, or Treatments—without further consolidation of scores for the criterion items. Nevertheless, an attempt will be made to describe briefly the results of this series of tables for all of the topics.

Table F.2 displays congruence with criteria for Chest Pain, a topic which was restricted to adult males. For this problem area it appears that physicians were more apt to inquire about the pain and its location, its onset, and history of previous experience with chest pain than they were to determine other historical aspects of the problem. They were more likely to take blood pressure and provide an ECG and working or final diagnosis than they were to include other laboratory or physical exam items in their work-up. As in the previous topic, hospital practitioners complied more closely with criteria than did physicians in private practice.

Table F.3 presents the degree of congruence with Hypertension items and it is immediately evident that very few items reached or exceeded the 50 percent level of compliance. Slightly more than 50 percent of the patients treated by physicians in both practice settings combined were asked for a complete history (as defined by the physician panel) or received an appropriate array of tests and procedures including ECG and lab work. Nearly two-thirds of the private physicians took and recorded blood pressure readings during patient visits. Hospital practitioners again appeared to be performing at a level which was more in line with the predetermined criteria; they obtained and recorded blood pressure readings on nearly three-fourths of their hypertension patients.

Table F.4 shows degree of congruence with criteria for Urinary Tract Infection (UTI) in adult female patients. As compared with performance in other adult diseases, hospital practitioners demonstrated better care for women presenting with UTI. Private practice internists also performed relatively well: they complied with the most essential criteria in treating over half of their patients. There are several indications of artifacts in the application of the scoring system for this topic (e.g., scores of 100 percent for color, turbidity, and clarity); as indicated in the footnote, these are not to be taken as representing perfect congruence with the criterion items. Another example of score inflation in this table is the criterion "signs and symptoms no longer present;" data for this item was to be abstracted on a follow-up visit. However, because of constraints experienced during the course of the study, it was not possible to pursue these cases further.

Degree of congruence with criteria for Pharyngitis is displayed in Table F.5. This topic is interesting for comparisons across all three specialties in both practice settings. One noteworthy item is the use of pharyngeal culture: this criterion was complied with in only 63 percent of all cases. Although this tabulation indicates that 54 percent of the private practice patients received penicillin as compared with 39 percent of the patients in the hospital setting, further analyses showed that private practitioners were more apt to dispense penicillin, erythromycin or other equivalents without a throat culture than were hospital practitioners. We also learned that the presence or absence of laboratory facilities alone did not explain these differences in care.

Table F.6 shows physician compliance with criteria for Otitis Media. Private practice patients seemed to receive analgesics and oral decongestants more frequently than did hospital patients. Hospital practitioners were more likely to refer Otitis patients to a higher level of specialty care, perhaps because of the availability of ENT clinics in most hospital sites. In contrast to the infrequent scheduling of follow-up visits for other topics, two-thirds of all Otitis Media patients were provided with follow-up instructions.

In Pediatric Abdominal Pain (Table F.7), care provided to patients appeared to be more congruent with criteria established by the panels than did care given to the adults with abdominal pain, as described above. Criteria were met more frequently by hospital practitioners than by physicians in private practice. Five items show compliance in treating more than 50 percent of all patients: "type of pain," "persistence of pain," "date of onset," "working diagnosis," and "symptomatic therapy."

Degree of congruence with criteria for Well-Infant Examination is presented in Table F.8. Keeping track of a patient's height and weight, providing scheduled immunizations and tuberculin tests all appeared to be done with relative frequency. Although parents are usually required to schedule visits to a hospital clinic well in advance, this was not the case for more than half of the children seen by general practitioners and pediatricians in private practice. It is surprising to note that pediatricians, who appear to be a psychologically sophisticated group of specialists, evinced less concern than expected for psycho-social items such as "development," "behavior under stress," "family history," and "living situation." These areas were covered more frequently with preschool children seen for Well-Child Examinations (Table F.9). In both of these topics, pediatricians appeared to render more complete physical examinations than did general practitioners.

Before using a relatively complex strategy to assist in interpreting the results of the application of the scoring mechanisms another simple method of looking at the data was used. Criteria developed by the panels for every disease and problem area were given to a physician consultant who placed them in clinical clusters or "lumps" (see Appendix F). The components of care into which criterion items were subdivided were the following: History, Physical Exam, Diagnostic Tests, Management, Follow-up, and Assessment. These clusters resembled, but were not identical to the components by which criteria were elicited from panel members during an initial interview. This was the first stage of criteria development. See Chapter 2 for more information.

As can be seen in Tables F.1 through F.9, the mere separation of items is some improvement over a simple sequential listing. For example, in the cluster of Diagnostic Tests used for Adult Abdominal Pain (Table F.1), it is apparent that internists were more likely than generalists to obtain a complete blood count and to arrive at and record a working diagnosis. However, this strategy did not clarify patterns of performance in large clusters of items such as the patient History.

Our attempts to reduce and add clarity to these data by using different formats are by no means exhaustive; for example, even smaller clusters could have been formed by the physician panels. However, Peterson et al. (1956) reported using factor analysis as a means of discovering order or structure in physician performance, and we were convinced

114 DETERMINANTS OF PERFORMANCE

that it might improve the quality of our analyses. Further, the use of a factor analytic technique seemed to be a more efficient method than reconvening the panels or using another advisory committee.

Observations of Private Practitioners

In order to validate the methods used to obtain measures of physician performance, in-person observations were instituted on a subsample of private practice pediatricians. As explained in Appendix A, the study design originally called for observations to be done in each site selected for study. The plan was to observe physicians while they were in the process of providing care and to compare the behaviors observed with notations made by the physicians (or staff persons) in the patient record. These activities were curtailed because of difficulties with project funding.

During the last phase of the field work, additional resources permitted us to pursue this aspect of the study. Private practitioners from all three specialties were sampled, but response rates of general practitioners and internists were prohibitively low. Nine pediatricians were selected for observation by an experienced family nurse practitioner who used a checklist to record all behavior relevant to the predetermined criterion items.

The degree of overlap between activities or behaviors observed and notations in the patient record is shown in Table 7.1. Items described in this tabulation are presented as they occurred in the Observation Checklists: i.e., by groups of items within each component of care. (An example of the Observation Checklist is provided in Appendix G.) The checklists were constructed to include all criterion items. Because the Abstract Form followed the same sequence in listing criteria, it was easy to compare the data from both sources.

Table 7.1 indicates a very high percentage of agreement between the two sources in every component except Instructions/Explanations. In the 33 cases of Pharyngitis observed, 93 percent of the History items actually performed by the pediatricians or staff persons were recorded on the patient charts. Ninety-six percent of the Physical Exam items, 98 percent of the Special Exam items (i.e., lab tests and special procedures), 100 percent of the Referral items, and 93 percent of the Therapy items were noted in the record. This does not replicate the findings of the Joint Committee on Quality Assurance (Thompson and Osborne 1974) which showed that, generally speaking, only 50 percent of activities done for the pediatric patient were recorded.

TABLE 7.1
Percentage of Criterion Items Complied with and Recorded by Pediatricians
Presented by Component of Care

Diseases or Problem Areas Observed	Number of Cases Observed	Components of Care Observed					
		History Items	Physical Exam Items	Special Exam Items	Referral	Therapy	Instruc- tions/ Expla- nations
Pharyngitis	33	93%	96%	98%	100%	93%	7%
Otitis Media	21	98	96	96	100	98	16
Well-Child Exam (Infant)	54	88	98	100	100	98	15
Well-Child Exam (Preschool)	27	85	98	98	100	96	5

NOTE: Results of observations on Pediatric Abdominal Pain will not be reported because only 7 cases were observed.

Marked differences were evident in recording behavior on Instruction/Explanation items. The highest percentage of agreement occurred in Otitis Media. Criteria required the physician to provide instruction to the patient regarding medications and to explain that a follow-up visit or phone call was necessary. Physicians or staff were more likely to arrange follow-up visits for Otitis and Well Examination patients than they were for their Pharyngitis or Preschool patients. The notation in the record or log of a follow-up visit implied that the appropriate instructions had been given for these sample cases.

The purpose of Table 7.1 is to show the level of agreement on items which were done as well as recorded by the physician rather than to show mean performance. It was not surprising to discover the large discrepancy in the Instructions/Explanations component. We did not expect to find that physicians would record their verbal interactions with their patients.

USE OF FACTOR ANALYSIS TO OBTAIN INDICES OF
PHYSICIAN PERFORMANCE

For each of the nine topics in the study, between 37 and 160 criterion items were developed for assessing the quality of care given to patients. The massive amount of data generated posed major problems when we tried to interpret how the quality of care differed according to various characteristics of physicians and their practices. For example, one way of examining differences in the treatment of Pharyngitis was to separate cases which were treated in private offices from those treated in hospital settings and make 37 comparisons between these two groups: i.e., one comparative statement for each of the 37 individual criterion items. While this strategy has the advantage of dealing with all available information, it also has obvious disadvantages: (1) the general incomprehensibility of the results of such a large number of comparisons; (2) the difficulties involved in making proper statistical inferences from these comparisons; and (3) the problem of interpreting the results obtained as indicative of general, pervasive aspects of physician performance.

Out of concern for these disadvantages, the technique of factor analysis was applied to the sets of criteria for each of the topics as a means of improving the quality of the analyses of differences in performance according to characteristics of the physicians and their practices. A more thorough explication of the rationale for factor analyzing the criteria sets is presented in this section of the chapter.

Reducing the Data

One purpose of factor analyzing the sets of criteria for each topic was to summarize interrelationships in a concise but accurate manner. This technique would reduce the full set of criteria to a much smaller set of clusters of criteria. Within each cluster the individual items would be internally consistent and each cluster would be different from all others. A single performance score could then be computed for each cluster of criteria. Factor analysis is an appropriate statistical technique for determining an empirical summary of the performance criteria. Reducing the mass of criteria to distinct groups added clarity to the process of examining differences in quality of care, since comparisons could then be made on a handful of factors (clusters) which represented the larger set of criteria instead of on the entire set. Furthermore, the clusters of criterion items obtained represent differential aspects of physician performance. These aspects indicate that the quality of care given in a physician-patient encounter is not unidimensional in nature, but multidimensional. A physician may perform a physical examination well or might be skilled at eliciting information from the patient regarding the onset and nature of symptoms, but he may interpret laboratory test results poorly or prescribe inappropriate medications.

Clarifying Statistical Inference

Differences in physician performance according to personal or organizational characteristics were examined by the use of statistical tests of significant differences or significant relationships. A problem can arise if there are a large number of criteria on which such tests are made. Because criteria are intercorrelated, the levels of statistical significance of differences or relationships cannot be interpreted in the usual way. Specifically, if compliance with certain criteria is correlated with compliance (or noncompliance) with other criteria, a series of statistical tests applied to these criteria would not be independent tests because of the intercorrelations present. "Significant" differences found in this way may be inflated.

A way of minimizing this problem of interpretation is to define clusters of criteria which, when taken together, are representative of the entire set. A single score representing performance on that cluster can be computed and used to assess differences related to various characteristics of physicians and their practices. Besides achieving an effective combination of highly correlated criterion items, the factor analytic procedure can also produce factors (or performance dimensions) which are relatively uncorrelated with one another. Therefore, performance on one dimension (e.g., physical exam) can be interpreted as being separate from performance on another dimension (e.g., interpretation of laboratory results). This ensures that statistical tests which involve these dimensions are independent of one another.

Generalizability

The performance factors derived in this study are a smaller set of variables which preserve almost all of the information contained in the original, much larger set of highly specific performance items. Reducing the large number of criteria in each topic to a more reasonable subset is useful beyond the simplification and clarification of these analyses.

The present study provides a good rationale for adopting a smaller set of variables (e.g., the performance factors obtained) when investigating differential physician performance in future research. In addition to simplifying the analyses, factors provide a more cost-effective method of assessing performance. Because the performance factors themselves accurately represent the larger sets of specific criteria, little is lost when the factors are used as the variables for comparing physician performance. And since these factors are at a higher level of abstraction than the specific criterion items, useful comparisons between similar studies of this type would be greatly enhanced. The assessment of physician performance on the basis of meaningful summary measures (i.e., not summarizing unlike tasks or procedures) would facilitate the integration of findings from various studies and thus contribute to the formulation of a systematic body of knowledge related to the quality of patient care and the manner in which it is delivered.

Procedures Used to Factor Analyze the Data

The first step in factor analyzing the criteria for each topic was to compute a correlation matrix depicting the interrelationships of performance on the individual items. Principal factors of the correlation matrix were extracted, using squared multiple correlations as the initial communality estimates with an iterative procedure used to further improve these estimates. (All factor analyses were done at the Yale University Computer Center using SPSS subprograms [Nie et al. 1975].) The principal factors were orthogonally rotated by the standard varimax method, a procedure which was used because of its tendency to produce highly interpretable factors. Following the initial factor analysis in which all principal factors with a characteristic root equal to or greater than one were rotated, a variety of subsequent factor analyses were performed for each topic in which the number of factors to be rotated were specified, ranging from two or three in number to about nine or ten. The factor loadings of the performance criterion items were examined for each of the different solutions.

Factor loadings represent the correlations of individual criterion items with each of the underlying factors. Groups of items which correlated highly with one factor while having low correlations with other factors were taken as defining that unique factor. As a rule, loadings of .40 or greater were regarded as being of sufficient magnitude to demonstrate a relationship between a variable and a factor.

Establishing the Factors

The selection of important factors of physician performance was based on the results of the multiple factor analyses of the criterion items for each topic. This involved a combination of statistical and judgmental considerations, with the intention of selecting factors which were both reliable (i.e., would be likely to appear again if the study were replicated) and valid (i.e., made sense logically, in terms of the items defining each one and the probability of their indicating differences in physician performance).

Reliability

One source of evidence regarding the reliability of factors appeared within the multiple factor analyses themselves. Factors which continued to emerge across analyses in which varying numbers of factors were rotated could be regarded as reliable factors. For example, when four to ten principal factors were rotated for a given criteria set and a factor associated with a group of physical exam criteria consistently appeared, that factor was regarded as reliable. Factors which emerged only at certain stages of the analyses and not others were considered to be unreliable factors.

Another method used to identify reliable factors was to split the full sample of cases in a topic into two subsamples and compute separate factor analyses for each subsample (Armstrong and Soelberg 1968). Comparisons could then be made between the results, and factors which appeared in both analyses could be considered reliable. To ensure the adequacy of this procedure, there must be a very large number of cases in a topic relative to the number of criteria for that topic. In fact, the ratio of cases to criteria should be at least 4:1 or 5:1; some recommend ratios as high as 10:1. Certain topics in the present study did not have sufficient sample sizes to meet ratio specifications (e.g., Chest Pain, Pediatric Abdominal Pain).

Validity

Two perspectives should be considered when assessing the validity of a factor obtained through factor analysis. One perspective is concerned with the internal composition of the factor: the nature of the items which comprise the factor should be logically consistent. Empirically derived factors which are made up of heterogeneous, diverse items are likely to be of questionable value since they have no inherent meaning. The assessments of the logical, internal validity of the factors derived in this study were made by physician experts.

A second perspective on the validity of an empirically obtained factor deals with the relationship of performance scores on that factor to other external variables. That is, if all performance factors related in an identical way to a set of independent variables (e.g., physician specialty, setting of the practice, size of the patient load), then there would be evidence that the factors were not reflecting separable dimensions but rather an overall view of physician performance. Scores on the performance factors used in this study did in fact display differential relationships to a variety of independent variables, thus providing additional supporting evidence that the factors reflected separable dimensions of physician performance.

A third way to assess the validity of the factors for a given topic was to examine how the extracted factors compared with the a priori categories of performance as designated by the physician panels responsible for developing the criteria used in the study (for a further discussion of this approach, see Armstrong and Soelberg 1968). These broad components (e.g., Physical Exam, History, Lab) were often quite similar to the empirical groupings of the criteria produced by factor analysis. The correspondence between empirical and logical groupings of items suggests that the factors represented meaningful dimensions of physician performance. If the factors did not resemble components, they were examined by physician experts to determine whether or not they were clinically meaningful. It is noteworthy that, when empirical factors reflected the panels' a priori divisions of the criteria, they often did so with significantly fewer items for each performance dimension.

Scoring Performance on the Factors

Once the reliability and validity of a factor have been confirmed, a score must be obtained on that factor to indicate the quality of care delivered. In the present study, this was done by computing the average score for compliance with the individual criteria which were associated with a particular factor. For example, if six specific criterion items were associated with a factor labelled "history," the average of the compliance scores for those six items became the score for the performance factor called "history." Each item which was strongly associated with a factor was given an equal weight of one (1.0); all other items were excluded from the calculation of a score for that particular factor.

An alternative to this approach, one which has been frequently used in research employing a factor analytic technique, involved the computation of a weight for each item based on the strength of association between that item and a particular factor. This weight (called a factor score coefficient) could then be applied to the compliance score for the item in the process of calculating the performance score for each factor. For the purposes of the present study, the unweighted strategy seemed preferable: (1) it is simpler and more economical; (2) evidence from other sources (e.g., Gorsuch 1974) has shown that there is very little net difference between factor scores produced by the weighted and the unweighted methods; and (3) if a differential weighting system had been used, the actual weights given to each criterion item for each factor would only have been applicable to the present study. The unweighted system of computing performance factor scores can be generalized for use in subsequent investigations since it identifies only the subset of criteria which are relevant to a performance factor and does not attempt to attach specific weights of importance to those items.

Concluding Remarks on the Use of Factor Analysis

The factor analytic approach adopted in the present study to establish viable dimensions of physician performance was an attempt to improve upon the two extreme ways of depicting physician performance. One extreme uses each and every criterion item in a topic as a basis for examining differences in performance according to major independent variables such as setting and specialty. To give an example, if this method had been used for Chest Pain, the result would have been 72 individual comparisons of performance according to setting, another 72 for examining the effects of specialty, and yet a third 72 for a consideration of the joint effects (interaction) of both setting and specialty. The contrasting efficiency of reducing the data to five performance factors is undeniable. By adopting the factor analytic approach and formulating performance factors from highly interrelated items, the liabilities of this one-item-at-a-time approach have been overcome.

At the same time, the factor analytic technique still permits summary measures to be made for physicians of different specialties and practice settings. For example, Tables 7.2a through 7.10a provide summary measures of performance for all primary care physicians on each factor as well as mean scores for practice setting and major specialty. A Global Category can be retained (as in Tables 7.2a through 7.10a) to show mean performance on all criterion items in a given disease or problem area; this global score has become a traditional way of demonstrating physician performance.

The strategy of factor analysis has been introduced as a useful technique to aid in the development of a multidimensional conceptualization of the process of delivering medical care. However, this statistical tool should not be relied upon to produce the ultimate in truth or validity. A factor analysis of any set of criteria of care will always yield factors (in the statistical sense), but the validity and importance of those factors as representing separable facets of the process of delivering care must be assessed in theoretical or logical terms. Furthermore, it must be recognized that the quality of the factors derived can only be as good as the composite quality of the pool of criterion items.

Factor analysis is a very flexible tool and can be used in many contexts. Hopkins, Hetherington, and Parsons (1975) employed this technique in an attempt to identify sets of services that were indicative of the quality of patient care. They were interested in obtaining very general subsets of procedures which could then be used to describe and measure the essence of medical care for virtually all diseases or conditions encountered by physicians. In the present study, performance criteria (or procedures) were factor analyzed for each particular disease or problem which differs from the larger scale objectives and analyses of Hopkins and his colleagues. Both studies, however, are in complete agreement on one thing: that quality of care is not defined along some unitary dimension but is most accurately conceptualized as a multidimensional process. Whether such dimensions are best specified within individual diagnostic categories or across all categories is an issue which requires further examination.

USE OF ANALYSIS OF VARIANCE AND T-TESTS ON PERFORMANCE FACTORS

Many variables can be viewed as potential determinants of the quality of care provided by a physician. Two of the most conspicuous are the setting in which care is delivered and the specialty of the physician. In one of the first sets of analyses undertaken, scores on each performance factor in each topic were analyzed in a two-way analysis of variance. Both setting and specialty were examined for their effects on physician performance; the analysis of variance approach allowed the effects of each to be analyzed separately as well as conjointly. In all cases, there were two levels or classifications of setting: private practice office and hospital outpatient clinic. Two or three levels of specialty were involved, depending on the topic. For example, in Otitis Media almost all patients were treated by general practitioners or pediatricians, providing only two levels of specialty. Cases of Pharyngitis were treated by physicians in all three specialties: general practice, internal medicine and pediatrics. Thus, all analyses of variance were of a 2 × 2 or 2 × 3 design. An example of a 2 × 3 design, used to analyze performance on each of the factors in Pharyngitis, is given below. If performance on the physical exam factor was being analyzed, then cell *a* would contain all physical exam performance scores for general practitioners in a private practice setting, cell *b* would contain all physical exam scores for general practitioners in a hospital setting, and so on for the remaining four cells.

Example of the Analysis of Variance Design Applied to Pharyngitis

Setting	Specialty		
	General Practice	Internal Medicine	Pediatrics
Private Practice	a	c	e
Hospital	b	d	f

The analysis of variance approach was not applicable to the Well-Child topics. Cases were handled by pediatricians in both private and hospital practice settings, but very few cases were treated by general practitioners in the hospital setting. Therefore, only three of the four cells in a 2 × 2 design could be filled, making it impossible to carry out the analysis of variance approach. For these topics, t-tests were performed between mean performance scores according to specialty.

Presentation of Findings

The results of the analyses of variance computed for each performance factor in Adult Abdominal Pain, Chest Pain, Hypertension, Urinary Tract Infection, Pharyngitis, Otitis Media, and Pediatric Abdominal Pain are shown in Tables 7.2b through 7.8b. These tables will be found on pages 138–139. Results of t-tests for the performance factors in the two Well-Child topics are displayed in Tables 7.9b and 7.10b.

There are two components to each of the first seven tables. Part *a* indicates the actual mean performance score on each factor in the topics, presented by specialty and practice setting. Part *b* presents a statistical summary of the analysis of variance for each factor. It contains the F value and the level of significance for the effects of setting and specialty and their interaction. A statistically significant effect on a performance score for setting would imply that there is a significant difference in the mean level of performance on that factor between hospital and private practice physicians. Similarly, a statistically significant effect for specialty shown in Part *b* of a table implies that there are significant differences in the performance of physicians by specialty.

When a statistically significant interaction exists between setting and specialty for a performance factor, the implication is that some unique combination of the two variables, setting and specialty, influenced performance in a way that could not be detected by examining the effects of either variable alone. Part *a* of the tables also reveals the mean performance score for a combination of specialty and setting. For tables 7.9 and 7.10, the mean levels of performance are reported in Part *a* and the t-value and its associated level of significance in Part *b*.

Part *b* of each table also includes a measure of the strength of the total effects of setting, specialty and their interaction on each performance factor. For Tables 7.2 through 7.8 this measure is based on the amount of variance in the performance scores which is directly attributable to the total effects of setting, specialty, and their interaction; it is presented in terms of the percent of variance in performance on each factor which can be accounted for by the setting and specialty conditions under which care was given. For the Well-Child topics (Tables 7.9 and 7.10) these measures represent the percent of variance in performance which can be attributed to the specialty of the physician performing the examination. Strengths of effects are reported because the occurrence of a statistically significant result implies only that some effect of setting or specialty exists, but it does not yield information about the magnitude of that effect. Furthermore, there are large sample sizes in the present study and this greatly enhances the likelihood of obtaining statistically significant results: the measure of the strength of effects is less affected by sample size. Thus, the measure of the percent of variance accounted for by the independent variables provides an additional bit of information in evaluating the influence of setting and specialty on physician performance. (For a further discussion of strength of effect measures, see Hays 1971.)

Part *a* of each table also contains a listing of the individual criterion items which go together to comprise each performance factor in the topics. While the actual descriptive labels given to the factors might seem somewhat arbitrary, this display of items adds a measure of concreteness and clarity to their interpretation.

Performance factors or categories called Residual and Global appear in every topic. These are not true factors in the same sense as all of the other factors of performance since they were not formulated in the same manner. The Residual factor is simply made up of all of the original criterion items which did not associate with a specific factor during the analyses of the criteria sets: they are "leftovers." Performance on these items is not related to performance on items comprising the true factors, nor are performance scores on any of the items within the Residual category interrelated. Unlike the true performance factors which reflect meaningful, homogeneous groups of individual criteria, the Residual items are a heterogeneous cluster, a diverse collection of criteria which do not represent a singular aspect of physician performance. Although these Residual items have been retained and performance scores computed for this category, no attempt has been made to interpret their meaning.

Criteria on which there was less than 9 percent or greater than 91 percent compliance were also excluded from the calculation of the levels of performance. During the process of factor analyzing the data, these items automatically fell into Residual, as might be expected. The extremes which approximate total noncompliance (or, rarely, total compliance) prevent the rational inclusion of these items in the assessment of differences in care.

The Global category reflects the overall, average performance score for all criteria in a topic, irrespective of the factor with which different items were associated. It is a grand summary measure of physician performance which ignores any differences in the various dimensions of performance. Such summary scores have been reported many times in other research on the quality of care (Payne and Lyons 1972).

Results of Analysis of Variance and T-tests

Adult Abdominal Pain. In examining Table 7.2 it is apparent that scores on the performance factors tend to be higher when care is delivered in a hospital setting. This was the case for five of the six performance factors—Abdomen, Bowel Movement, Nausea, Diagnosis and Lab—the one exception was History. The Residual and Global categories also reflected this trend of differences, which are significant at the .001 level. Table 7.2 also shows that specialists in internal medicine had significantly higher performance scores on all factors and categories except History. The only significant interaction ($p < .001$) appears on the Diagnosis factor; this shows that hospital internists had the highest performance score on this factor and it was enhanced by the hospital setting. However, their performance score was higher than could have been predicted by the additive effects of setting and specialty. The strength of effects of setting and specialty on performance in this topic are moderate, considering the rather broad nature of setting and specialty variables.

Chest Pain. On three of the five performance factors shown in Table 7.3—Physical Exam, Symptom 1 and Symptom 2—hospital physician performance surpassed that of private practitioners, and the performance of internists surpassed that of general practitioners on four of the five performance factors. The greatest differences in performance in this topic can be seen on the Symptom 1 factor, where the performance scores of internists in hospital settings were much higher than those of private practice general practitioners. On certain factors, such as Physical Exam and Symptom 1, the influence of setting and specialty on performance was quite strong.

Hypertension. Nine performance factors were developed for Hypertension, the largest number for any one topic (Table 7.4). The effects of setting and specialty on these factors are displayed in Part *b* of the table. On five of the nine factors—General Follow-up, First Visit, First Lab, Eyes and Blood Pressure Check—hospital physician performance scores were significantly higher than those of private practice physicians; there were differences on the other four factors. The effects of specialty are very consistent: performance scores of internists were significantly higher than those of general practitioners on seven of the nine factors. Significant interactions were found on two factors, First Visit and Eyes. These interactions indicated that the performance level of hospital internists was much higher than that of private practice general practitioners on these factors. Interestingly, the strongest effects of setting and specialty are seen on the factors which reflect the quality of care delivered during the initial patient-physician encounter (e.g., First Visit, First Lab, Eyes); the effects of setting and specialty are much weaker on factors which define the quality of care given on subsequent occasions.

Urinary Tract Infection. On four of the five performance factors in UTI (displayed in Table 7.5) significant effects were found for the influence of setting. On three of these factors—Pain, Lab, and Diagnostic History—performance in private practice was below the level displayed in hospitals. A reversal of this pattern appears for the Previous Treatment factor, where physician performance in private offices exceeded performance in hospitals. UTI is often recurrent and, since private practitioners tend to have a more stable patient population, they are perhaps more likely to incorporate information about previous treatment in the handling of a specific case of UTI. There are significant effects for specialty on each performance factor in this topic, with internists consistently scoring higher than general practitioners. As in Adult Abdominal Pain, an interaction existed on the Diagnosis factor such that internists in hospital settings displayed the highest level of performance on this factor. The effects in this topic are somewhat weaker than those displayed in other topics.

Pharyngitis. Pharyngitis is the topic which had the largest number of sample cases; therefore, one would expect to find many statistically significant effects. Table 7.6 demonstrates the usefulness of calculating and reporting a measure of the strength of effects of setting and specialty. Despite the heavier volume of cases, the strength of effects reported in Table 7.6b are comparable in magnitude to those reported for other topics. Examination of only the levels of significance and their frequency of appearance in each topic, followed by a comparison across topics, could be misleading. It would appear that setting and specialty were more important determinants of physician performance in Pharyngitis than in other topics because almost all effects were statistically significant in this topic. Overall, the results show that performance scores in this topic, on all factors, tend to be higher when care is delivered in hospitals than in private offices, and higher when delivered by internists and pediatricians than by general practitioners. The highest performance scores were obtained by internists and pediatricians treating cases in hospital settings.

Otitis Media. Performance factors for Otitis Media are presented in Table 7.7. Part *b* of the table shows that setting has a significant effect on four of the five factors. On three of these factors—Follow-up 1, Follow-up 2 and Disease—performance in hospitals surpassed the level displayed in the private practice setting. The reverse is true on the History factor. Only one performance factor revealed any significant differences in care according to specialty: performance scores of pediatricians were significantly higher on the Treatment factor than were scores of general practitioners. One significant interaction exists on the Follow-up 1 factor, which shows that pediatricians in hospitals received the highest performance scores for this factor and general practitioners in private practice the lowest. The effects of setting and specialty in this topic are noteworthy on Disease and Follow-up 1 but they are negligible on the other performance factors.

Pediatric Abdominal Pain. Six measures of performance in Pediatric Abdominal Pain were employed: four performance factors and the Residual and Global categories (Table 7.8). Part *b* of the table shows that specialty had virtually no effect on performance in this topic, as measured by the factors, but there were significant effects for setting on three of the four factors. As in Adult Abdominal Pain, the level of performance tended to be higher when care was given in a hospital setting. Again, there was one significant interaction, on the Vomiting factor, where hospital pediatricians displayed superior performance to physicians in other combinations of setting and specialty. The effect of setting and specialty are moderate in this topic.

Well-Child Examination (Infant).   Note that in this topic, as well as in the Preschool Examination, no data exist for cases encountered by general practitioners in hospital settings (Table 7.9a). Thus, the analyses performed in these topics differ slightly. Two sets of t-tests were performed in each. One set examined the difference in performance between two specialties in one setting, and the other examined the difference in two settings for one specialty.

For the Well-Infant Examination, as shown in Table 7.9b, significant differences were shown between general practitioners and pediatricians in private practice settings, with the latter group obtaining higher performance scores on four of the six factors. There was no difference in the other two. The effects of setting on physician performance could only be assessed for pediatricians. Consistent with findings in other topics, the hospital setting generally tended to have a positive effect on physician performance. Of the six performance factors, two show no difference in performance between pediatricians in private practice and pediatricians in hospital settings; however, the remaining four showed performance levels in the latter settings to be significantly higher. Note that the strength of effects reported in Table 7.9b as well as in Table 7.10b are slightly smaller than those reported in Tables 7.2 to 7.8. This is because the strength of effects measures in Tables 7.9 and 7.10 were calculated on the basis of only one variable at a time (specialty or setting), whereas the strength of effects measures reported in the previous tables were based on the sum of the effects of setting, specialty, and their interaction.

Well-Child Examination (Preschool).   The same analytical approach adopted in the Well-Infant Examination was used for the Preschool topic. Table 7.10b reveals significant differences in performance in private practice settings according to the specialty of the physician on three of the four performance factors—Physical Exam, History and Size—and no difference on Follow-up. Again, pediatricians received higher performance scores than general practitioners on these three factors. Within the pediatric specialty, the Physical Exam factor demonstrated the only significant difference in performance according to the setting in which the cases were encountered. The strength of effects reported in Table 7.10b are smaller than those reported in Table 7.2 to 7.8, as explained above.

Results in Residual and Global Categories

The Residual Category. The performance criteria found in the residual category are those which failed to associate with other groups of criteria when the full set of items was factor analyzed. The reason for categorizing these heterogeneous criteria was to display them with the performance factors for each topic. Although there are significant effects of specialty and setting on scores in this category for virtually all of the topics, it is not really meaningful to make an inference about differences in physician performance according to these effects.

The Global Category. A performance score in this category is the average performance of physicians on all of the criteria for the disease or problem area. That is, performance was assessed without regard for performance factors or other groupings of the criteria set. In this sense, the scores in the global category represent a grand summary measure of performance.

Performance scores in the Global category of each topic show significant differences due to the effects of setting and specialty, and it is interesting to compare this information with the results obtained when performance factors were used to assess physician performance. Using Chest Pain as an example, the contrast between the quality of information conveyed by reporting a summary measure of perform-ance and that which is conveyed by reporting scores on performance factors can be highlighted.

The Global score shows that performance in hospital settings was significantly more aligned with the criteria than was performance in private practice. Internists performed significantly better than general practitioners. This is meaningful information, but it falls short because the global score inherently regards physician performance as unidi-mensional. As discussed earlier, it is only logical to conceive of the delivery of medical care by a physician as a multidimensional process. The performance factors obtained in this study demonstrate the different dimensions of the process of patient care which make up the whole. A gross summary measure is less meaningful because it masks the different components of physician performance. It is more useful to know how performance differs than to know only that it does differ.

TABLE 7.2a

Performance Measures on Adult Abdominal Pain by Setting and Specialty

Performance Factors and Other Categories	Practice Setting						All Physicians
	Private Practice			Hospital			
	All Private	GP	IM	All Hospital	GP	IM	
Abdomen	.29	.22	.35	.59	.52	.65	.35
Bowel Movement	.19	.12	.13	.32	.25	.38	.22
Nausea	.21	.14	.27	.57	.50	.63	.28
Diagnosis	.41	.35	.46	.65	.59	.70	.44
History	.31	.29	.31	.30	.28	.31	.31
Lab	.26	.23	.29	.41	.38	.44	.29
Residual	.28	.24	.31	.41	.37	.45	.31
Global	.28	.23	.32	.47	.42	.51	.32
No. of Sample Cases	212	93	119	146	35	111	358

Abdomen Factor includes—abdominal rebound; abdominal guarding; abdominal tenderness; abdominal masses.

Bowel Movement Factor includes—rectal exam; diarrhea; melena; rectal bleeding; stool character.

Nausea Factor includes—nausea; vomiting; hematemesis.

Diagnosis Factor includes—constant pain; persistent pain; onset of pain; affecting factors; food and drugs; working diagnosis; pulse, blood pressure; pelvic exam; relationship of menses to pain; temperature; chest exam.

History Factor includes—history of studies; previous pain; history of surgery; history of injuries.

Lab Factor includes CBC and urinalysis.

Residual Category includes—type of pain; current events; other points of pain; location of pain; radiation; fever; *dyspepsia; abdominal distension; visual inspection of abdomen; bowel sounds; occult blood; final diagnosis; medication; new appointment.

Global Category includes—all criterion items in Abdomen Factor, Bowel Movement Factor, Nausea Factor, Diagnosis Factor, History Factor, Lab Factor and Residual Category.

*91 percent or more did not comply with this criterion item.

TABLE 7.2b

Results of Analyses of Variance on Performance Factors in Adult Abdominal Pain

Performance Factors and Other Categories	Setting		Specialty		Interaction		Strength of Effects: % Variance Explained
	F	Signif. of F	F	Signif. of F	F	Signif. of F	
Abdomen	184.75	.001	46.98	.001	1.52	ns	14.6
Bowel Movement	52.28	.001	81.81	.001	3.24	ns	9.0
Nausea	278.82	.001	44.48	.001	1.03	ns	19.2
Diagnosis	368.45	.001	82.50	.001	14.37	.001	24.7
History*	<1	ns	3.14	ns	<1	ns	0.3
Lab	37.30	.001	8.74	.003	1.81	ns	3.3
Residual	260.59	.001	120.58	.001	1.87	ns	22.0
Global	338.59	.001	117.66	.001	4.23	ns	25.2

*Only significance levels of .005 or lower were considered acceptable to be reported for these analyses.

TABLE 7.3a
Performance Measures on Chest Pain by Setting and Specialty

Performance Factors and other Categories	Practice Setting						All Physicians
	Private Practice			Hospital			
	All Private	GP	IM	All Hospital	GP	IM	
Physical Exam	.28	.12	.40	.51	.35	.63	.34
History	.26	.15	.33	.25	.16	.32	.26
Symptom 1	.12	.07	.15	.47	.42	.50	.21
Follow-up	.61	.53	.67	.63	.55	.69	.62
Symptom 2	.18	.05	.27	.34	.21	.45	.22
Residual	.21	.14	.26	.35	.28	.40	.25
Global	.28	.18	.35	.43	.33	.50	.32
No. of Sample Cases	62	29	33	70	12	58	132

Physical Exam Factor includes—murmur, gallop, rubs (friction, pleural, pericardial), organ size, auscultation of chest, percussion of chest, auscultation of abdomen, abdominal masses, heart rhythm, frequency.

History Exam includes—treatment for previous problem, history diagnosis for previous problems, history of prior restrictions, history previous experience, acceptance of prior restrictions, smoking history, history nitroglycerine effect, pain aggravated by time of day.

Symptom 1 Factor includes—temperature, fever, cough, pulse, respiration, chills.

Follow-up Factor includes—is condition improving?, is problem yielding to medication?, ECG.

Symptom 2 Factor includes—difficulty breathing, eructation, aggravated by exercise or physical activity, presence of dyspnea, vomiting.

Residual Category includes—*chest pain, †chest fullness, †chest ache, †chest pressure, †chest cramps, †gas, location of chest pain, radiation, onset, mode of onset, duration, quality, aggravated by body position or motion, aggravated by respiration or swallowing, diaphoresis, nausea, †hemoptysis, dizziness, †syncope, †dysphagia, abdominal pain, aggravated by stress or anxiety, history nitroglycerine prescribed, occupation, past chest injury, blood pressure, description of appearance, description of emotional state, fundoscopic exam, †description of sputum, neck veins distended, cervical nodes, †relation of pain to movement of neck, †chest wall tenderness, †location of apex beat, status venous circulation of legs, status arterial circulation of legs, hematocrit, urinalysis, final diagnosis, working diagnosis.

Global Catetory includes—all of the criterion items in Physical Exam Factor; History Exam Factor; Symptom 1 Factor; Followup Factor; Symptom 2 Factor; and Residual Category.

*91 percent or more did comply with this criterion item.
†91 percent or more did not comply with this criterion item.

TABLE 7.3b
Results of Analyses of Variance on Performance Factors in Chest Pain

Performance Factors and Other Categories	Setting		Specialty		Interaction		Strength of Effects: % Variance Explained
	F	Signif. of F	F	Signif. of F	F	Signif. of F	
Physical Exam	37.15	.001	98.04	.001	7.49	ns	28.6
History	3.53	ns	42.56	.001	<1	ns	9.0
Symptom 1	302.39	.001	<1	ns	11.36	.001	42.3
Follow-up	<1	ns	16.54	.001	8.66	.004	3.7
Symptom 2	17.00	.100	75.21	.001	2.89	ns	21.2
Residual	78.30	.001	61.06	.001	7.93	.005	29.6
Global	66.12	.001	135.04	.001	14.52	.001	37.2

Table 7.4a

Performance Measures on Hypertension by Setting and Specialty

Performance Factors and Other Categories	Practice Setting						All Physicians
	Private Practice			Hospital			
	All Private	GP	IM	All Hospital	GP	IM	
General Follow-up	.40	.39	.41	.59	.58	.60	.41
First Visit	.20	.10	.29	.49	.38	.57	.21
Follow-up Eye Exam	.03	.01	.05	.06	.04	.08	.03
First Lab	.25	.13	.34	.65	.53	.74	.27
Initial Eye Exam	.07	.02	.12	.36	.31	.40	.08
Family History	.15	.08	.20	.25	.18	.30	.15
Symptoms Follow-up	.04	.02	.05	.05	.03	.06	.04
BP Check	.26	.27	.26	.44	.45	.44	.27
Basics	.70	.65	.74	.77	.72	.81	.70
Residual	.28	.24	.31	.33	.27	.36	.28
Global	.23	.18	.27	.41	.36	.45	.24
No. of Sample Cases	654	265	389	102	4	98	756

General Follow-up Factor includes annual BP checks, annual symptoms review (visual disturbance, angina, nocturia, muscle cramps, sweating), 12 mo. neurology and chest exam, 12 mo. check for edema, ocular fundi, side effects from meds, repeat chest x-ray, repeat ECG, repeat urinalysis, repeat BUN/creatinine, repeat electrolytes, sugar uric acid, and ANF; follow-up blood pressure readings; heart exam (size, sounds, murmurs, rales).

First Visit Factor includes history of visual disturbance, angina, nocturia, urinary tract infection; exam for heart sounds, size, murmurs, rales; abdominal exam for bruits and masses; check peripheral pulses DTRS, check for pitting edema.

Follow-up Eye Exam Factor includes follow-up history of visual disturbance; follow-up eye exam including ocular disks, retinal vessels; check for hemorrhages and exudates.

First Lab Factor includes urinalysis, BUN/creatinine, hemoglobin/hematocrit, serum electrolytes, chest x-ray and ECG.

Initial Eye Exam Factor includes check retinal vessels for hemorrhages and exudates.

Family History Factor includes family history of hypertension, family history of neurologic disorder, family history of cardiovascular and/or renal disease.

Symptoms Follow-up Factor includes follow-up history of angina, nocturia, muscle cramps; follow-up examination of abdomen for masses, and peripheral pulses.

Blood Pressure Check includes recording of baseline and six month BPs.

Basics includes weight, urinalysis and notation of blood pressure.

Residual Category includes follow-up BP, follow-up check of retinal vessels and ocular discs for hemorrhages, annual urinalysis, *BP in all positions, *BP at current visit, *instructions for low salt diet and weight reduction, regularly scheduled follow-ups, *history of weakness, follow-up history of weakness, instructions to discontinue birth control pills if female.

Global Category includes all criterion items in all the above factors plus all items in the Residual Category.

*91 percent or more did not comply with this criterion item.

TABLE 7.4b
Results of Analyses of Variance on Performance Factors in Hypertension

Performance Factors and Other Categories	Setting		Specialty		Interaction		Strength of Effects: % Variance Explained
	F	Signif. of F	F	Signif. of F	F	Signif. of F	
General Follow-up	34.82	.001	1.49	ns	3.28	ns	1.1
First Visit	158.72	.001	679.63	.001	11.81	.001	20.9
Follow-up Eyes	3.90	ns	88.43	.001	<1	ns	2.7
First Lab	13.93	.001	484.82	.001	3.40	ns	18.4
Eyes	233.47	.001	121.41	.001	18.02	.001	10.3
Family History	7.19	ns	244.25	.001	2.36	ns	6.9
Symptom Follow-up	<1	ns	77.49	.001	<1	ns	2.1
Blood Pressure Check	28.67	.001	2.71	ns	<1	ns	0.8
Basics	2.65	ns	65.75	.001	2.00	ns	2.0
Residual	9.60	.002	327.91	.001	<1	ns	9.1
Global	179.33	.001	358.23	.001	7.64	ns	14.8

The results of the Chest Pain analyses reveal that the setting in which care is delivered has an effect on certain dimensions of physician performance (as reflected in Physical Exam, Symptom 1 and Symptom 2) but not on others (as reflected in History and Follow-up). Also, the specialty of the provider is seen to have a significant influence on four of the five performance dimensions.

The specificity of the multidimensional approach to the assessment of the quality of ambulatory care, as opposed to the unidimensional or summary score approach, has major implications for monitoring and continuing medical education. If deficiencies in quality of care are revealed in a medical audit, and the results of the audit are used in making policy decisions (such as those involving recertification, relicensure, etc.), these decisions are likely to increase in rationality (i.e., quality) as the specificity of information on which they are based increases. For example, the policy decisions made with regard to physicians whose performance is deficient on all of the dimensions of care for a given diagnostic category or disease are likely to be very different from those made about physicians whose performance is found to be deficient in only one aspect of care for that same disease or category. Only a multidimensional approach to quality of care would yield this type of information. Similarly, by knowing in which aspects of care physicians tend to be deficient and in which they excel, continuing medical education programs can be developed

TABLE 7.5a
Performance Measures on Urinary Tract Infection by Setting and Specialty

Performance Factors and Other Categories	Practice Setting						All Physicians
	Private Practice			Hospital			
	All Private	GP	IM	All Hospital	GP	IM	
Pain	.28	.17	.39	.50	.39	.61	.33
Previous Treatment	.30	.27	.33	.18	.15	.21	.27
Lab	.53	.45	.61	.88	.80	.96	.61
Diagnostic History	.31	.22	.40	.52	.43	.61	.36
Severe	.17	.09	.24	.17	.09	.24	.17
Residual	.24	.22	.26	.33	.31	.35	.26
Global	.30	.23	.37	.42	.35	.49	.33
No. of Sample Cases	69	35	34	73	15	58	142

Pain Factor includes pain with description; onset; location of pain; relation of pain to urination?; temperature; abdominal exam; CVA tenderness; signs and symptoms more severe.
Previous Treatment Factor includes hospitalization for urologic problems; surgery for urologic prob.; hx urologic problems; drug treatment for urologic prob.; recurrent episode?
Lab Factor includes urine culture; urinalysis; sediment exam.
Diagnostic History Factor includes other signs and symptoms present; onset and description of frequency; advise extra fluids.
Severe Factor includes fever; blood in urine; chills.
Residual Category includes onset of other signs and symptoms; drug allergies; vaginal discharge; description of bladder; pregnant; sulfonamides; *ampicillin; *Azogantrisin; why medicated; *need for continued surveillance; follow-up scheduled?, visit one week post-treatment with antibiotics; patient asymptomatic; *tetracycline; signs and symptoms no longer present; *color; *turbidity; *clarity; *description of kidneys; *nitrofurantoin; *cephalosporins; *urised; *explain common, benign nature of disease; *call if reaction to drugs; *call if fever, chills, back pain; *call if not well in 5–7 days.
Global Category includes all criterion items in Pain Factor, Previous Treatment Factor, Lab Factor, Diagnostic History Factor; Severe Factor; and Residual Category.

*91 percent did not comply with this criterion item.

TABLE 7.5b
Results of Analyses of Variance on Performance Factors in Urinary Tract Infection

Performance Factors and Other Categories	Setting		Specialty		Interaction		Strength of Effects: % Variance Explained
	F	Signif. of F	F	Signif. of F	F	Signif. of F	
Pain	28.77	.001	57.23	.001	5.48	ns	18.4
Previous Treatment	20.20	.001	10.32	.002	<1	ns	4.8
Lab	86.86	.001	10.13	.002	<1	ns	19.3
Diagnostic History	28.09	.001	36.47	.001	17.59	.001	14.3
Severe	3.29	ns	43.21	.001	9.16	.003	7.9
Residual	43.22	.001	3.05	ns	<1	ns	10.0
Global	42.78	.001	105.69	.001	15.66	.001	27.4

TABLE 7.6a
Performance Measures on Pharyngitis by Setting and Specialty

Performance Factors and Other Categories	Practice Setting								All Physicians
	Private Practice				Hospital				
	All Private	GP	IM	PED	All Hospital	GP	IM	PED	
Instruction	.00	.00	.03	.00	.05	.04	.08	.04	.01
Diagnosis	.48	.38	.52	.55	.92	.82	.96	.99	.53
Throat Exam	.58	.40	.74	.66	.82	.64	.98	.90	.61
Ear Exam	.24	.08	.37	.32	.64	.48	.77	.72	.29
Residual	.35	.33	.42	.33	.43	.41	.49	.41	.36
Global	.33	.24	.41	.37	.57	.48	.65	.61	.36
No. of Sample Cases	643	206	126	311	258	68	106	84	901

Instruction Factor includes explanation of vital concern for strep infection and need for culture.
Diagnosis Factor includes working diagnosis and final diagnosis.
Throat Exam Factor includes exam of tonsils, pharynx, cervical nodes, chief complaint, pharyngeal culture.
Ear Exam Factor includes exam of ear canal and tympanic membranes.
Residual Category includes cough, fever, *history of rheumatic fever, recurrent infection, history of smoking, allergy history, *rhinorrhea, *hoarseness, vomiting, temperature, skin rash, *diffuse adenopathy, cardiac auscultation, abdominal palpation, *CBC, *mononucleosis, *tetracycline, *sulfa, penicillin, *bicillin, erythromycin, other medication, follow-up scheduled?, second culture taken?, *notification of family members about strep.
Global Category includes all criterion items.

*91 percent did not comply with this criterion item.

TABLE 7.6b
Results of Analyses of Variance on Performance Factors in Pharyngitis

Performance Factors and Other Categories	Setting		Specialty		Interaction		Strength of Effects: % Variance Explained
	F	Signif. of F	F	Signif. of F	F	Signif. of F	
Instruction	47.52	.001	31.58	.001	20.97	.001	3.5
Diagnosis	446.26	.001	58.88	.001	4.76	ns	14.1
Throat Exam	218.49	.001	457.79	.001	37.46	.001	25.4
Ear Exam	315.48	.001	152.24	.001	18.67	.001	15.9
Residual	209.61	.001	176.93	.001	40.25	.001	15.6
Global	913.71	.001	400.77	.001	26.31	.001	34.4

TABLE 7.7a
Performance Measures on Otitis Media by Setting and Specialty

Performance Factors and Other Categories	Practice Setting						All Physicians
	Private Practice			Hospital			
	All Private	GP	PED	All Hospital	GP	PED	
Treatment	.20	.12	.22	.22	.14	.25	.20
Follow-up	.19	.17	.19	.52	.50	.52	.24
Follow-up 2	.03	.01	.03	.04	.02	.04	.03
Disease	.46	.48	.44	.81	.83	.79	.52
History	.05	.04	.05	.01	.00	.04	.04
Residual	.19	.16	.19	.29	.26	.29	.21
Global	.18	.15	.18	.30	.27	.30	.20
No. of Sample Cases	257	26	231	119	20	99	376

Treatment Factor includes penicillin; duration and dosage of medication.
Follow-up Factor 1 includes signs and symptoms worse 1st follow-up; no change 1st follow-up; asymptomatic 1st follow-up; mention signs and symptoms 1st follow-up; 1st follow-up improvement of signs and symptoms; follow-up; first follow-up visit; follow-up directions.
Follow-up Factor 2 includes no change 2nd follow-up; signs and symptoms worse 2nd follow-up; 2nd follow-up improvement signs and symptoms; asymptomatic 2nd follow-up; mention signs and symptoms 2nd follow-up.
Disease Factor includes tympanic membrane characteristics; chief complaint regarding ear; date of onset; other present respiratory illnesses and symptoms; pharynx description.
History Factor includes hearing problems; adenoidectomy, myringotomy.
Residual Category includes oral decongestants; *swimming; diagnosis; *drums bulging and painful at any time?; description of auditory canal; location of pain; *was there a referral to a specialist?; *ear drainage; *stapes or ossicles visible; past ear infections; *is hearing normal?; ampicillin; analgesics prescribed; *sulfa; *penicillin allergy.
Global Category includes all criterion items in the Treatment, Follow-up 1, Follow-up 2, Disease and History factors, and the Residual Category.

*91 percent or more did not comply with this criterion item.

TABLE 7.7b
Results of Analyses of Variance on Performance Factors in Otitis Media

Performance Factors and Other Categories	Setting		Specialty		Interaction		Strength of Effects: % Variance Explained
	F	Signif. of F	F	Signif. of F	F	Signif. of F	
Treatment	3.10	ns	11.28	.001	<1	ns	1.1
Follow-up 1	238.17	.001	7.52	ns	11.86	.001	16.7
Follow-up 2	8.01	.005	4.55	ns	1.21	ns	0.9
Disease	151.62	.001	<1	ns	<1	ns	11.4
History	10.18	.002	<1	ns	<1	ns	1.0
Residual	248.72	.001	33.11	.001	8.04	.005	18.2
Global	200.58	.001	19.36	.001	<1	ns	15.0

TABLE 7.8a
Performance Measures on Pediatric Abdominal Pain by Setting and Specialty

Performance Factors and Other Categories	Practice Setting						All Physicians
	Private Practice			Hospital			
	All Private	GP	PED	All Hospital	GP	PED	
Physical Exam	.21	.15	.21	.43	.37	.43	.29
Vomiting	.25	.20	.23	.59	.54	.57	.37
Ingestion	.00	.00	.01	.01	.01	.02	.00
Lab	.02	.00	.02	.10	.07	.10	.05
Residual	.16	.13	.16	.25	.22	.25	.19
Global	.13	.10	.13	.28	.25	.28	.18
No. of Sample Cases	52	20	32	53	19	34	105

Physical Exam Factor includes lungs normal, pharynx normal, tonsils normal, abdominal rebound, abdominal guarding, abdomen distended, abdominal masses, and jaundiced.

Vomiting Factor includes vomiting, recurrent vomiting, data of onset, hematemesis.

Ingestion Factor includes pica, foreign substances ingested, food eaten which was possible cause of pain.

Lab Factor includes discussion of tests, stool blood test, appearance of stool, change in appearance of stool, barium enema, blood chemistry, liver function repeat, repeat stool testing.

Residual Category includes type of pain, persistent pain, constant pain; affecting factor; previous pain; *pattern; *relief of pain; pattern change; *parasites; chronic diarrhea; *rectal bleeding; respiratory; urinary; current events; rectal exam; urinalysis; *parasite test; *stool culture; abdominal tenderness; *urine culture; *liver function test; *upper GI series; working diagnosis; referral; CBC; *repeat urinalysis; *repeat urine culture; additional x-rays; consultation; final diagnosis; symptomatic therapy; *discussion of condition; referral follow-ups; emergency room referral.

Global Category includes all criterion items.

*91 percent or more did not comply with this criterion item.

TABLE 7.8b
Results of Analyses of Variance on Performance Factors in Pediatric Abdominal Pain

Performance Factors and Other Categories	Setting		Specialty		Interaction		Strength of Effects: % Variance Explained
	F	Signif. of F	F	Signif. of F	F	Signif. of F	
Physical Exam	58.41	.001	1.85	ns	5.00	ns	16.0
Vomiting	4.58	.001	<1	ns	6.97	.001	26.4
Ingestion	5.56	ns	2.36	ns	3.75	ns	2.0
Lab	35.76	.001	5.22	ns	2.47	ns	13.9
Residual	68.62	.001	6.80	.001	5.87	.003	21.5
Global	176.94	.001	4.41	ns	6.77	.001	36.9

TABLE 7.9a
Performance Measures on Well-Child Examination (Infant) by Setting and Specialty

Performance Factors and Other Categories	Practice Setting					All Physicians
	Private Practice			Hospital		
	All Private	GP	PED	All Hospital	PED	
Physical Exam	.15	.03	.16	.54	.54	.18
Development	.36	.08	.37	.56	.56	.37
Birth	.68	.34	.70	.68	.68	.68
Follow-up	.15	.11	.16	.37	.37	.17
Family	.09	.10	.09	.23	.23	.10
Size	.97	.80	.98	.98	.98	.97
Residual	.28	.21	.28	.34	.34	.28
Global	.38	.24	.39	.53	.53	.39
No. of Sample Cases	476	21	455	125	125	601

Physical Exam Factor includes chest; abdomen; throat; nose; eyes; ears; heart; genitalia; reflexes; extremities.
Development Factor includes sleeping behavior; bowel pattern; feeding behavior; sensory and motor development; social development.
Birth Factor includes head circumference at birth; height at birth; weight at birth; description of pregnancy; type of delivery; chest circumference at birth.
Follow-up Factor includes detection of abnormality; follow-up done?
Family Factor includes family description; family history of illness and death; living situation.
Size Factor includes height and weight.
Residual Category includes *urination; *crying behavior; *hips; *common areas of herniation; *peripheral pulses; urine PKU; hemoglobin/hematocrit; immunization schedule met; tuberculin test; more than one abnormality; was visit scheduled?; *guidance to parent re: behavior; guidance re: feeding; *guidance re: discipline; *guidance re: toilet training; *guidance re: appetite; *response to separation from parents; and behavior in general.

*91 percent or more did not comply with this criterion item.

TABLE 7.9b
Results of T-Tests for Performance Factors in Well-Child Examination (Infant)

Performance Factors and other Categories	Specialty		Strength of Effect: % Variance Explained
	t	Signif. of t	
Physical Exam	10.76	.001	5.3
Development	21.74	.001	18.9
Birth	14.90	.001	9.8
Follow-up	1.34	ns	5.7
Family	<1	ns	0.0
Size	6.17	.001	0.1
Residual	12.77	.001	7.4
Global	14.71	.001	9.6

TABLE 7.10a
Performance Measures on Well-Child Examination (Preschool) by Setting and
Specialty

Performance Factors and Other Categories	Practice Setting					All Physicians
	Private Practice			Hospital		
	All Private	GP	PED	All Hospital	PED	
Physical Exam	.18	.07	.18	.81	.81	.19
History	.23	.05	.24	.26	.26	.23
Follow-up	.17	.16	.17	.22	.22	.17
Size	.95	.52	.97	.95	.95	.95
Residual	.22	.10	.22	.32	.32	.22
Global	.35	.18	.36	.51	.51	.35
No. of Sample Cases	333	13	320	21	21	354

Physical Exam Factor includes eyes; ears; nose; throat; chest; heart; abdomen; genitalia; extremities; reflexes.

History Factor includes bowel pattern; urination pattern; feeding; concern over physical or behavioral problems; speech development; sensory development; motor development; social development and interpersonal relationships.

Follow-up Factor includes detection of abnormality; follow-up done; more than one follow-up.

Size Factor includes height and weight.

Residual Category includes *common areas of herniation; blood pressure; vision; height/weight percentile; was this visit scheduled?; *reference to dental care; reference to school; *attention span, *coordination; *hips; *peripheral pulses; behavior in general; urinalysis; hematocrit; *hemoglobin; tuberculin test.

Global Category includes all criterion items in Physical Exam Factor, History Factor, Follow-up Factor, Size Factor, and Residual Category.

*91 percent or more did not comply with this criterion item.

TABLE 7.10b
Results of T-Tests for Performance Factors in Well-Child Examination (Preschool)

Performance Factors and other Categories	Specialty		Strength of Effect: % Variance Explained
	t	Signif. of *t*	
Physical Exam	4.78	.001	1.5
History	12.27	.001	9.2
Follow-up	<1	ns	0.0
Size	19.09	.001	19.7
Residual	12.06	.001	8.9
Global	12.58	.001	9.6

in accordance with the problems indicated, thus avoiding a blind and inappropriate allocation of resources.

SELECTION AND USE OF ORGANIZATIONAL AND PHYSICIAN CHARACTERISTICS TO EXPLAIN VARIANCE IN PERFORMANCE

From the 108 organizational and physician characteristics on which data were collected, 36 variables were selected as being most significant for the detailed analysis designed to explain differences in performance. There were several steps in the selection process. First, groups of items were rationally determined based on the original areas of investigation suggested by the study Advisory Committees. Examples of these constructs are the nature of the appointment system, management problems and the most gratifying aspect of medicine, which is sometimes referred to as a physician's orientation (i.e., helping or relating to patients, diagnosis, treatment, or teaching). A marker item was selected for each conceptual group of variables. Next, this rational selection process was checked empirically, using a very simple and rudimentary scaling approach. This empirical check suggested that several things could be done to improve the validity of the constructs based on items that were correlated at a .35 level or above, and it resulted in an improved list of variables.

In the initial round of analyses, 55 variables were introduced to explain variation in performance. Experience with use of these variables resulted in further culling until the number of characteristics was reduced to the 36 most explanatory variables. They are shown in Table 7.11 Summary Table of Organizational and Physician Characteristics. The analytical strategy was simple and straightforward.

AUTOGRP (Automated Grouping System) was the data analysis system selected for these analyses (Mills et al. 1976). This interactive system was used to perform nonsymmetrical branching based on variance reduction using the performance factors as dependent variables. The general strategy of AUTOGRP is to search for a set of predictors that increase one's power to account for the variance of the dependent variable. The system facilitates splitting the sample into distinct sets of subgroups which minimizes the unexplained variance of the dependent variable. The user can generate a split at any point in order to divide the particular group into any specified number of subgroups. In the analyses presented here, an upper limit of three subgroups was specified to facilitate interpretations of the findings. In contrast to traditional clustering techniques, AUTOGRP allows a high degree of flexibility and user input in group definition,

TABLE 7.11
Summary Table of Organizational and Physician Characteristics

Organizational Characteristics

Practice setting
Patient volume
Length of average office visit
Presence/absence of an assistant, secretary, nurse, etcetera
Nature of work delegation
Type of appointment system
Number of physicians in the practice
Presence/absence of laboratory facilities

Management problems (presence/absence):
—too much paperwork
—staff feeling overworked
—physician absent or out of the office

Physician Characteristics

Primary specialty
Numbers of years in practice
Number of years of education in U.S.
Type of internship
Country in which physician's medical school was located
Presence/absence of board certification
Presence/absence of faculty appointment
Professional membership in ASIM/AAPD
Type of continuing education, if any
Number of hospital committees in which physician participated

Percent of patient population known well
Frequency with which patients were discussed with colleagues
Extent of patient noncompliance
Extent of patient demands
Extent of trivial patient complaints

Extent of practice interfering with life outside the office/hospital
Most gratifying aspect of practice
Skill developed the most since graduation
Extent of problems with supervisory staff
Satisfaction with caseload
Satisfaction with the organization of practice
Extent of physician's autocratic behavior
Degree to which he/she encourages staff to work autonomously
Degree to which he/she provides (negative) feedback to staff on their performance

resulting in a partitioning that has both statistical and practical meaningfulness.

Percentage of Variance in Performance Explained by Physician, Organizational, and Patient Characteristics

Although the AUTOGRP analyses were conducted on every disease and problem area, only one set of detailed flow diagrams or trees will be discussed in the text (Figures 7.1–7.6). Accompanying each figure are tabulations which provide summaries of the variance partitioning, presenting the total sums of squares explained by each variable. The reader will find the summary tables useful in clarifying the results of the analyses.

Urinary Tract Infection (UTI). Figure 7.1 displays the results of the AUTOGRP analyses for urinary tract infection. Although all of the previously selected organizational and physician characteristics were included in this analysis, most were not significantly related to performance. Therefore they do not all appear in this series of diagrams. In the *pain factor* (Figure 7.1), the tree begins by showing all physicians, their mean performance score (.35), and the number of patients in the sample. Reading from left to right, the first branching of the tree was created by introducing the characteristic, practice

FIGURE 7.1
URINARY TRACT INFECTION
Partitioning of Variance in Performance on *Pain* Factor

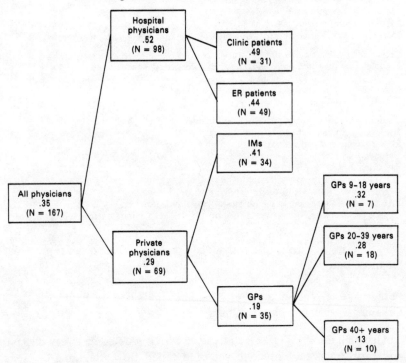

NOTE: Mean value for performance presented in each box.

TABLE 7.12
Order of Importance of Variables in Explaining Variation in Performance
in Urinary Tract Infection

Variable Name	Order of Importance	Variance Reduction*	Total Reduction in Variance
PAIN FACTOR			25.88%
Practice Setting	1	11.95%	
Specialty of Physician	2	8.95	
Number of Years in Practice	3	2.99	
Length of Appointment	4	1.99	
PREVIOUS TREATMENT FACTOR			12.73
Percent of Patients Known Well	1	9.00	
Practice Setting	2	3.73	
LAB FACTOR			40.27
Delegation of Work	1	19.35	
Practice Setting	2	17.89	
Physician Orientation	3	1.72	
Physician Status	4	1.31	
DIAGNOSTIC HISTORY FACTOR			26.97
Length of Appointment	1	13.77	
Practice Setting	2	9.23	
Specialty of Physician	3	2.44	
Physician Status	4	1.53	
SEVERE FACTOR			24.26
Physician Orientation	1	15.89	
Specialty of Physician	2	6.89	
Physician Status	3	1.48	
GLOBAL CATEGORY			39.65
Specialty of Physician	1	16.33	
Practice Setting	2	13.53	
Physician Orientation	3	6.62	
Delegation of Work	4	3.17	

*Variance reduction expressed as percent of Total Sums of Squares explained.

setting, the variable determined to explain the largest amount of variance, with other variables controlled for. Hospital physicians were then grouped according to the location in which they saw their urinary tract patients, while private physicians were branched on primary specialty. Finally, private general practitioners were grouped according to number of years in practice.

Table 7.12 summarizes the results of the variance partitioning process and specifies the order of importance of each of the variables. The relative magnitude of importance can be obtained by examining the last column which contains the percent of the total sums of squares explained by each variable.

Although the sample for urinary tract infection was comparatively small, there was fairly even distribution of cases between general practitioners and internists in private practice and between private and hospital practitioners. Criterion items in the *pain factor* called for both physical and history examination tasks. A description of the onset, location, and relation of pain to urination was required, as were the temperature and results of an abdominal examination. Hospital practitioners behaved more in accordance with criteria than private practitioners on this combined history and diagnostic cluster (see Figure 7.1). More comprehensive histories were taken on hospital patients, especially when they were seen in clinics.

In these analyses practice setting explained more of the variance than any other variables introduced. Internists in private practice received higher scores (.41) than private general practitioners (.19). Their histories resembled histories taken by hospital general practitioners. Generalists who had been in practice for more than 39 years demonstrated a low level of performance (.13). In fact, a decline in performance was observed among internists after their seventeenth year in practice. This pattern is similar to findings reported by Peterson et al. in the 1956 North Carolina study of private general practitioners.

The *previous treatment factor* (Figure 7.2) included criteria requiring a history of previous problems, surgery, and experience with medication. Practice setting was somewhat productive in explaining differences in performance but the degree to which private practitioners knew their patients was more explanatory. Private practitioners who reported knowing a few of their patients received lower scores (.19) as compared with physicians who reported knowing most of their patients (.39). This finding contradicted the working hypothesis of advisors to the study who maintained that doctors who really knew their patients would both provide and record less than doctors who did not know their patients well.

Physician specialty explained a very small portion of variance within the hospital practice and is not included in the Table. Internists and urologists conformed more to these UTI standard criteria.

The *laboratory factor* contained several of the most essential criteria items as determined by the physician panel weighting process. It can be seen from the flow diagram (Figure 7.3) that the population of patients seen by sample physicians is split into two groups based

FIGURE 7.2
URINARY TRACT INFECTION
Partitioning of Variance in Performance on *Previous Treatment* Factor

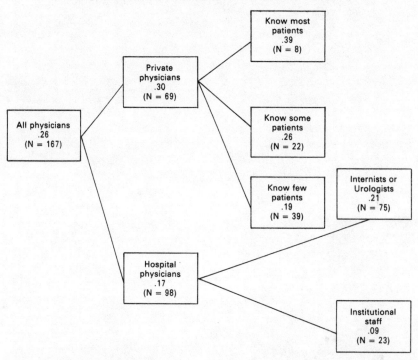

on practice setting. Hospital physicians perform at a higher level (.86) than private practitioners (.53). Difference in performance within private practice could best be explained by the extent and nature of work delegation. Laboratory technicians or other staff members who routinely performed these tasks received higher scores (.66) than physicians who did not (.14). In any event, it was better for a physician to delegate work to another staff member (.39) than it was for him to attempt to complete all of the tasks himself (.14). Fortunately, providers caring for patients presenting with urinary tract infection symptoms were very likely to delegate tasks to their nurses or lab technicians.

The orientation of the physician was also observed to be explanatory but not to the same degree as task delegation. Physicians who were treatment-oriented performed at a higher level (.87) than physicians who preferred the diagnostic process (.64). This finding emerged in accordance with our expectations that physicians who were treatment-

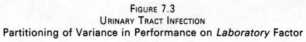

FIGURE 7.3
URINARY TRACT INFECTION
Partitioning of Variance in Performance on *Laboratory* Factor

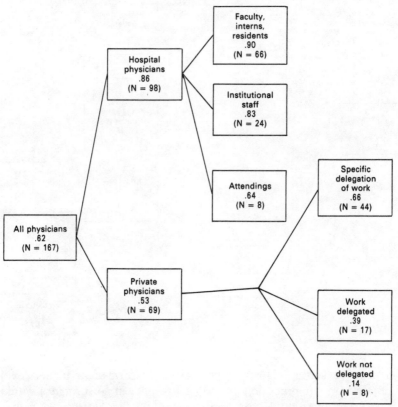

oriented would perform best in providing care for patients presenting with acute illness.

Going back to the earlier part of the tree, note that some variance in performance is explained by the physician's status in the hospital practice. A common occurrence is diagrammed here. Attendings usually do not perform at the same high level as interns and residents or their faculty. Institutional staff usually fall somewhere in between.

The UTI panel included a large number of history items when they developed the standards for this disease. The *diagnostic history factor* called for the history notation of other signs and symptoms present, and a description of the onset and frequency of painful urination (see Figure 7.4). This item cluster empirically included the

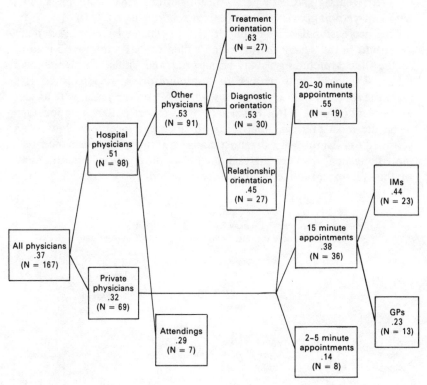

FIGURE 7.4
URINARY TRACT INFECTION
Partitioning of Variance in Performance on *Diagnostic History* Factor

criterion falling between the number of minutes per appointment and
the quality of care according to these criterion items. The longer
a physician spends with a patient, the more likely is the taking of
a more complete history. Note that private practitioners who spent
between two and five minutes per patient received rather low scores
(.14), whereas physicians who spent 15 minutes with their patients
received higher scores of .38. Physicians who spent 20 minutes or
longer with their patients were probably taking more comprehensive
histories. Additional variance was explained by the specialty of private
physicians. Internists received higher scores (.44) than general practitioners (.23).

The care provided to hospital patients was somewhat affected by
the status of the hospital physician. As we noted in the previous
factor, attendings do not perform as well as other physicians (.29

as compared with .53). Although the professional orientation of a physician was not highly explanatory in this factor, physicians who enjoyed treating patients performed "better" (.63) than physicians who enjoyed diagnosis (.53) or patient relationships (.45).

The professional orientation of the physician became extremely important in the *severe factor* which called for a symptomatic history of the illness including fever, hematuria, and chills. As depicted in Figure 7.5, physicians who were treatment-oriented performed at a higher level (.61) than physicians who preferred the diagnostic aspect of medical practice (.16). Physicians who report patient relationships to be the most gratifying aspect of their career received a low mean score (.06). Among the diagnosticians, internists' performance was more congruent with criteria than the behavior of general practitioners. In this factor, practice setting accounted for a very small amount

FIGURE 7.5
URINARY TRACT INFECTION
Partitioning of Variance in Performance on *Severe* Factor

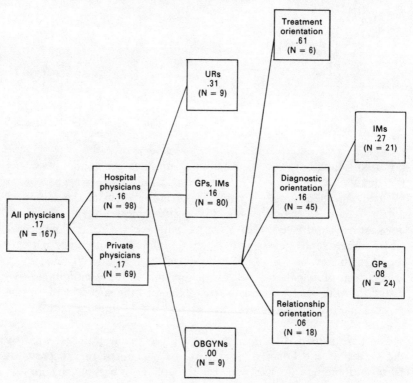

of variance: the split on practice setting was done mainly to provide a picture that could be compared among factors and across acute illnesses.

Hospital practitioners' performance varied widely depending on their specialty. Urologists performed "better" (.31) than general practitioners and internists (.16). Obstetricians earned the low score of .00 on this cluster of items. Physician status explained a very small amount of difference in performance in the hospital setting and was not included in the tree. Again, interns, residents, and their faculty earned higher scores (.29) than physicians of other status.

FIGURE 7.6
URINARY TRACT INFECTION
Partitioning of Variance in Performance on *Global Category*

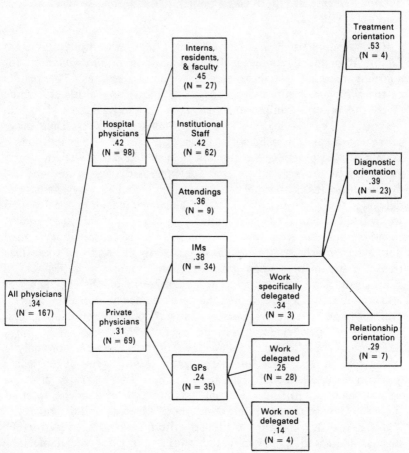

The *global category* includes all criterion items combined and can be viewed as an overall measure of performance. In this category, the residents, interns, and faculty among the hospital practitioners received scores of .45 which were somewhat higher than scores for institutional staff and much higher than attendings (Figure 7.6). Patients seen by treatment-oriented providers were apt to receive care which was more congruent with criteria than patients seen by diagnostic- or relationship-oriented physicians.

Within private practice, the most explanatory variables for the global category were primary specialty, physician orientation, and the nature and type of task delegation in private offices. Internists performed better (.38) than general practitioners (.24). Physicians who delegated work to specific staff also did relatively well (.34); physicians who did not delegate any performed poorly (.14) as compared with those who delegated (.25).

Adult Abdominal Pain. The *abdomen factor* was a physical exam factor. It included standards for examination of the abdomen for guarding rebound, tenderness, and abdominal masses. The results of the variance partitioning process are shown in Table 7.13 which gives the order of importance of each of the variables. Hospital practitioners earned higher scores in this cluster of tasks. Their mean score was .59 as compared with a mean of .29 for private practitioners. Within private practice, the element of task delegation was important as shown by the amount of variance explained. Physicians who did not delegate tasks routinely did not do as well as physicians who delegated tasks to other office staff. The importance of task delegation was related to improved performance, regardless of physician specialty.

In hospital practice physicians who were more seasoned performed better than interns and residents. In this setting an array of specialists treated patients presenting with abdominal pain; specialties ranged from obstetrics to radiology. The performance of obstetricians was less compliant with criteria than the performance of internists, general practitioners, or surgeons. Institutional staff (all general practitioners) and surgeons performed at the high level of .71.

The characteristic that explained most of the variance in our analytic framework in the *bowel movement factor* was the type of internship a physician had selected. This factor included a variety of criterion items which call for rectal exam, examination of the character of the stool, investigation to determine rectal bleeding and diarrhea.

Since the development of these criteria, there has been much discussion regarding the essentiality of looking for rectal bleeding

TABLE 7.13
Order of Importance of Variables in Explaining Variation
in Performance in Adult Abdominal Pain

Variable Name	Order of Importance	Variance Reduction*	Total Reduction in Variance
DIAGNOSIS FACTOR			35.55%
Practice Setting	1	21.80%	
Delegation of Work	2	5.47	
Specialty of Physician	3	4.74	
Physician Orientation	4	3.54	
NAUSEA FACTOR			24.23
Practice Setting	1	12.62	
Specialty of Physician	2	6.43	
Physician Orientation	3	3.60	
Delegation of Work	4	1.38	
BOWEL MOVEMENT FACTOR			14.67
Type of Internship	1	6.98	
Practice Setting	2	2.81	
Specialty of Physician	3	2.46	
Physician Orientation	4	2.42	
ABDOMEN FACTOR			20.81
Practice Setting	1	13.22	
Delegation of Work	2	4.26	
Specialty of Physician	3	3.33	
LAB FACTOR			15.45
Delegation of Work	1	6.00	
Practice Setting	2	3.58	
Specialty of Physician	3	2.57	
Physician Orientation	4	1.85	
Supervision	5	1.45	
GLOBAL CATEGORY			38.00
Practice Setting	1	17.93	
Delegation of Work	2	12.45	
Specialty of Physician	3	3.18	
Physician Orientation	4	3.08	
Physician Status	5	1.36	

*Variance reduction expressed as percent of Total Sums of Squares explained.

and conducting a rectal exam on patients presenting with abdominal pain unless the pain is recurrent in nature. It was not unexpected to find compliance with this item cluster to be rather low. Despite overall low compliance, physicians with training in medicine performed at a higher level than physicians who chose other types of internships.

Practice setting also explained a small amount of variance. Hospital physicians' performance was most congruent with criterion items. Private practitioners who reported preferring diagnostic aspects of their medical careers did not do as well as physicians who enjoyed helping or relating to their patients. This pattern differed from findings in urinary tract infection; it was expected that treatment-oriented physicians would have met more of the criterion items even in this factor.

The *nausea factor* included a variety of history items such as nausea, vomiting, and presence of hematemesis. Compliance with these criteria was lower than expected with private practitioners demonstrating a mean score of .21, as compared with a mean score of .57 for hospital practitioners. Within private practice a portion of variance is explained by the physician specialty with internists behaving more in accordance with standards than general practitioners. This time, physicians who were diagnostically-oriented received scores which were 20 points higher than physicians who preferred other aspects of medical practice. These findings contradicted results of the analyses of the abdominal factor. A significant but very small portion of the variance was explained by task delegation. Physicians who did not delegate work to their assistants, either because they did not employ other staff or because they did not use them appropriately, received a mean score of .05, in contrast to the score of .20 for physicians who delegated work.

The *diagnostic factor* was a mixture of physical exam and history items. Overall compliance with these criteria was a little higher perhaps because of the nature of the criteria included; compared with sets of criteria developed by other organizations or study groups, these items seem quite reasonable, with the exception of the requirement for a pelvic examination. A history of the nature and onset of the pain, possible contributing factors to the pain, a working diagnosis, pulse and blood pressure, are included in the cluster. Most of the variance in our analytic framework was explained by practice setting, with hospital practitioners receiving higher scores than their colleagues in private practice. Private practitioners performed more in congruence with criteria if they delegated tasks than if they tried to do everything themselves. Private internists received higher scores than general practitioners. Among the internists, those who were relationship-oriented did better than physicians who were diagnostic- or treatment-oriented.

Hospital physicians' performance differed somewhat with physician status, but status explained less than one percent of the variation.

The second *history factor* in adult abdominal pain included standards requiring data on previous studies of previous episodes of abdominal pain and previous surgery or injuries, which might contribute to these symptoms. Scores for practitioners in both settings in both specialties hovered around the thirtieth percentile (.30). Although practice setting and a physician's professional status within the hospital accounted for a very small amount of variance, it was cumulatively less than one percent. (For this reason, there is no table for variance reduction in the history factor.)

The *lab factor* included criteria requiring a CBC and urinalysis on all patients presenting with abdominal pain. Some variance in performance was explained by practice setting; as expected, CBCs and urinalyses were more likely to be routinely done for hospital patients. In private practice, most variance, in our analytic framework, was explained by the presence and extent of task delegation. Private practitioners who did not delegate work performed at the .03 level, whereas those who delegated tasks to other staff received higher scores (.24 mean). Physicians who employed laboratory technicians demonstrated higher mean performance (.44); in this case, work was specifically and routinely delegated to one person.

Within private practice, specialty accounted for a small portion of variance, with internists providing care which was most congruent with criteria. The professional orientation of the physician and the extent to which he was disturbed by supervisory problems also accounted for a small portion of the difference in performance. Physicians who were relationship-oriented earned somewhat higher scores than their colleagues who preferred diagnosis or treatment.

Practice setting and work delegation accounted for most of the explained variance in the *global category*. Compliance among hospital practitioners was much higher. Physicians in private practice who delegated work to a particular person, such as a laboratory technician, received scores which were higher (.46) than physicians whose tasks were not specifically delegated (.27). Physicians who tried to accomplish all of the work themselves received a noticeably lower mean score of .12. Major specialty was explanatory in both practice settings; the practice patterns of internists more closely approximated the criteria than patterns of general practitioners in either setting.

Overall, the results of introducing the variable, a physician's orientation (i.e., preference for relating to or helping the patient, treatment, diagnosis or teaching), produced a confusing picture. In some abdominal pain factors, physicians who were relationship-oriented performed better than physicians who were treatment-oriented. In the global category, the supportive, helping physician performed at a much higher level (.32) than the treatment-oriented physician (.00). This was also true in the bowel and nausea factors, which were clusters of patient history items. The relationship-oriented physicians also performed better in the diagnosis factor which was a combination of history and physical examination items, with the emphasis on history.

Chest Pain. One of the intentions of the panel which developed criteria for chest pain was to include branching criteria which would rule out sequentially acute myocardial infarction (AMI), pneumonia, and other prevalent illnesses which presented with symptoms of chest pain. The branching of these criteria was included in a series of complex "if . . . then" statements. Abstracting and coding was geared to the branching system so that physicians would not be docked if many of their patients presented with symptoms related to only one of the branches (i.e., pneumonia/pneumonitis/pneumothorax). For example, physicians were given credit if they did not inquire about history or nitroglycerin when there was good reason to suspect pneumonia. However, the panel felt that it was always important to rule out cardiopulmonary involvement. Physicians were required, in the *physical exam factor,* to search for heart murmur, gallop, rubs, and indication of organ size. Auscultation and percussion of the chest and pulse were also included in the physical exam factor.

Hospital practitioners complied with about half of the criterion items whereas private practitioners' compliance patterns were closer to 30 percent. Therefore, practice setting was an important predictor of performance. Physician specialty in both practice settings was also influential because internists generally performed 20 to 30 score points above general practitioners (see Table 7.14). The degree and specificity of task delegation was also rather important. When a staff member such as a laboratory technician had the responsibility for laboratory tests and procedures, the physician or the practice received much higher scores.

Patient volume (i.e., the number of patients seen) also affected care in this item cluster. Physicians did better on the physical exam if they saw a smaller number of patients. The mean score for practices which saw over 200 patients a week was .12 as compared with a .30 for practices that saw 100 to 150 patients per week. We are not suggesting here that the relationship between number of patients and performance is simple. Patient volume may not only relate to length of time a physician spends with the patients but also to the degree of task delegation present in the organization. A practice which is

TABLE 7.14
Order of Importance of Variables in Explaining Variation
in Performance in Chest Pain

Variable Name	Order of Importance	Variance Reduction*	Total Reduction in Variance
PHYSICAL EXAM FACTOR			43.35%
Specialty of Physician	1	16.04%	
Practice Setting	2	13.09	
Delegation of Work	3	9.78	
Patient Volume	4	2.27	
Percent of Patients Discussed	5	2.17	
HISTORY FACTOR			27.90
Managerial Style of Physician	1	10.48	
Specialty of Physician	2	10.14	
Years of Education in U.S.	3	7.28	
SYMPTOM 1 FACTOR			48.34
Practice Setting	1	42.18	
Specialty of Physician	2	4.19	
Type of Internship	3	1.97	
FOLLOW-UP FACTOR			22.74
Participation in Hospital Committees	1	8.63	
Interference with Life Outside	2	8.29	
Specialty of Physician	3	5.82	
SYMPTOM 2 FACTOR			32.57
Specialty of Physician	1	16.21	
Delegation of Work	2	9.21	
Practice Setting	3	5.56	
Number of Years in Practice	4	1.59	
GLOBAL CATEGORY			49.42
Specialty of Physician	1	21.76	
Practice Setting	2	16.84	
Number of Years in Practice	3	6.35	
Board Certification	4	2.57	
Physician Orientation	5	1.90	

*Variance reduction expressed as percent of Total Sums of Squares explained.

characterized by routine and appropriate delegation of work could easily accommodate many more patients than, for example, a solo practice.

Within hospital practice, physicians who reported discussing their patients with others received higher scores on the physical exams. This finding may be related to professional status. That is, physicians in training who consult with their preceptors do better than institutional staff. It is evident in this and other problem areas that trainees often perform at the same high level as their faculty.

The results of the chest pain analyses are different in two respects from other adult diseases. First the analyses were based on a set of branching criteria. Second, criteria were designed with low emphasis on laboratory tasks. Most of the criteria required a physician to perform certain history of physical examination tasks. In the *history factor* criteria called for a history of previous problems, diagnoses, restrictions, and effects of medication on the pain. Physician specialty was a very important variable in explaining difference in performance. Internists always earned higher scores in both private and hospital practice. Internists who allowed their staff persons to function more autonomously took better histories than internists who tended to be autocratic. Those who delegated work and then interfered were likely to do poorly (.25) in comparison with colleagues who did not interfere with their staff (.79). The mean score for general practice was much lower (.18) than it was for medicine (.34).

Within general practice, the degree to which physicians knew their patients well, and the extent to which they discussed them with other practitioners, were nearly as important as the length of time they had studied in this country. Physicians with more education in the United States performed somewhat better than general practitioners who spent only two years studying in the U.S. General practitioners with over three years of training in the U.S. performed at a mean level of .71.

In hospital practice, physician specialty was associated with some difference in performance, with internists performing better than institutional staff (i.e., general practitioners) or other specialists.

As we mentioned before, a physician caring for a patient with chest pain was to rule out alternative diagnoses to heart disease, especially to AMI. One of the alternatives was pneumonia or pneumonitis. Explanations of variation in performance on the *Symptom 1 factor*, a cluster of respiratory items, was dominated by the characteristic, practice setting. An enormous difference in performance was explained by this single attribute. Apparently, hospital practitioners were four times more likely to investigate the possibility of pneumonia than physicians in private practice.

A physician's primary specialty was important in explaining variance in both settings but especially in a private practice. There, specialty entered the picture in two ways. First, it appeared in the type of internship a physician chose. General practitioners who took an internship in medicine performed at a higher level than generalists who did not. Second, it emerged in the usual pattern of internists receiving higher scores than generalists.

Specialty was also explanatory in hospital care but the pattern was different. Institutional staff performed more in accordance with criteria (.61) than the hospital internists (.45). They may have seen more pneumonias or were more anxious about treating a patient with chest pain and, therefore, took more detailed histories.

The chest pain panel developed criteria which called for a follow-up to determine whether or not the condition was improving and the problem was yielding to medication. The panel also specified under which circumstances a follow-up would be appropriate. A high score on the *follow-up factor* in chest pain is a reflection of the number of cases in which a follow-up was not appropriate according to the panel's instructions. Even so, private internists performed more in accordance with criteria than private general practitioners. Among the private generalists, it appears that participation in professional activites such as hospital committees is serving as a form of continuing medical education (CME). In several problem areas these activities appear to provide professional stimulation and awareness. General practitioners who did not participate in committee activities received a score of .36 as compared with .80 for those who participated in several.

An interesting finding occurred among the private internists. Those who reported that their practice interfered greatly with their lives outside of the office performed at a low level (for internists) of .33, as compared with those who felt that their practice interfered with their private lives very little (.90).

Little of the variance in performance could be explained in hospital practice. However, institutional staff, who were always general practitioners, seemed to be taking more comprehensive histories than other physicians, as in the Symptom 1 factor.

The other symptom constellation that concerned the chest pain panel was named the *Symptom 2 factor;* these criterion items called for a history that would rule out hiatus hernia. Apparently, hospital interns were much more likely to search for this problem than other groups of physicians.

In both private and hospital practice internists complied more closely with criteria than other specialists. In fact, when one looks at the performance of internists in this disease as compared with other selected conditions, internists do quite well. The high scores of internists may result from using branching criteria as well as from the predominance of history items. Although work delegation was not a crucial characteristic in the global category, it appeared a second time in this cluster of items. Internists who delegated work to particular staff received higher scores than internists who did not.

Within the hospital setting, there was a small amount of difference explained by the number of years in practice, which is probably suppressing physician status. We usually observed that the younger physicians performed like their faculty or preceptors; the Symptom 2 factor was an exception. Interns and residents earned scores of .18 while faculty and attendings together received a mean score of .28.

The importance of physician specialty in explaining variation in performance was highlighted in the *global category*. As we emphasized previously, internists performed quite well in this disease in both practice settings. The next most explanatory characteristic was practice setting, demonstrating the usual pattern of relatively high compliance with criteria among hospital physicians. Two characteristics which were probably suppressing the presence of a faculty appointment were significant in explaining difference in performance in these analyses. The first was presence of board certification and the second was the orientation of the physician. Doctors who reported enjoying teaching activities more than other aspects of their professional lives perform "better" in this disease. Physicians who were board certified received higher scores than physicians who were not. As we have noted previously, board certification is very highly correlated with the presence of a faculty appointment. However, we cannot explain why the faculty appointment variable did not emerge as it should have.

Work delegation items did not explain any of the variance in this category. This may be a result of the very small number of laboratory and other tests and procedures included in the criteria. Further, sample physicians probably felt that many of the tasks called for in these standards had to be done by the physician himself.

In summary, the picture of performance in chest pain is indicative of the contribution of education and training and continuing education activities to the patterns of patient care. Physicians who were involved with their colleagues on hospital committees, in teaching relationships, or in a practice setting which favors discussion of patients with colleagues, performed more in accordance with criteria than physicians who were relatively isolated.

Hypertension. Even with the very large number of cases of hypertension in the sample, the results of these analyses were disappointing. With the exception of the *basic factor* there was very low compliance with criteria in both practice settings, and it was especially low in private practice. Because of the influential position of the chairman who was known for his research on underlying causes of hypertension, these criteria were the most stringent set of standards in the study. A related problem was the difficulty of deciding on the appropriate factor solution. The nine-factor solution yielded too many subsets of items, but a smaller number of factors produced clusters of items that were, in the opinion of our physician advisors a hodge-podge of tasks that were clinically unrelated. Additionally, low compliance together with the large number of factors hindered the process of interpretation.

The first factor which included a very large number of criterion items was the *general follow-up factor.* It encompassed all of the criteria requiring an annual review of the patient's condition; this annual review included physical examination, laboratory and x-ray procedures and many other tasks. Variance in performance which could be accounted for by our analytic framework was minimal (see Table 7.15). Practice setting explained only a very small portion of the variance. The performance of private practice physicians deteriorated with number of years in practice, starting to drop off after the eleventh year.

The *first visit factor* included a combination of history and diagnostic criteria calling for listening to the heart and abdomen, checking peripheral pulses, deep tendon reflexes (DTRs), and checking for pitting edema. The most explanatory variable in these analyses was physician specialty. Specialists in private practice out-performed generalists by .24 mean score points. Private practitioners who delegated work to their staff performed at a higher level than physicians who did not delegate tasks. In this factor it was the internists whose performance noticeably diminished with years in practice.

Practice setting accounted for some variance in performance but not a great deal. All that can be suggested is that patients are likely to receive better care if they go to hospitals. If they choose a private practitioner, they are better off with a practitioner who delegates work to his staff and who has been in practice for less than twelve years.

The *follow-up eye exam factor* included a follow-up history of visual disturbance and an examination of ocular discs and retinal vessels, checking for hemorrhages and exudates. Compliance on these items

TABLE 7.15
Order of Importance of Variables in Explaining Variation
in Performance in Hypertension

Variable Name	Order of Importance	Variance Reduction*	Total Reduction in Variance
GENERAL FOLLOW-UP FACTOR			4.14%
Number of Years in Practice	1	2.87%	
Practice Setting	2	1.27	
FIRST VISIT FACTOR			26.90
Specialty of Physician	1	15.00	
Practice Setting	2	6.22	
Number of Years in Practice	3	4.26	
Delegation of Work	4	1.42	
FOLLOW-UP EYE EXAM FACTOR			3.17
Board Certification	1	3.17	
FIRST LAB FACTOR			26.02
Delegation of Work	1	13.51	
Practice Setting	2	7.99	
Specialty of Physician	3	2.82	
Trivial Complaints	4	1.70	
INITIAL EYE EXAM FACTOR			12.35
Practice Setting	1	7.30	
Patient Volume	2	3.73	
Physician Status	3	1.32	
FAMILY HISTORY FACTOR			13.66
Delegation of Work	1	9.41	
Years of Education in U.S.	2	4.25	
SYMPTOMS FOLLOW-UP FACTOR			6.86
Delegation of Work	1	4.80	
Length of Appointment	2	2.06	
BASICS			13.66
Delegation of Work	1	9.59	
Interference with Life Outside	2	4.07	
BLOOD PRESSURE CHECK			1.49
Physician Orientation	1	1.49	
GLOBAL CATEGORY			20.44
Specialty of Physician	1	8.54	
Practice Setting	2	6.60	
Physician Orientation	3	3.15	
Number of Years in Practice	4	2.15	

*Variance reduction expressed as percent of Total Sums of Squares explained.

was very low; the private practice mean score was .03 and the hospital mean score was .06. A small amount of variance in performance was explained by the presence of board certification. Physicians who were board certified in internal medicine received a score of .05 as compared with physicians who were not board certified (.01). Although this finding was statistically significant, it has no educational or social relevance. Board certification was partly suppressed by specialty. However, it was not enormously explanatory even when specialty was controlled for.

The *first laboratory factor* was a little more interesting. Work delegation explained a modest amount of the variation in performance. Private practitioners who did not delegate work received a mean score of .09 as compared with .24 for private practitioners who did delegate. Practice setting was also explanatory, and in the usual manner, with hospital practitioners performing more in accordance with criteria than private physicians. In private practice, internists performed more congruently than general practitioners. Also, a very small portion of variance was explained by the extent to which physicians were disturbed by patients' trivial complaints. Those who were really troubled by these trivia did not perform as well as physicians who were only annoyed.

In analyses of the *initial eye exam factor* practice setting explained some of the variance in performance. Physicians in private practice who saw more than 40 patients did not perform as well as practitioners who saw a smaller number of patients. Hospital practitioners performed more in accordance with criteria. Hospital institutional staff were the most likely to comply with standards developed for examining the eyes.

Performance on the *family history factor* was unexpectedly low, e.g., a mean score of .15 for private practice and .25 for hospital care. This item cluster required physicians to collect data on family history of hypertension, neurologic disorder and cardiovascular and/or renal disease. Internists did not record this information unless they specifically and routinely delegated work to their staff. Nothing in hospital practice was explanatory.

Mean performance scores on the *symptoms follow-up factor* were close to zero. These criteria called for a history of angina, nocturia and muscle cramps plus some odd follow-up examination items. The extent of task delegation in the private office and the length of the average office visit were the only variables in our framework which explained more than one percent of the variance. A physician who gave longer appointments to patients performed a little bit better on these rather incompatible items.

Although mean compliance scores on the *blood pressure check* were somewhat higher than on other factors, there was little difference in performance among private practitioners or hospital and private practice. Even the amount of variance explained by practice setting was less than one percent. There was a tenuous indication that physicians who enjoyed helping and relating to patients were more likely to collect and record baseline and/or six-month blood pressure readings.

The *basics factor* was so named because it was thought to include the very basics of an office visit for hypertensive patients. The criteria require providers to take a patient's weight, perform a urinalysis, and to note the results of the blood pressure check. Performance was very high in both practice settings on these items. Hospital practitioners were somewhat more likely to collect these data routinely, but practice setting explained less than one percent of the variance. Physicians who delegated work to a particular staff person were much more likely to perform and record the results of these tasks. Physicians who were only mildly satisfied with their case loads were less likely to obtain or routinely record this information. This group of physicians could be described as feeling somewhat resentful toward their patients; they reported that their patients were excessively demanding and that their practices interfered with their lives outside of the offices.

The picture presented in the *global category* was a recapitulation of themes suggested by analyses of the other performance factors. First, physician specialty explained some variance in performance, with internists behaving more in accordance with criteria as expected. The mean performance score for internists in private practice was .27 as compared with a .19 for general practitioners. Practice setting was also noteworthy because hospital practitioners routinely received higher scores; their mean was .40 as compared to a mean score of .23 for all private practitioners.

Physicians who enjoyed helping patients performed somewhat better than those who were diagnostically- or treatment-oriented. The performance of private practitioners dropped off after twelve years in practice and continued to deteriorate over time.

Pharyngitis.   Pharyngitis was the only disease in which we had the opportunity to compare performance among all three physician specialties (i.e., general practice, pediatrics, and internal medicine). Although differences were noted in the characteristics of pediatricians and internists, the difference in performance between these two groups was not statistically significant in explaining variation in the AUTOGRP analyses.

There were few noteworthy findings in the *instruction factor* because of a problem of missing data. As mentioned previously, the provision of instructions and explanations to patients was the one area of performance in which a very low correlation was discovered between provider behavior and provider documentation. Physicians who provided instructions to patients rarely recorded them. However, these findings did indicate that physicians who were patient-oriented were more likely to record instructions than were physicians who preferred diagnosis and treatment.

In the hospital setting, physician status explained a small portion of variance in performance. Faculty were twice as likely to record instructions provided to the patient as were other hospital staff. A small portion of variance in performance was explained by the characteristic, practice setting, because of the high scores of physicians with faculty appointments (See Table 7.16).

Criteria in the *diagnosis factor* required the physician to record a working and/or final diagnosis. As one might expect, practice setting was the most important characteristic in explaining variance with hospital practitioners who recorded diagnoses in 92 percent of the cases. Private practitioners did not believe it was essential to have this information available, and recorded diagnoses on only half their cases. Internists and pediatricians were more likely to record these data than were general practitioners, but this difference did not explain variation in performance.

As one might expect, patient volume explained some variance. The more patients a physician saw, the less likely he was to record working and/or final diagnosis. Private practitioners were less likely to record this information if they saw a patient for a short time. Patients who had appointments shorter than five minutes received less care (mean score .15) as compared with patients whose appointments were 15 minutes (.37) or between 20 and 30 minutes (.55).

In the opinion of panel members, the *throat factor* contained the most essential criterion items in pharyngitis. This item cluster included examination of the pharynx, tonsils and cervical nodes, as well as the recording of chief complaint and the results of a pharyngial culture. The physicians on the panel showed a regional difference in their lack of concern for false positive cultures. They rarely saw positive cultures in asymptomatic patients even in special screening programs in the schools. For this reason, they strongly recommended the throat culture as a useful diagnostic tool.

Pediatricians used throat cultures more often than internists or general practitioners. Pediatric practices frequently invested in laboratory equipment that enabled them to do their own throat cultures.

TABLE 7.16
Order of Importance of Variables in Explaining Variation
in Performance in Pharyngitis

Variable Name	Order of Importance	Variance Reduction*	Total Reduction in Variance
INSTRUCTION FACTOR			10.61%
Physician Orientation	1	4.59%	
Physician Status	2	4.12	
Practice Setting	3	1.90	
DIAGNOSIS FACTOR			24.81
Practice Setting	1	13.15	
Patient Volume	2	6.29	
Length of Appointment	3	3.06	
Number of Years in Practice	4	2.31	
THROAT EXAM FACTOR			42.16
Specialty of Physician	1	19.95	
Delegation of Work	2	9.61	
Practice Setting	3	6.95	
Laboratory Facilities	4	3.87	
Managerial Style of Physician	5	1.78	
EAR EXAM FACTOR			19.43
Specialty of Physician	1	9.30	
Practice Setting	2	8.36	
Patient Volume	3	1.77	
GLOBAL CATEGORY			48.02
Practice Setting	1	21.13	
Specialty of Physician	2	15.45	
Number of Years in Practice	3	4.53	
Patient Volume	4	3.97	
Delegation of Work	5	2.94	

*Variance reduction expressed as percent of Total Sums of Squares explained.

The presence of laboratory resources seems to have influenced their performance. The additional amount of variance in performance accounted for by the presence of laboratory facilities in the private office supports this premise.

Private general practitioners were least likely to examine the pharynx, tonsils and cervical nodes; their mean score for this cluster was .40. Although the performance pattern of internists resembled that of pediatricians, internists were more likely to examine cervical nodes and pediatricians were more likely to obtain the results of a throat culture.

The delegation of work influenced provider behavior in two ways. First, improved performance was associated with the specific delegation of work. In general practitioners who delegated routine tasks to particular staff members performed at a much higher level (.86) than practitioners who preferred doing everything by themselves (.27). Second, the effects of supervisory style, another important aspect of work delegation, explained a small amount of the variance in performance and indicated that physicians who interfered with their staff were less likely to get good results. Personnel in private practice often complained to researchers that physicians delegated work to them and later interrupted them, completing the task themselves. Although generalizations should not be made from this example, here is an indication that private practitioners would do best to delegate work to their staff and leave them alone to get the job done.

The outcome of the analyses of performance in hospitals was unremarkable. Care provided by primary specialists was somewhat more congruent with criteria than care provided by physicians in other specialties.

The results of the AUTOGRP analyses of the *ear exam factor* resembled findings for the diagnosis factor. Once more, a reasonable amount of variation was explained by physician specialty, with internists and pediatricians performing better (.34) than general practitioners (.07). Physicians in hospital practice (.64) included and recorded the results of an examination of the ear canal and tympanic membrane more often than physicians in private practice (.24).

An inverse relationship appeared between patient volume and performance in private practice. This pattern was unmistakable within general practice offices; general practitioners who saw 70 or 80 patients a day performed poorly in this cluster of items. In fact, the high-volume and solo general practices demonstrated extremely low performance in all diseases and problem areas.

Performance in the *global category* resembled the individual item clusters. Practice setting explained a fair amount of variance in performance. As usual, hospital practitioners performed more in accordance with the criteria than physicians in private practice. Internists and pediatricians in both practice settings received higher scores than general practitioners.

In private practice, an inverse relationship existed between number of years in practice and performance. The longer a physician had been in practice, the lower was his performance. The dropoff began in year eleven, as in the North Carolina study (Peterson et al. 1956), and fell continuously from year 12 to year 45. The mean score of physicians who had been in practice from 20 to 45 years was .35 as compared with the .51 mean score of physicians who had been in practice for less than 12 years. Difference in care provided by private practitioners was also explained by patient volume. Physicians who saw 25 or fewer patients per day earned higher scores than did those who saw over 40 patients. Private practitioners, and especially general practitioners, who delegated the same tasks to the same staff members achieved scores which were twice as high as their colleagues who did not delegate work.

Otitis Media. The pediatric topics were unique because findings lent themselves to sociological speculation. The predominance of variables such as satisfaction with the clinical caseload, stress from worried-well patients, professional orientation, and years in practice, in otitis media and well-child preschool exam was dramatic.

The first factor in otitis media was the *treatment factor* which included the administration and notation of drugs prescribed as well as the duration and dosage of medication. Results of the otitis media analyses were unusual because practice setting did not influence performance. (See results of analysis in Table 7.17.) Physicians who were happy with their clinical caseloads performed much better (.22 score points higher) than physicians who were only satisfied with their caseloads. Private physicians who have more contact with their peers in hospital committees received higher scores than physicians who did not participate in any of these activities. However, performance dropped when they participated in four or more committees, probably because they spent so much time away from their offices. Private pediatricians who were extremely satisfied with their caseloads performed better than their colleagues. Pediatricians who had a faculty appointment did better than pediatricians who had no such appointment.

As in most adult diseases, attendings in hospitals were less apt to comply with criteria than were trainees and their faculty. Not surprisingly, faculty received higher performance scores than trainees in this disease. Interns, residents and fellows who were aware of and bothered by trivial complaints did better than those who reported not being disturbed by inappropriate patient demands. It is possible that trainees who report not being bothered do not wish to acknowledge the extent to which trivial complaints upset them because they still feel that it is wrong to have negative feelings toward patients (Groves 1978).

Criteria developed by the physician panel for otitis media included

TABLE 7.17
Order of Importance of Variables in Explaining Variation
in Performance in Otitis Media

Variable Name	Order of Importance	Variance Reduction*	Total Reduction in Variance
TREATMENT FACTOR			19.91%
Satisfaction with Clinical Caseload	1	7.66%	
Faculty Appointment	2	4.39	
Specialty of Physician	3	2.71	
Physician Status	4	1.85	
Participation in Hospital Committees	5	1.80	
Trivial Complaints	6	1.50	
FOLLOW-UP FACTOR 1			22.53
Practice Setting	1	14.55	
Numbers of Years of Education in U.S.	2	6.47	
Physician Status	3	2.63	
Specialty of Physician	4	1.88	
DISEASE FACTOR			43.61
Supervision	1	22.88	
Practice Setting	2	14.91	
Physician Orientation	3	5.82	
HISTORY FACTOR			7.47
Supervision	1	6.29	
Practice Setting	2	1.18	
GLOBAL CATEGORY			38.17
Practice Setting	1	14.71	
Faculty Appointment	2	10.96	
Number of Years of Practice	3	4.46	
Managerial Style of Physician	4	3.97	
Physician Orientation	5	3.31	
Physician Status	6	1.76	

*Variance reduction expressed as percent of Total Sums of Squares explained.

two follow-up factors. The *first follow-up factor* included criteria calling for a physician to bring back the patient and conduct a follow-up examination. According to the panel, practitioners should follow up all cases of otitis media. In fact, the panel felt they should conduct a second follow-up if there were positive findings in the first. The vast majority of Connecticut practitioners did not use a second follow-up. A few did bring patients back for a first follow-up and noted whether or not signs and symptoms were the same, had worsened, or had disappeared.

In the *first follow-up factor,* practice setting made a difference in physician performance. Hospital practitioners were much more likely to bring patients back for a first follow-up, and the patients cooperated. Interns and residents were less likely to bring patients back for a first follow-up than attendings and faculty. Faculty were most likely to follow-up their patients, setting a good example for their students. The faculty reached a performance level of .72 in this factor. Trainees in the primary specialties (internal medicine and pediatrics) were more likely to conduct a follow-up than trainees in other specialties. Perhaps the most encouraging finding in this disease was that physicians were successful in bringing patients back for a second visit. The next unexpected result was that the general practitioners received slightly higher scores than pediatricians in both private and hospital practice.

The *disease factor* included many of the most essential criterion items. Characteristics of the tympanic membranes, chief complaint regarding ear pain or ear ache, date of onset, examination of pharynx and other respiratory problems were required. The findings suggest that in order to obtain the necessary information on these essential criterion items, a physician must be skillful in supervising his staff. Physicians who were more skillful in supervision, reporting a low level of tension, received scores which were 20 points higher than physicians who reported great difficulty in supervision. The crucial aspect of supervision in patient care seemed to be the ability to successfully delegate work. The supervision variable was probably suppressing task delegation. But we were unable to document this.

Private doctors who enjoyed the helping and supportive aspects of medicine performed better on this combined history and physical exam factor (.52) than their colleagues who preferred diagnosis (.32). A low plateau of performance was observed among pediatricians in the middle of their careers (18 to 28 years in practice) but did not explain a significant amount of variation in performance. In this factor, the mid-career depression could have been related to difficulties with supervising staff because pediatricians in the middle of their careers employed more staff than their colleagues.

The *history factor* in otitis required the physician to take a history of previous hearing problems, adenoidectomies, and myringotomies. This was a rather specialized history factor and Connecticut physicians did not routinely do these tasks. It is unfortunate that low scores were received on history of hearing problems, but it is important to remember the very low incidence of adenoidectomies and myringotomies in the entire pediatric population. Additional variation in performance in private practice was explained by the extent to which a physician found supervision difficult for him. Physicians who reported considerable stress from supervisory tasks were less apt to perform in accordance with standards than physicians who reported no difficulties with supervision.

A very small amount of difference was explained by practice setting. It was more common for hospital practitioners to investigate these problems than private practitioners. The assumption of several study advisors was that hospital patients are sicker than private patients; if this were true, the difference could be attributed to more frequent adenoidectomies and myringotomies in children presenting to hospitals.

Often the *global category* in relation to previous factors provides findings which are somewhat unclear with respect to physician performance. Other times, as in UTI and chest pain, analyses in the global category are quite interesting. In this disease, the results of the analyses for the global category included quite a bit of noise. For example, whether or not a private physician had a faculty appointment made a difference in performance. This finding was probably related to a physician's board certification status and the number of hospital committees and other professional groups in which he was active. Physicians with a faculty appointment were much more apt to conform to criteria than physicians who had no such appointment. If the process of criteria development had been dominated by medical school faculty (who spent the majority of their time in teaching activities) it could be argued that because faculty established the criteria, they were more like to conform to them. Physicians who developed criteria for otitis media had faculty appointments, but they were much more involved with their own practices and spent close to 95 percent of their time in private pediatrics.

Most of the variance that could be explained in this analytic model was explained by practice setting; hospital practitioners' care was more congruent with standards than care provided by private practitioners.

Pediatric Abdominal Pain. The first factor in pediatric abdominal pain was the *ingestion factor* which included criteria calling for a history of ingesting foreign objects or foods which were possible causes of the symptoms. There were no noteworthy findings within private practice. Apparently, private practitioners did not regard the ingestion of foods or foreign objects as an important part of the patient history in this problem area. In hospital practice, a very small portion of variance in performance was explained by physician specialty (see Table 7.18). Pediatricians were more likely to include ingestion items than providers with other specialties.

The *physical exam factor* called for an examination of the abdomen for tenderness, rebound, and abdominal masses. Physician specialty accounted for less than one percent of the variance, probably because of the very small sample of patients from general practices. Setting was the most explanatory characteristic, with hospital physicians adhering to the standards more often than their colleagues in private practice. Within private practice, physicians who reported knowing

TABLE 7.18
Order of Importance of Variables in Explaining Variation
in Performance in Pediatric Abdominal Pain

Variable Name	Order of Importance	Variance Reduction*	Total Reduction in Variance
INGESTION FACTOR			3.02%
Specialty of Physician	1	3.02%	
PHYSICAL EXAM FACTOR			34.96
Practice Setting	1	15.26	
Percent of Patients Known Well	2	14.85	
Physician Status	3	2.99	
Extent of Patient Demands	4	1.86	
VOMITING FACTOR			35.18
Practice Setting	1	26.19	
Number of Years in Practice	2	5.37	
Physician Status	3	1.92	
Managerial Style of Physician	4	1.70	
LAB FACTOR			25.16
Practice Setting	1	11.67	
Type of CME	2	8.70	
Faculty Appointment	3	2.40	
Specialty of Physician	4	2.39	
GLOBAL CATEGORY			42.81
Practice Setting	1	35.32	
Percent of Patients Known Well	2	3.68	
Specialty of Physician	3	2.50	
Physician Status	4	1.31	

*Variance reduction expressed as percent of Total Sums of Squares explained.

more than 60 percent of their patients received mean scores of .25. Those who reported knowing almost all of their patients reached the fiftieth percentile. These findings again suggest that the better a physician knows his patient population, the more comprehensive will be his physical exam. He also seems to be more thorough in recording the process of providing care.

In the hospitals, attendings did not perform as well as physicians with faculty appointments or institutional staff. Interns and residents joined their faculty in demonstrating a higher performance than attendings. It was not unexpected to find students imitating behavior of their preceptors.

In the *vomit factor* the large differences according to practice setting may have occurred because more comprehensive histories were taken in hospitals. The criteria in this cluster of history items included inquiring about vomiting, recurrence of vomiting, date of onset, and hematemesis. When patient histories were taken by hospital institutional staff, they were more likely to include questions regarding vomiting than were histories taken by attendings, faculty, and trainees.

Within private practice, the number of years a physician has been working accounted for some of the variance in performance. Once more, a dip in performance occurred in the middle years (12 years to 28 years in practice); this pattern emerged even when size or volume of the practice was controlled for. A little of the variance in performance could be attributed to the private practitioner's supervisory style. Physicians who allowed their staff to work more autonomously were likely to do better. The more work physicians delegate, the more time they have to spend taking a patient history.

Even though laboratory items were designated essential by private practitioners, there was very low compliance with the standards in the *lab factor*. As is often the case when there are very low scores on performance factors, the results are puzzling. Practice setting explained part of the small amount of variance found in this cluster of items. Hospital physicians' practice patterns more closely approximated the criteria. Hospital physicians who participated in clinical courses and rounds (considered a form of continuing education) were more likely to receive higher scores than those who reported no such activities.

In the *global category* the most important characteristic in explaining variance was practice setting. Provider behavior in hospitals came closest to the process of care described by performance standards. A small portion of variance in the behavior of hospital physicians could be explained by physician status, with attendings receiving lower scores than the rest of the staff. Private pediatricians demonstrated more congruent performance than private general practitioners. Private physicians who reported knowing over 60 percent of their patients well earned the highest scores.

Well-Child Infant Examination.   Factor analysis produced six factors for this pediatric problem area. The first factor, the *physical exam factor,* required a thorough systems review. Physician specialty was not an important characteristic in this problem area because of the very small number of cases treated by general practitioners. An average of only 21 well babies were seen by the generalists during the two-week log periods.

Concepts or variables which were most explanatory of physician performance in the Well-Child Infant Exam were the number of hospital committees to which a physician belonged, patient volume, and practice setting (see Table 7.19). A private physician who belonged to one or two committees performed more in accordance with standards than a physician who belonged to three or more hospital committees. In private pediatric practice, an inverse relationship existed between the number of patients seen and physician performance. In other words, physicians who were seeing between 162 and 751 patients weekly had a mean score of .04 as compared to a mean score of .76 for physicians who saw between 32 and 58 patients per week. Results of the AUTOGRP analyses for this topic also showed that private practitioners who allocated less time to their patients were unlikely to perform in accordance with criteria developed by the physician panels.

Because of the small sample of well-baby exams in the hospital setting (125 as compared to 476 for private practice), and because there was no statistically significant variation in performance among hospital pediatricians, no remarkable differences emerged.

The *development factor* included criteria requiring the collection of social and behavioral data on the well baby. Standards included inquiring about sleeping and feeding behavior, as well as social development. As expected, pediatricians scored higher than general practitioners. Physicians who had chosen pediatric or medical internships performed more in accordance with standards than physicians in rotating or other kinds of internships. Private doctors whose primary professional gratification was helping their patients demonstrated higher performance than physicians who reported enjoying treatment or diagnosis. The performance of physicians who had faculty appointments was even more impressive.

TABLE 7.19
Order of Importance of Variables in Explaining Variation in Performance in
Well-Child (Infant) Exam

Variable Name	Order of Importance	Variance Reduction*	Total Reduction in Variance
PHYSICAL EXAM FACTOR			41.68%
Participation in Hospital Committees	1	21.00%	
Patient Volume	2	11.74	
Practice Setting	3	8.94	
DEVELOPMENT FACTOR			46.57
Trivial Complaints	1	15.66	
Type of Internship	2	9.13	
Faculty Appointment	3	8.18	
Number of Years in Practice	4	6.84	
Physician Orientation	5	3.77	
Practice Setting	6	2.99	
BIRTH FACTOR			23.43
Number of Years in Practice	1	10.31	
Specialty of Physician	2	9.34	
Satisfaction with Clinical Caseload	3	3.78	
FOLLOW-UP FACTOR			5.19
Practice Setting	1	2.62	
Type of CME	2	2.57	
FAMILY FACTOR			22.06
Supervision	1	9.54	
Practice Setting	2	3.42	
Number of Years in Practice	3	2.94	
Net Annual Income	4	2.14	
Percent of Patients Known Well	5	2.06	
Physician Status	6	1.96	
SIZE FACTOR			7.53
Specialty of Physician	1	6.61	
Delegation of Work	2	1.92	
GLOBAL CATEGORY			38.46
Number of Years in Practice	1	12.49	
Practice Setting	2	10.46	
Specialty of Physician	3	7.99	
Length of Appointment	4	4.65	
Percent of Patients Known Well	5	2.87	

*Variance reduction expressed as percent of Total Sums of Squares explained.

The most interesting findings in this factor emerged while investigating the relationship between the number of years a private physician had been in practice and his performance. The cohort phenomenon which had emerged previously in several acute diseases showed up again in the Well-Infant Examination. Generally speaking, pediatricians in practice for less than 12 years and pediatricians for 40 years or more performed very well in accordance with standards, whereas pediatricians in the middle of the range did not. This mid-career slump was evident even when patient volume was held constant.

The extent to which physicians were able to cope with the trivial complaints of their patients also seems to effect their performance in obtaining data on child development. Physicians who were able to put up with a great deal of this professional stress performed best in obtaining a developmental history.

Findings in hospitals were unremarkable. There was little variation in performance among hospital practitioners. Moreover, physician status explained less than one percent of the difference in performance.

The *birth factor* included standards which called for the height and weight at birth, the head circumference, and the nature of the delivery. Again, physicians in their middle years of practice (in this case, between 18 and 39 years) received the lowest scores. Their mean score was .31 as compared with .74 for younger, or .74 for older private pediatricians. Physician specialty was a significant attribute also. Private practice pediatricians demonstrated higher performance (.70) as compared to private general practitioners (.35); however, it must be noted that the private general practice sample was small and these findings should not be generalized.

Younger pediatricians who were extremely satisfied with the quality of their clinical caseloads received higher scores (.78) than their colleagues who reported that their cases were just all right.

Results of the AUTOGRP analyses of the *follow-up factor* were negligible due to a very low compliance with criterion items such as "detection of abnormality" and "follow-up of patient." These criteria appear overly stringent because of the low probability of finding an abnormality in an infant. More abnormalities were noted in the hospital population. This may indicate only that there are differences in health status of the private practice and hospital pediatric population. Involvement in continuing education programs was related to higher scores (i.e, 30 score points) among hospital providers, even though overall compliance with criteria requiring follow-up was low.

The most important concept in explaining performance variation among private practitioners in the *family factor* was a physician's comfort with staff supervision. Physicians who reported extreme difficulty with supervision received much lower scores than physicians who reported only mild supervisory problems. Possibly, physicians who had great difficulty supervising their staff were unable to delegate work. Appropriate work delegation would have given them more time for the patient history. The importance of appropriate task delegation has already been demonstrated in previous diseases and problem areas.

It is difficult to interpret the meaning of net income in relation to performance in providing care. Although patient volume was controlled for in these analyses, the variable income continued to emerge. Physicians who earned over $30,000 demonstrated lower performance than physicians who reported earnings between $20,000–$30,000 per year. One fifth of the general practices scheduled very large numbers of patients (80 per day). These general practitioners reported the highest net incomes of all physicians in the sample (over $100,000). When gross income was calculated according to charges for the average visit, two of these one-person practices were grossing over $250,000 annually.

As in the previous history factor, the development factor, physicians who reported knowing 50 percent or more of their patients well received higher scores than their colleagues. The mid-career drop in performance appeared again in this cluster of patient history items.

Little is explanatory in the hospital setting but physician status. For some reason, interns received higher scores (.53) than other providers (.19).

Analysis of performance on the *size factor* did not explain very much. Nearly all physicians elicited and recorded information on the height and weight of the child. Pediatricians were somewhat more careful to collect these data than general practitioners. A slight amount of variance in performance was also explained by the extent to which physicians delegated tasks to their assistants. Physicians who appropriately delegated work performed better even in the size factor than solo practitioners or physicians with staff who tried to do everything themselves.

The results of the *global category* were productive because they highlighted findings of the performance factors. The cohort phenomenon or mid-life crisis recurred. Physicians who had been in practice for 18 to 39 years performed at a much lower level (.31) than their colleagues who were younger (.41) or older (.48). Our data do not provide reasons for this mid-life crisis among private pediatricians. These findings could be the result of a peculiarity in the sample. On the other hand, the rise in scores after 38 years might occur because low performers who were less satisfied with their profession retired early, while pediatricians who found their work intrinsically satisfying stayed in practice.

As in all diseases and problem areas, practice setting was paramount in predicting difference in performance. Hospital practitioners, all of whom were pediatricians, received higher scores (.53) than their private practice colleagues (.38). Also, physician specialty was positively related to good performance; pediatricians complied with a greater proportion of criterion items than general practitioners. The more patients physicians reported to know well, the higher were their scores.

The length of time a private physician spent on the average Well-Baby Examination influenced the quality of care provided. Pediatricians who spent 15 minutes or less with their patients had much lower mean scores than physicians who spent more time with their patients. An interesting finding in this factor was that physicians who reported knowing over 50 percent of their patients well scored higher than physicians who reported knowing only a few of their patients well.

Well-Child Preschool Examination. In Well-Child Preschool Examination, generalizations that could be made about performance of general practitioners are again limited by the small sample size. Only 13 cases presented to general practice offices during the two-week log.

In the *physical exam factor* which includes criteria calling for an extensive systems review, the length of time a physician spent with a patient explains most of the variation in performance in these analyses (see Table 7.20). Physicians who allocated from two to five minutes to each child performed at a much lower level (.12) than physicians who spent 15 minutes or more with their patients (.90). The positive relationship between length of appointment and performance is less than perfect across all topics because the relationship is mitigated by other contingencies such as the appropriateness of task delegation and difficulties with supervision. Here the finding is logical because a physician who spends more time with a patient can do a more complete systems review in accordance with standards developed by the well-child panel.

Performance was also influenced by practice setting. Hospital practitioners demonstrated a mean score of .54 as compared with private pediatricians whose mean score was .16. Private physicians who enjoyed the diagnostic aspect of their work performed better than physicians who preferred helping or treating their patients.

TABLE 7.20
Order of Importance of Variables in Explaining Variation in Performance in
Well-Child Preschool Exam

Variable Name	Order of Importance	Variance Reduction*	Total Reduction in Variance
PHYSICAL EXAM FACTOR			30.72%
Length of Appointment	1	18.10%	
Practice Setting	2	5.48	
Physician Orientation	3	4.70	
Number of Years in Practice	4	2.44	
HISTORY FACTOR			50.73
Trivial Complaints	1	31.57	
Physician Orientation	2	12.64	
Managerial Style (autonomy)	3	3.91	
Number of Years in Practice	4	2.61	
SIZE FACTOR			23.36
Specialty of Physician	1	19.46	
Physician Orientation	2	2.73	
Satisfaction with Clinical Caseload	3	1.17	
GLOBAL CATEGORY			23.26
Specialty of Physician	1	9.28	
Length of Appointment	2	8.47	
Practice Setting	3	2.88	
Delegation of Work	4	2.63	

*Variance reduction expressed as percent of Total Sums of Squares explained.

The mid-life or mid-career slump appeared again among pediatricians who had been in practice between 12 and 38 years. Participation in hospital committees was somewhat indicative of better performance; physicians who did not belong to any hospital committees did not score as well as their more participative colleagues.

In preschool examination, the *history factor* included an array of social and developmental items. The most important concept in explaining variation in performance was the private practitioner's tolerance of patients with trivial complaints. As in Well-Child Infant Examination, a physician's ability to tolerate minor or trivial complaints from the patient or the patient's family was positively related to performance. It was not unexpected to find that physicians who enjoy helping and supportive relationships scored rather high in this factor; most of the items are relationship-oriented.

The importance of a practitioner's supervisory skill is demonstrated

here by the presence of one of the leadership variables. The extent
to which a private physician allows staff to work in an autonomous
fashion is positively related to his performance. A doctor who is
able appropriately to delegate work to other staff can spend more
uninterrupted time on a social history. In this factor, physicians who
are in their fourth decade of practice did not perform as well. Perhaps
this is because the social and behavioral components of pediatric
practice were not emphasized during their medical training.

It can be noted from an inspection of Table 7.10a that compliance
with the criteria for following up the preschool child was minimal.
Because so few practitioners found it necessary to follow up their
patients, there were no differences found according to practice setting,
major specialty, or any other physician or organizational characteristic.
For this reason there were no findings to report on the *follow-up
factor*.

The *size factor* included a cluster of criterion items related to the
height and weight and the relationship between the height and weight
of the preschool child. Specialty was by far the most explanatory
characteristic, with pediatricians obtaining and recording data on nearly
all of their patients. General practitioners recorded this information
on less than half of their preschool patients. Another concept that
was useful in explaining difference in performance was the orientation
of the private pediatrician. Physicians who enjoyed helping or relating
to patients and their families performed at a higher level than physicians
who preferred diagnosis and treatment, or who had no preference.
There was no significant difference found when practice setting was
introduced.

As is often the case, not all of the characteristics which explained
variation in performance in previous factors showed up in the *global
category*. In preschool examination, the most explanatory attribute
was physician specialty; pediatricians performed more in accordance
with standards than general practitioners. Difference explained by
practice setting was statistically significant but less important than
length of appointment or delegation of work. The length of time a
physician spent with an average well-child visit also affected performance. The longer a physician spent with his patient the higher was
his score. The ability of a private practice physician to appropriately
delegate work was also associated with better performance. There
was a prior indication of this finding in the history factor, where
the physicians who allowed staff to function with considerable autonomy performed better than physicians who did not.

SUMMARY

As mentioned previously, it is not possible to summarize physician performance across diseases and problem areas using the performance factor. Although there are common elements in, for example, history and physical exam factors, in all of the selected conditions, a history in hypertension does not require the same skills and resources that are used in obtaining the history of a pharyngitis patient. In a similar fashion, the treatment and management components of hypertension are much more complex than treatment in pharyngitis, which requires only a simple set of explanations to the patient and a short course of antibiotics. It would only be appropriate to make summary statements across performance factors if the same items appeared in each one.

However, a few comprehensive and comparative statements can be made about attributes affecting physician performance across diseases and problem areas by using the Global Category (see Table 7.21). This tabulation displays variables which explained significant amounts of variation in performance. Their rank or order of importance is enumerated for each of the selected conditions. Practice setting is the attribute which is most powerful in explaining difference in performance in five of the nine topics. It is significant in all nine. Hospital practitioners received higher scores for care given to their patients throughout the study because their performance was more compliant with criteria.

Physician specialty was the next most important characteristic and was significant in all conditions except Otitis Media. The performance of internists and pediatricians was more congruent with criteria in eight of the nine topics. The orientation of the physician was also an important variable. Physicians who were patient-oriented (i.e., who enjoyed the relationship aspect of their practice) usually received higher scores than physicians who preferred to be involved in diagnosis and treatment. Physicians who preferred teaching activities, which also has a relationship component, were high performers in Chest Pain.

The number of years a physician had been in practice entered the global categories of the various diseases in two ways. In pediatric problem areas, physicians who had been in practice for less than 12 years or more than 40 years received high scores even when patient volume or the length of time spent with the average patient was controlled for. In adult diseases, the pattern was different. As in

TABLE 7.21

Variables which Explain Variation in Performance Across Diseases and Problem Areas in the *Global Category* by Order of Importance

Variables	Urinary Tract Infection	Adult Abdominal Pain	Chest Pain	Hyper- tension	Phar- yngitis	Otitis Media	Pediatric Abdominal Pain	Well-Child Exam (Infant)	Well-Child Exam (Preschool)	No. of Topics in which Variables are Significant
Setting	2	1	2	1	1	1	1	2	3	9
Specialty	1	3	1	2	2		3	3	1	8
Physician Orientation	3	4	5	3		5				5
No. of Years in Practice			3	4	3	3				4
Work Delegation	4	2			5			1		3
Physician Status*		5				6	4			3
Length of Appointment								4	2	2
Percent Patients Known Well							2	5		2
Faculty Appointment						2				1
Board Certification			4							1
Managerial Style						4				1

*Pertains to hospital physicians only.

the work of Peterson et al. (1956), performance of general practitioners deteriorated with the length of time they had been in practice.

The extent to which a physician delegated work to his private office staff was positively related to his performance according to criteria developed for this study. Physicians who delegated work always performed better than physicians who tried to do all the work themselves, regardless of their hiring practices. In some offices, physicians had a full complement of personnel who were not active in providing care to patients. Physicians who delegated work to specific staff persons received even higher scores. Although the variation in performance explained by work delegation was not always statistically significant, the positive relationship emerged in all selected conditions.

The professional status of a physician in private practice was always the same but there were marked differences in hospital practice. A difference in status often explained some of the difference in performance. Interns, residents, and their faculty always received higher scores than attendings, and usually performed more in congruence with criteria than hospital institutional staff. Physician's specialty also explained difference in performance in this practice setting. As expected, interns and pediatricians received higher scores in most problem areas. They also ordered many more tests and procedures than the generalists.

The degree to which physicians reported knowing their patients well and the length of time they spent in an average office visit were positively related to performance in all selected conditions. However, the difference explained in performance was only significant in several areas. Physicians who were board certified and/or had faculty appointments were more compliant with criteria, as one might expect. These were always specialists who had more than four years of education in the U.S. Physicians who allowed staff to operate more autonomously received higher scores. Findings on a physician's leadership style complemented results of analyses using the extent to which he was comfortable with supervising staff. Physicians who reported having little difficulty with supervision were less controlling and more likely to delegate work to staff, allowing them to complete their tasks without interference.

Although the Global Category is an averaging out across all criterion items, it only allows for sweeping generalizations. These kinds of summary statements do not show the importance of each characteristic in the individual factor. For example, the item work delegation is usually most significant in a laboratory factor where clear and complete delegation of work can occur. The laboratory factor in urinary tract infection is a good example (see Table 7.12). Work delegation is very important in this lab factor, but does not appear in the lab factor for Chest Pain, where decisions of which tasks to delegate are much more difficult. Again, in UTI, the percent of patients known well is important in the previous treatment factor. Physicians who know their patients well are probably more cognizant of previous infections and related problems. Similarly, within the Diagnostic History factor, the length of time spent with the patient is quite important. Physicians who spend more time with their patients have a better opportunity to get a complete history.

8

Summary of Findings and Methods Used in Evaluating Care

This study was an interdisciplinary approach to evaluating the quality of care provided by primary care physicians in private and hospital practice. Performance assessment was based on criteria developed by physician panels for nine selected diseases or problem areas. Performance was measured on care given to patients presenting with conditions which were frequently seen by generalists, pediatricians, and internists in both settings.

CRITERIA, SAMPLING AND INSTRUMENT DEVELOPMENT

Criteria of care were established by a process which included interviews with individual panel members and group meetings of the panels in which the lists of suggested criteria were reviewed. In the final stage of this process, numerical weights designating the relative importance of each item were assigned to all criteria selected. The resulting lists of Essential criteria (i.e., those which should be complied with in every case) were later validated by means of a Criteria Checklist administered to the private physicians who participated in the study. The agreement between these sample practitioners and the panel members was very high.

A stratified random sample of 162 solo practitioners was selected from a master list of all primary care physicians licensed to practice in the greater Hartford and greater New Haven areas. Previous research had demonstrated that these geographic areas include approximately three-fourths of all internists, pediatricians, and general practitioners licensed to practice in Connecticut. Hospital physicians were chosen from a sample of hospitals with the largest outpatient services in both areas. A sample of several thousand patients was selected from hospital sites and the 153 physicians responsible for care of these patients were interviewed. A total of 4,280 case abstracts were included in the sample of private and hospital practice primary care patients. Participation from both types of setting was very good for this kind of study, i.e., 68 percent for solo practitioners and 100 percent for hospital practitioners.

Instruments were developed to collect identical data from sample physicians in both practice settings. Major categories of information obtained were the following: (1) data on professional and personal characteristics of the practicing physician; (2) data on characteristics of the practice setting including organizational resources such as personnel, laboratory facilities and their utilization; (3) basic data on the patient population in all sites for a two-week period; (4) abstracts of the medical records of the 4,280 sampled patients in selected problem areas which provided information on the specific care rendered to patients; (5) information on volume of the private and hospital practices; (6) data from physician participants on their individual preferences for essential criteria of care; and (7) information on a physician's performance while providing care obtained from observations of a subsample of patients during treatment.

Lists of criteria generated by the physician panels were used to develop Abstract Forms with accompanying detailed instructions. Abstractors were trained in an intensive two-week seminar conducted by the medical director with assistance from a medical records staff. In the first year of field work half of the abstracts were spot-checked by field coordinators to ensure that reliability of the abstracts was kept at the 98 percent level.

In addition to the major interview schedules used to collect data on physician and organizational characteristics, private physicians and their staff were given a self-administered questionnaire on managerial style. This instrument yielded descriptive information on the leadership skills of the practitioners and their manner of interacting with their staff.

A nonrespondent questionnaire was mailed to all physicians who refused to participate in this study of ambulatory patient care. Findings showed that nonrespondents did not differ significantly from participants on those personal and professional characteristics that later emerged as important variables in determining the quality of physician performance.

Characteristics of the Physicians

General practitioners in our sample were older than internists and pediatricians; 52 percent were 60 years of age or older, as compared to 16 percent of the pediatricians and 20 percent of the internists. General practitioners were also twice as likely to have received medical degrees from foreign schools than the primary specialists. They reported fewer years of training, low frequency of board certification and few faculty appointments. The major reason for lack of board certification among general practitioners is the absence of specialty boards. A specialty board in the field of family practice was not available until 1970. Only three doctors in the sample described themselves as family practitioners. Two of the three were board certified in family practice and one in surgery. Both of the board certified family practitioners had faculty appointments.

Overall, physicians reported that they were moderately satisfied with their careers. A surprisingly small proportion of private and hospital practitioners were extremely satisfied with their jobs. There was some indication that hospital practitioners' dissatisfaction was related to the very large volume of patients they treated. Hospital general practitioners (i.e., institutional staff) saw between 61 and 350 patients in one week; we were unable to separate the emergency room cases as to severity and type. Most internists reported fewer than 60 outpatient contacts per week; the average for pediatricians was slightly higher. Pediatricians frequently mentioned that their modest satisfaction with their practice was partly due to their low net annual incomes relative to practitioners in other specialties. The level of satisfaction reported by physicians in all three specialties could be related to the very routine work that they customarily perform.

Internists and general practitioners acknowledged that they were often quite irritated by trivial complaints and patient noncompliance. They also reported that their training had not prepared them for dealing with problem patients and other aspects of practice which require a high level of interpersonal skill. However, most pediatricians differed from their colleagues on this point. They felt that developing relationships with patients and patients' families was one of the most gratifying aspects of their profession. Internists decidedly preferred the diagnostic and treatment aspects of medical care. General practitioners were less homogeneous in their statements of preference.

When asked to comment on the current problems facing the medical profession, most physicians expressed concern about the rising cost of care. Another major issue frequently mentioned was the fear of being sued.

Almost all private practitioners were involved in one or more kinds of continuing medical education (CME) activities. Their definition of continuing education rarely included self-assessment or evaluation programs and was more likely to denote participation in clinical courses or rounds. Internists who reported participating in self-assessment programs offered by the American Society of Internal Medicine (ASIM) performed at a higher level in treating acute diseases than other internists or general practitioners. Institutional physicians with training in general practice reported a higher level of participation in clinical courses and rounds than did hospital internists or pediatricians.

Characteristics of the Practice Setting

Findings from the Organizational Characteristics Interview Schedule indicated that office and hospital staff had difficulty dealing with patient complaints that were unrelated to the presenting problem. In both practice settings patients often expressed their dissatisfaction with telephone communications. Private patients also complained to staff about the inability to speak with physicians directly, long waits receiving care, billing errors, and parking problems. Medium-sized practices seemed to receive a greater share of these complaints. Although patients seeking care in large practices still complained about long waits, many of the other patient-management problems had already been successfully dealt with by these practices as their increase in size dictated. The types of appointment systems used by private practitioners (an organizational feature directly related to the waiting problem) are not very effective. The length of the appointment appeared to vary with the number of patients seen in the given practice day, regardless of how appointments had been scheduled. Although 15 minutes was the average time reported for an office visit, approximately one-fifth of the general practice offices showed us that they were scheduling patients for two- and three-minute visits. Several of these offices saw over 85 patients a day. Patients were booked at five-minute intervals, allowing the physician a minute or so in between patients. Staff members in these offices complained to us about the heavy caseloads.

Nearly half of the practices surveyed reported that more than 15 percent of their patients were not physically ill. Most staff and many physicians perceived these trivial complaints as inappropriate demands. Staff in private offices complained bitterly about increasing amounts of paper work, difficulty with third-party payers, and rising overhead. Institutional administrators had similar complaints. Several stated that the paper work was burdensome but routine; others admitted to large backlogs.

Despite the recent outcropping of forms and other printed materials especially designed for the collection of patient data, very few private practices used questionnaires which could be filled out by the patient. The average patient record was kept on 5×8 index cards. A common alternative was a combination of preprinted forms used to collect biographical data on the patient and handwritten notes on $8\text{-}1/2 \times 11$ sheets of paper. Internists in private practice were most likely to use preprinted forms for recordkeeping.

In our Connecticut sample, most private practices were solo practices: 88 percent of the general practitioners, 74 percent of the internists and 67 percent of the pediatricians were in one-physician offices. Less than one-half of the private practices hired registered nurses who did not always work full-time. Physician assistants and pediatric nurse practitioners were very rarely employed by the private practitioners. Licensed practical nurses were usually retained on a part-time basis. With few options for delegating work to other staff, private practitioners had to assume responsibility for tasks that could easily have been left to other medically trained health professionals. Differences in hiring practices between specialties were not significant. Patient volume seemed to be a better indicator: general practitioners who saw more than 80 patients per day employed more ancillary staff than their colleagues with smaller practices.

The Clinical Caseload

An examination of the caseloads handled by primary care physicians indicates that diseases of the circulatory and respiratory systems and a high proportion of undefined conditions accounted for most of the presenting problems of private practice patients. Very few general practitioners in Connecticut seem to be providing obstetrical care. This finding differs from profiles of general practices in other states. Physicians in hospitals treated more patients who presented with diseases of the respiratory system and, as anticipated, a greater proportion of injuries and other problems requiring emergency care.

Methods of Scoring Physician Performance

The basic analyses describe the performance of physicians in terms of their compliance with the predetermined criteria. Degree of congruence with criteria is reported for each disease and problem area according to practice setting and major specialty. The quality of performance is then related to various salient characteristics of providers and organizational features of their practices. After reliability indexes had been developed for the panel members who had assigned weights to the individual criterion items, three alternative scoring mechanisms were devised.

System One was the simplest method of scoring performance. It did not use the weights and all items were viewed as being of equal importance. Whenever there was evidence that a particular criterion item had been met—e.g., information was included in the patient record on a particular aspect of the Physical Exam—the physician received a score of one (1) for performance on that item. If there was no record of compliance, the physician was given a score of zero (0).

System Two was more complex because it incorporated information on the relative importance of each criterion item. Relative item importance was established by taking the average reliable weight given to each item by the panel of physician experts. Assigned weights could have ranged from zero to one hundred, or .00 to 1.00. As in *System One* each item was scored independently regardless of performance on any other item. In other words, *System Two* was *System One* with the addition of item weights assigned by the panels.

System Three was developed and implemented by physician consultants and involved more astute "clinical" judgment. It is *System Three* that took into account the presence or absence of other information on the record as well as the quality of that information. In this way, data on the individual case was included in the process of making a judgment about performance on each item.

No statistically significant differences emerged among scoring systems used to measure the performance of physicians in any of the nine diseases or problem areas. Thus, *System One,* which was simple, straightforward and inexpensive, was shown to be as effective as the more costly, more cognitively complex *Systems Two* and *Three.* *System One* was used for all of the subsequent analyses.

Preliminary Analyses

In the first series of analyses, performance measures for physicians in hospital and private practice for all three specialties—general practice, internal medicine, and pediatrics—were displayed for each criterion item. With findings produced in this manner it was barely

possible to see differences in performance according to major characteristics of the physicians or their practice settings. However, a very
low degree of compliance or congruence with criteria was indicated
across all diseases and problem areas.

Concern for low congruence with criteria made it mandatory to
implement the original plan of validating performance measures obtained from the patient record with direct observations of physician
behavior. (Observations of a subsample of both private and hospital
practitioners were not carried out on schedule because of limited
project resources.) Since performance in private practice appeared
less congruent with criteria than performance in the hospital setting,
a subsample of private practitioners was selected for observation of
care given to patients presenting with the diseases chosen for study.
Less than one-third of the internists and general practitioners consented
to these observations. Most of them stated that they were too busy
to explain the presence of the observer to their patients. However,
all pediatricians sampled agreed to participate. Although observations
were confined to pediatric diseases or problem areas, there was no
reason to believe that the recording practices of pediatricians were
unique. The use of factor analytic technique in the principal analyses
allowed comparisons to be made while isolating or eliminating the
criterion items which referred to the recording of instructions or
explanations of treatment procedures.

Physicians were observed while in the process of providing care
and, when the observations were later compared with abstracts of
the patient records, an extremely high degree of similarity was noted
between actual behavior and data recorded. The observations were
conducted by an experienced and well-trained nurse practitioner. A
form of the Criteria Checklist was designed by a physician consultant
to enable efficient collection of data by the observer. There was
at least 90 percent agreement between behavior observed and data
recorded in four of the five broad components of care: history, physical
exam, special exams such as laboratory tests and procedures, referral,
and therapy. The exception was in the recording of instructions or
explanations of treatment procedures. Compliance with criteria in
this component was minimally reflected in the records: that is, such
verbal behavior was recorded less than 10 percent of the time.

Use of Factor Analyses to Obtain Indices

For each disease or problem area between 36 and 110 criterion
items were developed by panel physicians for assessing the quality

of care given to sampled patients. Such a massive number of criteria presented major problems for determining how the quality of care differed according to the various characteristics of physicians and their practices. While the strategy of using all criteria separately had the advantage of dealing with all available information, it also had obvious disadvantages: (1) the general incomprehensibility of the results of such a large number of comparisons; (2) impediments to proper statistical inferences made from the comparisons; and (3) the problem of interpreting the results obtained as indicative of general, pervasive aspects of physician performance.

Out of concern for these disadvantages, the technique of factor analysis was applied to the sets of criteria for each of the nine diseases/problem areas as a means of improving the quality of the analyses of differences in performance according to characteristics of the physicians and their practices. Reducing the massive number of criteria to distinct groups added clarity to the process since comparisons could then be made on a handful of factors which represented the larger set of criteria instead of on the entire set. The clusters of criterion items obtained reflected different aspects of physician performance, thus indicating that the quality of care given in a physician-patient encounter is not unidimensional but multidimensional in nature. A physician may perform a physical examination well or be skilled at eliciting information from the patient regarding the onset and nature of symptoms, but he may interpret laboratory test results poorly or prescribe inappropriate medications.

All performance factors were scrutinized for validity and reliability. The empirical factors were often found to be consistent with clinical interpretations of components of care such as history, physical exam and treatment. The clinical validity of the statistically derived factors was determined by physicians who reviewed the criterion items comprising the factors for clinical consistency.

Once factors were derived, performance scores were calculated for each case treated by a physician in each disease or problem area. The performance factors and a global or summary measure which reflected the average performance score for all criteria in a given topic, were related to setting and specialty by an analysis of variance approach. There was a significant difference in physician performance by practice setting in nearly every performance factor for all topics. Overall, hospital practitioners provided care which was more congruent with criteria than that provided by private practitioners. Except for pediatric abdominal pain and otitis media, the performance of primary specialists (i.e., internists and pediatricians) was found to be much more congruent with study criteria than was the performance of general practitioners.

Variables selected for second level analyses included characteristics of the physicians and their practice settings suggested by previous research, the study Advisory Committees, and the experiences of staff in the various sites. AUTOGRP, an interactive system of data analysis, was used to perform nonsymmetrical branching based on variance reduction when performance factors or the global category were used as dependent variables. A reduced set of physician and organizational characteristics were chosen for use as independent variables to explain variation in performance beyond that accounted for by major specialty and practice setting. The reduced set of variables included the following physician attributes: specialty, type of internship, most gratifying aspect of medicine, degree to which trivial patient complaints disturb the practice routine, type of continuing education, years of U.S. education, and number of years in practice. Organizational characteristics employed included practice setting, number of physicians in the practice (for private practice only), physician's style in relating to office staff (for private practice only), length of appointment or patient visit, flexibility of appointment system, delegation of tasks to other staff in the practice setting, presence or absence of laboratory facilities, and the extent to which staff felt overworked.

In this summary, emphasis will be placed on the analyses of the most important performance factors (i.e., those composed of criteria which were assigned the highest item weights by physician panels) and the global category which summarizes performance on all criterion items in a given topic. The global category is a summary measure which has traditionally been used in this kind of research. The performance factors which we have introduced in this study show differences in care provided according to different broad components such as history and physical exam.

PROVIDER AND ORGANIZATIONAL ATTRIBUTES AFFECTING PERFORMANCE

The working assumption of the CACS Advisory Committee, the Technical Committee, the panels, and the investigators was that predetermined process criteria should be used as indicators of the quality of care provided. Physicians whose performance was congruent with criteria developed by the panels were considered to be providing "better care" to patients than physicians whose care was not congruent with the criteria. Problems in using criteria for assessing the quality of medical care have been well-documented and are known to exist whether process or outcome measures are employed.

There are several attributes of the provider or the organization in which care is given which affect the quality of care, regardless of disease or problem area. Practice setting had a highly significant effect on care provided in all diseases but Otitis Media. Overall, hospital practitioners provided better care according to the criteria developed by the physician panels. In most diseases/problem areas, internists and pediatricians provided better care than did general practitioners within the same practice setting; private general practitioners, especially those in one-person practices, provided care which was minimally congruent, whereas general practitioners in hospital practice demonstrated better overall performance than private internists or pediatricians. A third variable indicative of better care for all private practice patients was appropriate use of ancillary staff. Private practitioners providing a higher level of care generally delegated laboratory work to lab technicians or specially trained assistants; these tests were done either in their own offices or specimens were sent to outside laboratories.

Several explanations could be offered for the higher level of performance demonstrated by hospital physicians. In *Doctoring Together* (1976), Friedson suggests that physicians who work together are more likely to be aware of the quality of each other's work. They reported finding out about colleagues through informal conversations, listening to patients who had been treated by these colleagues, sharing cases, covering for them or by checking their records. Our findings suggested that physicians who had little or no contact with colleagues performed relatively poorly in all of the diseases and problem areas. These practitioners tended to be dissatisfied with the organization of their practices and disillusioned with their careers. Informally, they complained to project staff about the kinds of patients they disliked but had to treat and about difficulties they experienced in relating to them. Some of these doctors appeared to be alienated and embittered.

One important finding that appeared throughout the study was that physicians who demonstrated managerial competence performed better according to standards developed. In the words of one Advisory Committee member, "we found that physicians who managed their practices better, practiced better medicine." Several indicators of managerial competence were used in the study. Appropriate delegation of work to other staff was one of the most important concepts. Physicians who delegated tasks to others spent more time with their patients, obtained better histories, and performed better on the physical exams. Physicians most frequently delegated laboratory work (including the collection of specimens) and minor physical exam tasks (such as height and weight) to their staff. Rarely did they share the more difficult or interesting work with them. If they had, it seems highly likely that their performance would have been improved; this was indicated by the in-person observations of several pediatricians who delegated one-third to one-half of their workload to ancillary staff.

Another indicator of managerial skill was the extent to which a physician felt comfortable with the supervisory responsibilities in his practice. Although this was not a finding of great significance, physicians who were at ease supervising staff generally performed better than physicians who reported feeling uncomfortable when supervising others. A questionnaire given to physicians and their office staff (The Leadership Opinion Questionnaire) provided other indicators of the way in which physicians related to staff. One of the described characteristics included in findings from this questionnaire was the extent to which a physician provided task leadership. Physicians who gave a great deal of direction (i.e., controlling or autocratic) or who were reluctant to let staff function autonomously did not perform as effectively as their colleagues.

In most problem areas the duration of the appointment influenced physician performance. Physicians who spent 15 minutes or longer with their patients provided better care than physicians who spent five minutes or less. Although this finding was statistically significant only in private practice, there were indications of a similar pattern in care given to hospital clinic patients.

The orientation of the physician (i.e., the aspect of his practice that he liked best) was also associated with differences in performance. Physicians who were relationship- or patient-oriented performed more in congruence with criteria in all conditions except Chest Pain and Urinary Tract Infection. In these two acute adult diseases, physicians who were treatment-oriented or who preferred teaching activities to patient care received higher scores. In the pediatric abdominal pain analyses no significant findings were noted with regard to orientation. However, physicians who reported knowing many of their patients well received higher scores than their colleagues.

It may be that treatment of these acute illnesses requires a physician to use more technical and fewer interpersonal skills. Physicians who enjoy diagnosis and treatment planning are, therefore, more likely to do well in treating common acute diseases which require quick decisions, immediate action, and less time than interviewing and/or educating the patient. The current cultural stereotype of the physician as a life-saving man of action clearly supports this type of role behavior. These doctors may find the treatment of chronic disease or health examinations boring and unrewarding. On the other hand, physicians who enjoy relating to patients are perhaps better suited for preventive tasks or health maintenance because they find satisfaction in interacting with patients. These practitioners are able to tolerate the trivialities of daily practice because they are more person- or relationship-oriented. Both types of physicians (the technical, task-oriented and the relationship-oriented doctor) may be good managers because both delegate work to others. The reasons for delegating work could be different. The task-oriented physician may delegate work because he dislikes it, whereas the relationship-oriented physician may delegate certain tasks to give him more time to spend interviewing or educating the patient.

The major predictors of different levels of quality (i.e., agreement with the standards) within the hospital were major specialty and the status of the physician. Faculty and their students usually provided better care across all problem areas than attendings or institutionally-based physicians with training in general practice. A more detailed description of findings within each problem area is provided below.

Adult Abdominal Pain.   In adult abdominal pain most of the variance in performance was accounted for by practice setting. More congruent care was provided by hospital practitioners and especially by hospital internists or any internists who had faculty appointments; these internists had higher mean performance scores than physicians in other categories. Within private practice, patients treated by physicians who delegated work to staff provided care which was most congruent with criteria. The global mean performance score for private practitioners treating Adult Abdominal Pain was .28. General practitioners received a score of .23 and internists, .32.

Difference in performance among private practitioners was also related to the aspect of medical practice the primary care physician enjoyed the most. Private practitioners who reported preferring diagnostic aspects of medical care to instituting treatment received lowest scores on adult abdominal pain; the relationship-oriented physicians received higher scores. This was a surprising finding because of the nature of this acute topic which requires the use of diagnostic skills to determine the cause and origin of the pain.

In private practice physicians who demonstrated a very low level of congruence with criteria practiced alone and performed laboratory tests in their own laboratories; they did not hire or train assistants to do these procedures for them.

Chest Pain. Care provided for chest pain patients in private practice was much less congruent with criteria (.28) than care provided in hospital practice (.43). Private physicians treating one-third of all chest pain cases received a mean score of zero on the physical exam factor. Criteria in this factor called for notation of results of listening to the heart, percussion and auscultation of the chest, heart rhythm and frequency, and auscultation of the abdomen. Criterion items in this factor were assigned the very highest item weights by the panels of physician experts indicating that they were considered to be the most essential criteria of care for a patient presenting with Chest Pain. All cases (approximately 100) with scores in the lowest quartile on the Physical Exam Factor were found in one-person general practices. These physicians reported being moderately disturbed by trivial patient complaints and saw their patients for a very short time; 20 percent spent less than five minutes in the average office visit.

Physicians whose care was most congruent with criteria were all internists who enjoyed diagnosis and treatment equally. About half were in practices which included more than one physician. Over two-thirds of physicians providing congruent care were board certified; all spent 15 minutes or more with the patient during an average visit. None of the private internists performed laboratory tests themselves. One-third employed laboratory technicians or assistants who were specially trained for lab work.

In hospital practice the picture was not very clear, showing only a significant difference in performance according to major specialty. Hospital physicians with higher mean performance scores in chest pain in the hospital setting were interns, residents, and their faculty.

Hypertension. A very low level of compliance on most of the criterion items complicated the analyses of physician performance in this chronic disease. As compared with the other diseases and problem areas, variance in performance explained by the variables included in the framework was minimal. Even practice setting was minimally significant in explaining differences in care.

Overall, delegation of work and the specialty of the physician were most explanatory. A few internists who received very high scores (.85) used their laboratory facilities appropriately and delegated diagnostic tests and procedures to particular staff members. The number of years a physician had been practicing was also important. Performance in both specialty groups dropped off after twelve years in practice and did not improve with time.

Urinary Tract Infection. Treatment of urinary tract infection in private practice was less compliant with criteria than treatment in hospital practice. Within private practice large differences were shown according to specialty; internists received higher mean scores than general practitioners. Physicians whose care was most congruent with criteria were internists who found the treatment aspects of medical practice to be more gratifying than relating to patients. This same group of internists usually hired laboratory technicians or trained assistants to perform routine tests and procedures. As in other acute diseases physicians with higher scores did not perform routine tests and procedures themselves; they were comfortable with delegating such tasks to their staff. These findings do not indicate that internists hire more staff. Indeed, general practitioners were somewhat more likely to hire more personnel but not laboratory technicians or physician's assistants.

In hospital practice very large differences in care were found according to physician specialty. Surgeons provided outstanding care (in accordance with study criteria) followed by internists. General practitioners in the hospital setting performed at a level similar to internists in private practice. Within the hospital setting it was also notable that patient care in clinics was more congruent with criteria than it was in the emergency room.

Pharyngitis. Ninety-seven percent of the physicians who received low scores in pharyngitis were general practitioners who had been in practice for over 30 years. These physicians rarely delegated work to their staff. A large group of private practitioners complied with all of the very highly weighted criterion items appearing in the throat factor (mean score .82). These items were considered by the panels to be the most essential tasks to be done for the pharyngitis patients. Eight percent of private practitioners in this high scoring group were internists who reported that they preferred the treatment aspects of medical practice to diagnosis or relating to the patient.

Within private practice most of the variance in performance in pharyngitis was explained by specialty; internists and pediatricians provided care which was most congruent with the criteria. The number of years a physician had been in practice and the extent to which he delegated work to staff assistants explained smaller portions of the variance. The duration of the appointment, and the total patient volume also explained some of the variance in performance, especially within the diagnostic factor.

In the hospital setting little difference in performance by physician specialty was noted. Care provided in the hospital was excellent according to the most essential items selected by the physician panels.

Hospital physicians were twice as likely to examine the ears of
pharyngitis patients as physicians in private practice.

Otitis Media.   This topic was unusual as compared with the other
acute diseases. For example, no significant differences emerged by
practice setting. Physician specialty was less important in explaining
variation than other variables such as the length of time the physician
was in training or his comfort with supervision. Private and hospital
physicians with faculty appointments received significantly higher
scores.

In private practices some variance in care provided was related
to the managerial style of the physician. Satisfaction with the types
of cases seen also predicted a higher level of performance. Hospital
physicians, especially those with faculty appointments were most likely
to follow their otitis patients.

Pediatric Abdominal Pain.   Pediatric abdominal pain proved to be
an unusual topic because of the extremely low compliance with criteria
developed. Global mean scores were .13 for private and .28 for hospital
practitioners. In private practice, physicians whose performance was
most congruent with criteria were very young or older pediatricians
who reported knowing most of their patients well. The managerial
style of the private physician and his susceptibility to the inappropriate
demands of his patients also affected his performance.

Practice setting was most explanatory with hospital practitioners
providing more congruent care. In the hospital setting physician
specialty accounted for a substantial mean difference. Criteria which
contributed to a large amount of the variance included examination
of the abdomen and the upper respiratory system. Pediatricians (.43
mean score) provided care which was better than care provided by
the general practitioners (.37). Hospital practitioners were not more
likely to obtain the specified laboratory test and procedures than
private physicians. This finding was unexpected because of previously
documented high utilization of tests and procedures by hospital
physicians.

Well-Infant Examination.   A very large number of well-infant
examinations were picked up in the private practices. Nearly three-
quarters of the private pediatrician's caseload consisted of well-child
exams. Few well babies were seen by general practitioners. Some
variation in performance was shown by physician specialty; another
powerful variable in predicting performance was practice setting.

Younger and older pediatricians performed better than colleagues who had been in practice for more than 12 and less than 40 years. This finding also appeared in the preschool exam analyses. Physicians who spent an appropriate amount of time with their patients (i.e., five minutes or more) also received higher scores. The percent of patients that a physician knew well was also important; pediatricians who know over 60 percent of their patients performed in a more compliant manner.

Well-Child Preschool Exam. Findings on the well-child preschool exam resembled the well-infant exam in many respects. Private practice pediatricians were more likely to comply with criteria than general practitioners. Again it was evident that a substantial portion of the variance was explained by the physician's orientation. Younger and older pediatricians who were relationship-oriented received the highest scores. This finding complements previous data on pediatricians who reported that relationships with patients and patients' families was the most gratifying aspect of their medical careers. All private practice physicians providing well-child care were likely to perform better if they delegated work to their staff. Physicians who spent longer with their patients demonstrated greater compliance with criteria for the Well-Infant Exam.

IMPLICATIONS OF FINDINGS

Continuing Education Needs

Throughout the CACS, the Advisory Committe stressed the importance of the CSMS taking an active role in continuing medical education (CME). Although the experiences of previous groups which used data from quality assessment have been mixed, several have been successful. Nelson (1977) stressed the importance of special projects which he suggested are more likely to be successful in improving physician performance.

Commonly stated objectives of CME are the following: (1) transmitting new knowledge; (2) refreshing old knowledge; and (3) building upon knowledge received during undergraduate and postgraduate training. Most experts in CME feel that physicians do know how to provide care which is technically adequate. However, some physicians may never have learned how to relate to patients well enough to develop the interpersonal skills necessary to obtain the information they need to solve the patient's problem. Our findings indicate that the ability to relate to patients and their families is related to higher levels of performance in health supervision and care for hypertension.

Physicians must perform competently in a number of roles: as clinician, teacher, and manager. Our findings show that the physicians who are able to delegate tasks, to supervise other staff, and to schedule patients appropriately are more successful in providing care to their patients. A physician's performance is affected by his ability to organize or manage his practice. Few medical schools even touch on managerial skills, even though a physician spends most of his career as an administrator. Administrative or supervisory skills are important for both hospital and private practitioners alike. The hospital physician must learn how to work in a large and complex organization and the private practitioner needs to know how to run a small business. Managerial skills training could easily be included in the undergraduate or graduate curriculum.

Although it might be more difficult to introduce some practicing physicians to new ways of organizing their practices, many physicians and office managers expressed an interest in learning about more efficient or cost-effective methods.

Workshops on management problems in everyday practice could be sponsored by various organizations. Physicians and their staffs or co-workers could participate in these workshops to learn how to solve problems as a team.

The Advisory Committee also recommended that enough time be scheduled for interviewing each patient. Unless the practice is managed in such a way as to allow a physician to spend an appropriate amount of time with each patient, he cannot acquire enough data to treat them effectively. Training in alternative kinds of scheduling could easily be provided in workshops for the office team.

Another inestimable source of information is the patient record. Our findings agree with previous research which has shown a positive relationship between good record-keeping and good care (Lyons and Payne [1974] and Starfield and Scheff [1972]). The worth of alternatives to the 5 × 8 cards should be formally explained to many practicing physicians. They may already be familiar with standard forms which have been developed by ASIM and AAPD which, with encouragement, could be used as is or modified.

Research Methods

Many of the significant findings were made in the area of research methods. Our experience indicates that it is somewhat inefficient to develop long lists of detailed criteria. Physician panels in the CACS generated lists of 36 to 110 criteria for the selected problem areas. When criterion items were weighted, a much smaller number were empirically designated as essential to good care (i.e., were assigned high item weights by all raters). Many reliable lists of criteria have been developed and used throughout the country. Recent research has shown a high degree of similarity among all lists. It would be more efficient for organizations involved in review to revise existing criteria rather than to develop completely new standards. In a study of this nature, it is important to include only the most essential criteria. Tasks which are desirable to do for patients under ideal conditions (i.e., with time and energy permitting) are not done in daily practice. Because these optimal criteria are not usually complied with, performance comparisons will be difficult to execute.

Once a short list of essential criterion items has been combined for an evaluation of practice, difficulties in obtaining measures of behavior will continue. Our observations on a randomly selected subsample of pediatricians showed that information in the medical record accurately reflected actual performance in providing care in the following components: History, Physical Exam, Treatment and Specialized Procedures including Laboratory Tests. However, explanations and instructions provided to the patient were rarely recorded. Evaluation which stresses outcome is especially vulnerable to problems of this nature. Outcome measures on a patient for whom the physician prescribed appropriate medications without providing instructions, would be poor; there would be no way of correctly explaining this poor outcome without information on instructions given to the patient. Further investigators would do well to observe or record the actual patient encounter in order to give the physician full credit for aspects of care which are verbal or relational and not easy to measure from commonly used records.

Panels of physician experts have been generating criteria of good medical care for several decades. One of the reasons for developing criteria using a group or modified Delphi method has been to involve practicing physicians. The assumption based on research in the behavioral sciences is that physicians who take part in the design will feel more committed to change. In this research we have demonstrated that there is a great gap between theory and practice. Criteria generated in groups or artificial settings were theoretical criteria and differed from criteria used by physicians in actual practice. For example, in their answers to a questionnaire, participants agreed with panel members who stated that a pharyngeal culture is essential, but in actual practice they reported using other means of determining whether or not the patient had a streptococcal infection (i.e., visual inspection). A similar lack of correspondence in word and deed is described by social psychologists who have observed that there is often a great discrepancy between a person's attitude and his behavior. These findings have obvious implications for CME activities. The reasons for the deviations from accepted standards must be fully understood in order to mount a program with effective and permanent benefits.

Measuring Physician Performance

In this study, three methods of scoring provider behavior were instituted; they are described earlier in this chapter. The simplest and a widely used scoring procedure is recommended as the method of choice. *System One,* a simple designation of one score point for criterion complied with and zero for criterion not complied with was found to be just as effective as a scoring procedure which used individually weighted items (*System Two*) or included an element of clinical judgment based on other information in the record (*System Three*). However, this last system of scoring might be more appropriate in some applications, and has been proposed by some investigators for routine screening (Greenfield et al. 1975).

The technique of factor analysis was used to define clusters of criteria or clusters of tasks which were done by the physician for the patient. Factoring of the criterion items allowed us to identify which of the specified tasks were likely to be performed together. These dimensions of performance included, for example, all physical exam items related to the presenting problem. In pharyngitis, a physician who examined the pharynx and tonsils was also very likely to examine the cervical nodes and to obtain a pharyngeal culture. Using this strategy, it was shown that a physician can be evaluated on one or more dimension(s) of care. Most physicians will perform better on some dimensions than on others. Differential performance among components of care is hidden by the Global or summary measure which we have shown to be an averaging out of performance strengths and deficiencies. The implications for continuing education are that certain components of care can be identified as being in need of improvement and designated as high priority areas for change.

This study has succeeded in identifying a number of attributes associated with differential performance, some of which are more amenable to change than others. It also has described a number of concerns such as the need for a better understanding of the reasons for departure from self-professed criteria, and the factors contributing to the apparent change in practice patterns with increasing time in practice. Until these issues are added to the agenda for future research, our attempts at behavioral change will be less than effective.

APPENDIX A

Instrument Development and Field Methods

APPENDIX A

Instrument Development and Field Methods

The central focus of the present inquiry was directed toward measuring the quality of care provided by physicians in both hospital and private practice settings. The basic standards used for evaluation were the criteria developed by panels of physician experts for each of the nine study topics as described in Chapter 2. Since our major source of information on the degree of congruence between physician performance and the predetermined standards was the data which appeared in patient charts, the medical records abstract was the primary instrument of the study. Concerns for validity of the criteria and reliability of the medical records prompted the development of two additional instruments: (1) the use of a Criteria Checklist to compare the preferences of participating physicians with those of panel members, and (2) a series of observations instituted to determine the extent to which the records were a reliable indicator of physician performance. In order to identify the factors influencing differential performances in the practice settings, instruments were also developed for the collection of data on the characteristics of providers, their organizations, and their clinical case loads.

Several elements influenced the selection of additional variables for study. Previous research in the field done by Peterson et al. (1956) and Clute (1963) demonstrated that it was not sufficient to investigate the impact of training and background when assessing physician performance in treating patients. Personal characteristics such as attitude toward patients, the amount of time spent in patient care activities, and referral networks all had to be explored. Because the present study was designed to assist the practicing physician in continuing his/her training, it was important to know the personal and professional attributes of physicians who did not comply with the normative criteria. This approach would give the medical society information on potential target groups of physicians who were most in need of retraining or continuing medical education.

However, it was not expected that the characteristics of the providers would explain most of the variance in performance. Organizational theory suggests that much of the variation in worker behavior can be explained by properties of the work setting. Overall effectiveness in reaching production goals is influenced by many factors. Riedel and Fitzpatrick (1964) and Donabedian (1968) have described how structural characteristics of an organization can affect provider behavior. Successful acquisition of resources such as personnel and equipment, utilization of these resources, and adaptation to environmental demands are several concepts that were examined in organizational research. Interaction with the client population is another important indicator of provider performance; this suggested the need to gather basic information on the characteristics of patients who were presenting to the various sites.

DEVELOPMENT OF INSTRUMENTS FOR DATA COLLECTION

Figure A.1 shows the variety of instruments and interview schedules used to collect data in the field. This appendix describes the development and pretest of the instruments, the training of staff, and problems encountered in the actual field work. A description of the development and implementation of coding schemes for data collected is also included.

Patient Log

In order to obtain a master list of all patients presenting to selected sites, a Patient Log form was designed to collect information for two specific purposes: (1) to provide a sampling frame for selection of patients presenting with one of the problems chosen for study, and (2) to obtain basic data on the characteristics of the entire patient population. The two-week log included space for recording the patient's name or identifying number; if names were used, the forms were never removed from the site without permission of the physician. Office staff were asked to record the presenting complaint in the patient's own words. In actual practice, they frequently recorded their own or the physician's best approximation of the condition that occasioned the visit: namely, a working diagnosis. This entry later posed problems for the coders.

The log design was simple. Instructions were printed on the reverse

FIGURE A.1
Instruments Used for Data Collection

Instrument	Description
Patient Log	Provided a record of all patients presenting to selected sites during a two-week period; included information on presenting complaint as well as age, sex, and address of the patient.
Medical Record Abstract	Provided data on the specific care rendered by providers to patients in selected diseases and problem areas.
Criteria Checklist	Presented data from the physician participants on their individual preferences for the essential criteria of care.
Observation Checklist	Direct observation of patient care behavior for comparison with recording behavior of the physician. The instrument was used on a subsample of participants who were treating patients with selected conditions.
Physician Characteristics Interview Schedule	Provided detailed information on the personal and professional characteristics of the physician.
Leadership Opinion Questionnaire	Elicited data on the managerial style of the physician in relation to staff.
Organizational Characteristics Interview Schedule	Provided information on characteristics of the practice setting, availability of organizational resources such as personnel and laboratory facilities, and managerial policies and practices.

side of the form so that a log could be easily maintained by office staff, even without supervision by a research assistant. Medical records of all patients presenting with selected conditions for study were examined; cases were defined as appropriate for inclusion using screening criteria developed by physician panels for each disease or problem area.

Medical Record Abstract

Sample patients whose records were to be abstracted were chosen from among those presenting with one of the nine diseases/problem areas selected for study. The abstracting of data on the type of care given to these patients was a painstaking process which was conducted with great attention to accuracy and reliability.

The development of an Abstract Form began with the final list of criteria designated Essential by the panels for each selected topic (see Chapter 2). Criteria were translated into items which could be easily interpreted by the field staff, and key words from each item were used as cues or reminders to the abstractors. The key words on the Abstract Form were followed by codes for "data recorded," "item not mentioned," "negative," "not ordered," "dosage," etc. Detailed instructions were compiled into an abstractor manual which was used to direct the search for information and which specified what should be done if relevant data were present or absent from the record (see Appendix B.)

Guidelines provided in the manual included descriptions of the type of illness specified by each topic, the parameters established, the focus of criteria developed by the panels, and cautionary remarks about potential problems which might arise. There were also specific instructions on abstracting procedures. For example, in the hospital setting, when an inpatient record was involved, only the summary sheet was used in the data search; when an illness was prolonged, certain history items were required only in the initial visit.

The development of the instructions for finding and recording information on the individual criterion items was a project shared by the medical director and the two team leaders who had had much previous experience with information systems. Two different styles of abstract packets were developed and pretested. Abstractors were encouraged to try out the different instruments in the pretest site and to report preferences to senior staff. Based on their experience, a decision was made to use the abstract which had the most instructional material included on the form itself. Although this choice might have contributed to inter-abstractor agreement and to the overall reliability of the abstracting, the form was not well-suited for coding of the data.

The medical record was the primary source of data on physician performance. Compliance or noncompliance with preestablished criteria was determined on the basis of medical record information. Kroeger et al. (1965) and others have maintained that the medical record is an adequate source of data for evaluating the quality of patient care. They reported that two-thirds of their random sample of internists had recorded sufficient material in their office medical charts to enable nonphysicians to abstract this information for review. In their concluding remarks they recommended using both explicit criteria developed by physicians and abstracts of the medical record. Several studies have documented a relationship between good record-keeping and good practice. Donabedian (1968) suggests that these behaviors are conceptually related. Empirical relationships have been demonstrated by Lyons and Payne (1974), Clute (1963), and Peterson et al. (1956). However, an equal number of studies, such as the one conducted by Fessel and Van Brunt (1972) support the contention that there is little or no relation between what a physician does for a patient and what is subsequently recorded.

Observation Checklist

In order to validate our reliance on the medical record in the present study, direct observations of physician performance were conducted on a subsample of private practitioners. Physician consultants designed Observation Checklists for the nine selected topics. They included all criterion items present on the Abstract Form as well as additional items that had not been specified by the panels. The items were grouped into sets of activities or tasks that might normally be done together in the process of providing care. For example, in the Well-Child Examination Checklist, all items pertaining to History were assembled under that heading. Physical Exam items were grouped in the order of a "typical systems review"—all items pertaining to the neck were grouped together, as were items pertaining to the chest and back. Our assumption was that most physicians had an internalized checklist of their own.

The use of a checklist was compared with both free-form note taking and the use of a cassette recorder during the pretest period. All who used the checklist preferred it to other forms of data collection because it gave them an opportunity to check off tasks which complied with criteria, while observing and describing other activities in their marginal notes. Free-form notes were found to be inaccurate or incomplete. The use of cassettes or other recording equipment in the examining room was distressing to the patient; physicians frequently alluded to the Watergate incidents.

Criteria Checklist

As a further substantiation of the validity and relevance of our standards of evaluation, a Criteria Checklist was developed and used to compare the preferences of sample physicians with those of the panel members. A complete description of this instrument has been provided in Chapter 2. Standards culled from several sources were compiled for each topic and the criteria selected by CACS panels were dispersed throughout these lists in random fashion. The physicians were asked to designate criteria which they considered to be essential to good care and used consistently in their own practices.

Physician Characteristics Interview Schedule

There were several stages in developing an interview schedule for the collection of data on physician characteristics to serve as independent variables in the study. First, a review of the literature was conducted to determine which areas had been investigated by previous research and which had proved important. The review also provided valuable information on schedules and questionnaires which had been used in earlier studies. At the same time, a Physician Characteristics Committee was organized to assist staff in the development of the interview schedule. Participants on this committee included three physicians (one with extensive experience in health services research), two sociologists, and the CACS staff. A number of meetings were held to discuss the objectives of the interview. The following areas of concentration were identified by the committee: physician's attitude toward diagnostic activities, therapeutic activities, and medical record-keeping; the referral process and use of physician consultants; attitudes toward patients, the role of counseling, patient education; participation in professional societies; background and training; and hospital privileges.

The instrument was designed to obtain characteristics in four broad categories: (1) graduate medical education, (2) style of practice and professional activities, (3) background, and (4) attitudes. Members of the special Advisory Committee were heavily involved in generating items for all components. Once items had been developed for the first three areas, which have been traditionally covered by studies of this nature, attention was focused on the physician's attitudes toward patients and practice. Several drafts were presented to the committee. The second draft, which contained 175 items, was approved after pretest.

The interview schedule was pretested on ten physicians who were members of various study Advisory Committees. They represented the three primary specialties and both practice settings. Several minor problems were identified in the pretest period. Physicians had difficulty providing answers to several questions; either these were reworded or the response categories were modified. Items which were found to be offensive or seemed to have little face validity for the interviewee were dropped from the schedule. The process of pretesting this and subsequent instruments with physician advisory committee members and physician friends of staff proved to be an invaluable aid in learning to anticipate and deal with many of the problems encountered in the field.

Leadership Opinion Questionnaire (LOQ)/Leader Behavior
Descriptor Questionnaire (LBDQ)

During the course of the committee meetings on the physician
interview schedule, concern was expressed about the lack of sensitivity
of previous research to a physician's personal style of interacting
with staff and patients. Research staff were asked to collect data
on ways in which physicians exhibited empathy or took the initiative
in encouraging staff to perform activities. The original Leadership
Opinion Questionnaire was administered to physicians (the superiors)
and adapted for use in private practice and hospital samples. The
Leader Behavior Descriptor Questionnaire was used as a collateral
instrument and was given to subordinates or to the staff persons
who knew the physician best.

Although the LOQ/LBDQ was presented as part of the physician
characteristics schedule, its central focus was on the leadership or
managerial style of the physician. Both the LOQ and the LBDQ
were self-administrable questionnaires containing 29 items each. (See
Appendix C for a sample of these questionnaires.)

Organizational Characteristics Interview Schedule

The Organizational Characteristics Interview Schedule was designed
to gather information on structural, management, and psycho-social
aspects of the organizations in which care was delivered. The plan
for developing the interview schedule was similar to the procedure
used for the physician characteristics schedule. First a review of
the literature was conducted. Then an Organizational Characteristics
Committee was assembled; it included primary care physicians and
nurses, administrators, and experts in health care management. A
remarkable variety of interests and concerns were expressed by this
group. Several drafts of the instrument were pretested before the
final draft was approved by the committee members.

The committee identified a number of specific functional areas which
warranted investigation:

1. Characteristics of the Physical Plant: equipment; presence
   or absence of structures such as laboratory and X-ray; adequacy of space; telephone facilities; parking; and supplies
   used (gowns, instruments, etc.).
2. Employee Characteristics and Managerial Practices: patterns
   of task delegation; supervision of staff; assignment of salaries,

bonuses and other extrinsic rewards; hiring practices; job satisfaction and job turnover.
3. Reimbursements: billing; fees for services; insurance coverage and related problems.
4. Relationship with Other Agencies: police and rescue services, ambulance services, mental health facilities and drug dependency programs; and relationship with specialists outside of the primary care system.
5. Relationship with Patients: scheduling of appointments; patient management problems; perception of patient socio-economic status.

In its original form the Organizational Characteristics Interview Schedule contained over 200 data items. After a lengthy pretest on nonsampled practices, the schedule was reduced to less than half of its original size. (Appendix D contains selected items from this schedule.)

Basic Data on Patient Population

The second objective of the Patient Log was to collect basic data on all patients presenting to sample sites during the two-week log period. The forms included space to record the patient's age, sex, and address. After census tracts had been assigned on the basis of residence, patients were categorized according to socio-economic characteristics such as education, income, occupation, race and ethnicity. It was hypothesized that treatment of patients would vary with the characteristics of the social areas. In other words, patients coming from lower socio-economic areas were expected to receive poorer care (measured in terms of low compliance with criteria) than those from higher socio-economic areas. Similar findings were anticipated in relation to race and ethnicity of the patients.

Staffing Patterns and Special Training

The staffing plan for the field work was organized around two data collection teams, one for hospital sites and one for private practices. Each team consisted of one team leader, either an information systems specialist or a medical record analyst, and four or five abstractors. The medical director rotated between both teams providing consultation and supervision on an as-needed basis. The field teams were responsible for maintaining the Patient Log and for abstracting data on charts that had been screened by the team leader in cooperation with the project physician. Senior research assistants were responsible for administration of the Physician and Organizational Characteristics Interview Schedules and worked around the teams and at the convenience of the respondents. The research director (senior author) remained available for trouble-shooting and solving special problems that arose in the implementation of the field work plan.

Training of the Abstractors

The personnel hired to abstract the medical records had varied backgrounds and credentials, ranging from a doctorate in anthropology to assorted bachelors degrees in the arts and sciences. Staff members were trained for records abstracting by the medical records analyst and the medical director, who had had previous experience with an office audit. They conducted a two-week seminar for the abstractors in abbreviations, prefixes and suffixes commonly found in medical terminology and medical English. A complete glossary of abbreviations and drug names was provided in the abstractor manual. This material was further elaborated and periodically updated by the anthropologist who took a special interest in this aspect of the work. The manuals were assembled in loose-leaf binders to facilitate additions and revisions of the contents.

The medical director was available to all personnel in the field teams for consultation on special problems involved in the data collection. Throughout the pretest he worked with the abstractors in a local hospital where he supervised a careful trial of all instruments and accompanying instructions. During this period all field staff, including the medical director, abstracted the same records and participated in two daily seminars to discuss differing interpretations of information found. The pretest hospital was very supportive and allowed staff to remain there for six weeks. Training continued until estimates of reliability among abstractors had reached 98 percent.

The training of the abstractors was an ongoing process. It continued throughout the data collection period, which extended for approximately two years. Team leaders checked a 50 percent sample of all cases abstracted for the first year. When errors were found, abstractors were given immediate feedback on their performance. Staff members whose error rates consistently rose above the 5 percent level were excused from employment. After the first year only 10 percent of all abstracts were checked by the field coordinator. By this time abstractors had developed their own system of checking each other's work.

THE FIELD WORK PLAN: PROCESS AND PROBLEMS

Different strategies were used in negotiating with and collecting data from the 110 private practices and 5 hospitals. For this reason, the process of data collection is described in separate sections, beginning with the private offices.

Private Practices

After the private practitioners had been successfully recruited (see Chapter 3), an initial visit was arranged to introduce all members of the research team to the physician and staff of the sampled practice. This meeting involved the medical director or the research director, both team leaders, and all research assistants responsible for conducting the interviews. The purposes of this initial visit were:

1. to negotiate with staff the appropriate arrangements for the conduct of research operations at the sample site;
2. to assess the condition of the medical records at the site as a basis for time allocations of the abstractors;
3. to request the specific allotments of time from physician and staff for their interviews;
4. to ensure that the sample physician would be available to interpret standard abbreviations or handwriting if the medical director or team leader was unable to do so; and
5. to determine the approximate incidence of selected topics by inspecting appointment books or other daily logs kept by the organization.

After collecting data in the first ten offices, it was possible to predict the amount of time required to complete abstracting on the basis of our initial assessment of the site.

The second visit to sampled practices was more difficult to arrange because of the number and intensity of the data collection activities in this phase. Either private practice office staff or, in one-person practices, the physicians themselves, were asked to maintain the Patient Log. During the two-week log period, research assistants spot-checked or supervised the logging to make sure that presenting complaint and other patient data were entered accurately. In some offices, research assistants obtained information on patient age, sex, and address by reviewing the charts. In practices which handled a larger volume of patients per day, the log had to be completed prior to abstracting in order to provide a master list for sampling the total number of patients presenting with selected conditions.

Only two physicians who participated in the study requested that patients be contacted first to obtain their permission for a review of their own medical record. Staff in both of these offices were willing to distribute or mail permission forms to their patients. A covering letter from the sample physician encouraged them to sign and return the form. Less than 1 percent of these patients failed to comply with the request.

All of the major instruments for collecting data were introduced in this phase of the work, which lasted for three days in the average office. The Physician Characteristics Interview Schedule was administered by the research assistant who had developed it. It was given to each of the private practitioners and usually required an hour and fifteen minutes of the physician's time. Participants were then requested to complete the Leadership Opinion Questionnaire, which could be done in about seven minutes.

The Organizational Characteristics Interview Schedule was administered to senior office staff or office managers in 93 practices and to the physicians themselves in 7 practices. (This schedule was not completed in all of the sample offices; 10 physicians did not wish their staff to spend any more time on the project.) The major problem with the schedule was its length—the respondent had to spend approximately one hour and thirty minutes with the interviewer. Since this could not always be done in one sitting, several sessions were scheduled to avoid interrupting the work flow in the office. Following the administration of the organizational schedule, the Leader Behavior Descriptor Questionnaire was given to the office staff persons who worked most closely with the sample physician. Both physicians and office personnel reported enjoying this short questionnaire.

During this phase of the field work, there was always at least one research assistant available to answer questions that office staff might have regarding data to be entered in the two-week Patient Log. The most frequent problem found on patient logs was the use of both presenting complaints (reported in the patient's own words) and statements of working diagnoses entered by the sample physician or the physician's staff. This created difficulties for coders in the ensuing months.

At the conclusion of the abstracting, the project physician administered the Criteria Checklist to 100 private practitioners. This was done after data collection had been completed in the given site so that it would not affect the recording behavior of the participant. The medical director sat with most of the respondents to be available for questions and to encourage them to consider each item carefully. It usually required about forty minutes to fill out the questionnaire. Some of the general practitioners preferred not to complete the pediatric section because they were treating very few children.

Direct observations of a subsample of private physicians during patient visits were conducted in the third phase of the field work. According to the original plan, these would have been coordinated with the records abstracting so that observations of the encounter could have been compared with the medical record of the patient sample observed. Funding problems forced a number of decisions regarding research priorities, and this component of the study had to be modified accordingly.

The following procedures were used to select a subsample. First, private practitioners who had already participated in the study were stratified by major specialty on a master list. Every third name was chosen from a random start in each of the three strata. Letters were sent to all of these practitioners by the senior research assistant who had conducted the physician interviews. Her letter reintroduced the study and asked for the cooperation of the physician in its final stage. Practitioners who did not respond within ten days were contacted by phone. The response rates for internists and general practitioners were extremely low, but all of the pediátricians were willing to participate. A family nurse practitioner was engaged to conduct these observations. Besides her years of clinical experience and graduate training, she was extremely skilled in dealing with people.

Physicians were observed for a period of six and one-half to eight hours. A half-hour adjustment period was allowed for the diminution of reactivity to the observer; the half hour was based on pretest experience which indicated the average length of time before a physician appeared oblivious to the observer. It would have been preferable to have spent much more time with these practitioners, but the main objective in these observations was to determine whether record-keeping behavior was representative of actual care provided to the patients. (Their charts were subsequently reviewed for purposes of comparison.) It was necessary to remain in the office for at least six hours to get an adequate sample of patients presenting with selected diseases. All relevant cases were included, and every pediatric topic was observed except Pediatric Abdominal Pain which occurred infrequently. The observer reported no remarkable changes in physician behavior during the six to eight hour period.

The nurse practitioner found the Observation Checklist easy to use and flexible enough to incorporate additional date. She had previously had considerable experience conducting observations and had often been observed herself while working in the new primary care unit of a major teaching hospital. Resources were not available to check the reliability of her observations.

When results of the Observation Checklists were compared with the patient records, they were discovered to be almost identical; however, the provision of instructions and explanations to the patient were an exception. Physicians were observed giving instructions which they did not record. It is understandable that the recording of instructions and explanations might seem superfluous to the busy practitioner. An alternative explanation is the reactivity to the observer. Instructions may have been provided to the patient simply because the physician was aware that he or she was being evaluated.

Hospitals

The coordination of data collection in hospital sites was more difficult due to the size and complexity of the organizations. In the initial visit, all members of the CACS staff who were involved in recruiting, interviewing, or abstracting were introduced to medical records personnel. Without the cooperation of the people in medical records, it would have been impossible to complete the abstracting in any of the hospital sites.

The Patient Logs were a troublesome instrument in this practice setting. Either there was no room for the research assistant who was logging patients in the emergency room and clinics, or it was disruptive to have someone copying the information from already existing logs. Several hospitals xeroxed their logs for us at convenient times of the day. This turned out to be the most efficient way of collecting the necessary data. However, this method had its drawbacks. In one hospital much of the handwritten log was illegible even to some of the staff in the unit in which care had been rendered. It was usually possible to enlist the help of staff to decipher both the presenting complaints and the signatures of physicians who were providing care to the patients sampled; however, 8 percent of all emergency room visits in one hospital were lost because staff were too busy to help.

Once the logging had been completed, a patient sample was selected from among those presenting with one of the nine topics chosen for study. Then the search for patient records in the various parts of the organization began. The hospital with missing log information was also the setting in which approximately 20 percent of the records for sample patients could not be found. Some effort was made by hospital staff to recover these records, but after six months the search had to be terminated. Patients whose charts could not be located during that period were dropped from the study. These missing records were proportionately distributed among the diseases and problem areas.

The medical director's supervision of the abstractors was especially important in the hospitals. When a patient presented with more than one disease which had been selected for study (for example, Otitis Media and Pharyngitis), the simple rule was to abstract for both topics. It was not unusual for patients in these sites to present with multiple complaints. After charts had been pulled, screening decisions were made by the medical director or by the team leaders who were carefully trained and supervised. When presenting complaint was undecipherable on the log form, the record was pulled and examined for presence of a selected condition. If there was a large number of illegible or missing complaints, a sample of these was selected and the corresponding records were checked.

Procedures for abstracting in the hospital sites were similar to those employed in private offices, with the same concern for supervision and checking. The process of abstracting continued for a period of one to three months.

The hospital practitioners designated for the Physician Characteristics Interview were those who were primarily responsible for providing care to sampled patients. This included attendings, residents, interns, institutional staff (who were called general practitioners but provided only emergency care), and several medical school faculty. The complete schedule was administered to 127 hospital primary care practitioners and a shorter form to 47 physicians in other specialties; the shorter form contained only the most essential data items. Although sampled patients were often cared for by surgeons, radiologists, and gynecologists, findings are not presented for this peripheral group.

The Organizational Characteristics Interview was administered to a variety of professionals within each hospital, such as the hospital administrator responsible for ambulatory services, several clinic directors and senior nurses with administrative responsibilities. It was expected that the set of responses for a given site would be fairly similar, but this was not always the case. Because it was impossible to reinterview one or more of the respondents in each hospital, the most common (i.e., most frequently given) answer to a question was used as the response for the entire hospital. In addition to these data problems, many of the administrative staff proved very difficult to interview and required a more experienced member of the research team.

Neither the LOQ/LBDQ nor the Criteria Checklist were administered to hospital physicians. Although these participants were initially very cooperative, they were often distracted by paging or other stimuli in the hospital setting. Occasionally interviews had to be conducted in corridors or waiting areas. We did not feel that respondents could bear to submit to additional demands on their time.

Observations of the hospital physicians in the process of caring for sampled patients were prohibited by diminishing project resources. We continually regret not being able to implement this component of the design.

Coding of Data

Coding sheets were developed for abstracted data in each disease or problem area. Two-character alphabetic codes were assigned to each criterion item on the abstract sheets. Coding manuals included very elaborate instructions for coding procedures on each criterion item. Different coding mechanisms were devised for the different scoring systems which were developed to quantify physician performance. (Alternative scoring procedures are described in Chapter 3.) A special numeric coding scheme was developed in a later stage of the coding to simplify the alphabetic codes for the third scoring system. This coding system was developed and implemented by consulting physicians who used all information on the case abstract to make appropriate clinical decisions regarding the sampled physicians' performance. An experienced registered nurse was hired to manage the extremely complex coding for Essential Benign Hypertension, but all other coding for the first two scoring systems was handled by research staff. With the exception of the Well-Child Exams, each coding scheme for each scoring system was implemented by one coder. Consulting physicians were always available to interpret abstracted material.

Answers to questions on the Physician Characteristics Interview Schedule regarding training were verified using the American Medical Association Physician Directory and several specialty board directories. The coding was carefully reviewed by a trained coder for completeness, accuracy, and appropriate categorization of responses (Fine 1978).

The coding for the Organizational Interview Schedule was handled in a similar fashion. However, four research staff were assigned to this task. Extreme care was taken to ensure reliability among the coders. This stage of the coding was supervised by the research director who had administered the hospital schedule and interviewed solo practitioners or staff in the more difficult private office settings.

Abstract-Instruction Packet (Pharyngitis)
Results of Criteria Validation
with Sample Physicians

APPENDIX B

Instructions for Abstracting Pharyngitis

INITIAL DEFINITION CHECK

Topic covers both adults and children and will include any visit for a "sore throat" as a complaint or any diagnosed case of pharyngitis.

GENERAL INSTRUCTIONS

This is an acute problem. Therefore, the audit will cover the sampled episode, i.e., during the log period. The criteria are focused primarily on streptococcal and viral pharyngitis; secondary consideration is given to infectious mononucleosis.

When abstracting you must keep in mind the patient's age because a lot of the criteria are for children or adults only. Children are considered 16 and under and adults are considered 17 and older.

PHARYNGITIS

I. *HISTORY*—Search the history section of the initial visit note only.

   Item 1   Record all the complaints and their corresponding time of onset.
   Item 2   Look for any mention of being present.
   Item 3   Look for any mention of patient reporting temperature above 99°, chills or just feverishness.
   (Items 4–7 Scan the record to find this information.)
   Item 4   Look for any mention whether present or not. Check the systems review list if there is one. ARflF = acute rheumatic fever.
   Item 5   Check the record to see if he has been treated within the last year for similar symptoms or a notation that he was treated by another physician. Record the number of episodes. A new episode is indicated if there is a month's time span between the two visits.

PHARYNGITIS—continued

Item 6   Look for any mention of smoking.
Item 7   Look for any reference to presence or history of allergy in the patient or his family including drug allergies or drug reactions.
Item 8   Look for any mention of rhinorrhea, nasal discharge, runny nose and coryza.
Item 9   Look for any mention of hoarseness, thickened voice, and dysphonia.
Item 10   Look for any reference to vomiting or emesis.

II. PHYSICAL EXAMINATION—Search the initial visit note for this spell.

Item 11   Record the actual reading or indicate no mention.
Item 12   May be described as clear skin, no evidence, or mention of macular, papular, erythematous, morbilliform, or scarlet form of rash.
Item 13   Look for notation of impacted cerumen, wax, color, or any appearance of the auditory canal such as swollen, inflamed, infected, ears negative, ears normal, light reflective, et cetera.
Item 14   Tympanic membrane (TM) is another name for eardrum. May be described as to the exact color, presence or absence of injection of fluid, Shrapnell's membrane, thickened, dull, et cetera.
Item 15   Look for any statement regarding pharynx, nasopharynx or throat in regards to exudate, swelling, color, ulceration or lymphatic tissue hyperplasia. Tonsils wnl, inflamed, no exudates ok for #16 and #17.
Item 16   Look for any statement regarding the tonsils or tonsillar pillars and their appearance or the absence of the tonsils. Must mention area even if tonsillectomy is mentioned.
Item 17   Look for any mention of the tonsillar, submandibular, or sublingual cervical lymph nodes.
Item 18   Look for any mention of diffuse enlargement of the lymph nodes in any of the following areas: axillary, iliac, inguinal, supraclavicular, epitrochlear. A + or more preceding or following a particular node indicates Yes adenopathy is present. Accept nodes normal.
Item 19   Look for any notation that the cardiac exam was normal or positive findings such as presence of murmurs, gallops, cardiorespiratory negative, et cetera.
Item 20   Look for any notation of a normal or negative abdominal exam, no splenomegaly, or listing of findings. Usually related to the LKS.

III. LABORATORY—Search the lab sheets and progress notes matching dates to this acute spell. Check the filing system used by the office.

Item 21   This should be found on a microbiology or bacteriology lab sheet. Record the results.
Item 22   Record the specific results that are listed.
Item 23   May be indicated as negative result and labeled as heterophile or mono spot test.

IV. MEDICATION—Search the progress notes and drug list log sheet if one is used. If there is a contradiction between the Dr.'s note and the nurse's note accept the Dr.'s prescription.

Items 24–28 Just mark No if it was not ordered or record the dosage (DO) if it was ordered.
Item 29   Record the name of the drug and dosage.

PHARYNGITIS—*continued*

V. *IMPRESSION AND DIAGNOSIS*

Item 30 Record any impression that physician has for the initial visit.
Item 31 Record the impressions or diagnoses made after the initial visit.

VI. *INSTRUCTIONS*—Search all the progress notes for this episode.

Item 32 Look for an indication that the patient was told why the culture was needed.
Item 33 Look for an indication that the patient was told of consequences of untreated strep infection and consequences of not completing full course of medication.

VII. *FOLLOW-UP*—Search lab sheets, logs and progress follow-up notes.

Item 34 Look for any indication that a second visit was scheduled.
Item 35 Record the data if a second culture was taken. Mark the first NA if there is no evidence of a follow-up visit or the follow-up visit hasn't occurred yet.
Item 36 Check the follow-up notes for notations like, family contacts okay, call if other family members become ill.

PHARYNGITIS ABSTRACT

Setting I.D. # _____   Sex _____
Physician I.D. # _____   B.D. _____
Patient I.D. # _____   Initial Visit Date _____
Demographic Code _____   Date of Abstracting _____

I. HISTORY

1. Chief complaints with onset			NM	D
2. Cough	Y	N	NM	
3. Fever	Y	N	NM	
4. History of rheumatic fever	Y	N	NM	
5. Is this a recurrent infection		N	NM	D
6. Does or has the patient smoked (LTA)	NA	Y	N	NM	D
7. Allergy History (LTA)	NA		N	NM	
8. Rhinorrhea	Y	N	NM	
9. Hoarseness	Y	N	NM	
10. Vomiting (LTC)	NA	Y	N	NM	

II. PHYSICAL EXAM

11. Temperature			NM	D
12. Skin rash (LTC)	NA	N	NM	D
13. Appearance of ear canal		N	NM	D
14. Appearance of tympanic membranes		N	NM	D
15. Description of the pharynx		N	NM	D

					Hgb. B.	Hct. L.	M.	WBC E.	S Baso.
16. Description of the tonsils		N	NM	D					
17. Cervical nodes		N	NM	D					
18. Diffuse adenopathy			NM	D					
19. Cardiac auscultation (LTC & adult under 25)	NA		NM	D					
20. Abdominal Palpation (LTC & adult under 25)	NA		NM	D					

III. *LABORATORY*

21. Pharyngeal culture	NO	NA	D	
22. CBC	NO	NA	D	
23. Mononucleosis	NO	NA	D	

IV. *MEDICATION*

24. Was tetracycline prescribed?	NO	DO
25. Was sulfa prescribed?	NO	DO
26. Was penicillin prescribed?	NO	DO
27. Was bicillin given?	NO	DO
28. Was erythromycin prescribed? Ilosone	NO	DO
29. Other	NO	DO

V. *IMPRESSION*

30. Working diagnosis	NM	D
31. Final Diagnosis	NM	D

PHARYNGITIS ABSTRACT—*continued*

VI. *INSTRUCTIONS*

32. Need for culture to guide therapy	Y	NM
33. Vital concern for streptococcal infection	Y	NM

VII. *FOLLOW-UP*

34. Was a follow-up scheduled?		N	NM	Date
35. Was a second culture taken?	NA	NO	NA	D
36. Notation about family members if strep	Y	N		

Initial: _____

RESULTS OF CRITERIA VALIDATION

TABLE B.1
Essential Criteria for Adult Abdominal Pain

Criteria Designated Essential by CACS Panel	Percent of Private Physicians Designating Item Essential[1]		
	GP	IM	Both
Refer or hospitalize if signs of acute abdomen are present: e.g., rebound tenderness, hematemesis or melena.	97%	100%	99%
Obtain a detailed description of duration, type and character of the pain including factors affecting pain: e.g., position, movement, life events.	94	97	96
Note presence/absence of tenderness, guarding and rebound.	97	95	96
If pain is located in the lower abdomen, note findings of rectal and pelvic exams.	97	97	97
Record working diagnosis for initial visit.	72	87	80
Provide follow-up directions instructing the patient to contact the physician.	94	90	92
Describe the location and radiation of pain.	97	97	97
Inquire about associated gastrointestinal signs and symptoms: e.g., nausea, vomiting, character of the stool.	97	100	99
Schedule follow-up visit for continued observation if the problem is chronic.[2]	—	—	—
Perform urinalysis.	88	72	79
Assess temperature, pulse and BP.	81	92	87
Obtain history of previous pain, surgery and trauma to the abdominal area.	91	97	94
Inquire about relationship to menstruation.	75	79	77
Inquire about associated temperature elevation.	81	79	80
Provide symptomatic relief with appropriate drug(s); narcotics or antibiotics without a specific diagnosis are contraindicated.	88	64	75
Number of Sample Physicians	32	39	71

[1] This topic was not applicable to pediatricians.
[2] Added by AAP Panel at a later time; not included in Criteria Checklist.

TABLE B.2
Essential Criteria for Chest Pain

Criteria Designated Essential By CACS Panel	Percent of Private Physicians Designating Item Essential[1]		
	GP	IM	Both
Describe in detail presenting complaints such as chest pain, fullness, ache, pressure and/or cramps, "gas," difficulty breathing.	97%	95%	96%
Describe in detail location, radiation, duration, quality and frequency or mode of onset of pain.	97	95	96
Describe aggravating factors including: (1) body position or motion, (2) exercise or physical activity, (3) stress or anxiety, (4) time of day, or (5) relationship to respiration or swallowing.	91	100	95
Perform or obtain results of an ECG.	72	79	76
If fever and chills present, or pain pleuritic in nature, include or obtain the following: (1) the vital signs—temperature and BP, and (2) description of the sputum.	91	90	89
Indicate results of auscultation of the chest.	88	100	94
Provide a general description of the patient's appearance and emotional state.	56	82	70
Provide a description of the location of the apex beat, heart rhythm; note presence/absence of murmurs, gallops and friction rub.	81	92	87
Describe results of auscultation and palpation of the abdomen for bowel sounds, organ size and masses.	59	69	64
Assess levels of serum cholesterol, triglycerides and FBS.	33	46	40
Include the results of a chest X-ray.	66	82	75
Establish a diagnosis within 2 months of initial visit.	81	51	65
Record instructions given to patient.	60	78	70
Diagnosis of hiatus hernia should be based on more than a positive X-ray.	66	74	70
Obtain smoking history.	72	69	70
If chest pain is sharp or shooting and radiates to the neck, shoulder, extremities or torso, obtain results of an X-ray of the cervical and thoracic spine.	59	81	71
Include results of UGI and gallbladder series with gastrointestinal symptoms.	75	80	78
If sharp, stabbing, eccentric pain or distress aggravated principally by body motion or position, describe presence/absence of chest wall tenderness and the response of the neck to movement.	94	97	96
Number of Sample Physicians	33	39	72

[1] This topic was not applicable to pediatricians.

TABLE B.3
Essential Criteria for Hypertension

Criteria Designated Essential by CACS Panel	Percent of Private Physicians Designating Item Essential[1]		
	GP	IM	Both
Perform a complete urinalysis.	83%	99%	92%
Obtain results of ECG.	67	98	84
Assess body weight.	81	98	90
Obtain results of chest X-ray.	70	86	79
Control hypertension within 12 months of the initial visit.	100	94	97
Assess complications within 12 months of the initial visit.	94	94	94
Describe completely heart size and cardiac sounds; include presence/absence of murmurs and pulmonary rates.	94	100	97
Perform BUN or creatinine.	81	89	85
Obtain blood pressure readings from monthly follow-up visits until condition is stable; then obtain readings 2–3 times annually.	88	88	88
Obtain and record results of the following tests and procedures every 12 months: BUN/creatinine, ECG, urinalysis, and chest X-ray.	56	73	65
Note presence of peripheral edema.	22	87	58
Obtain results of IVP for sustained hypertension.	75	89	83
Review medications prescribed with patient on each visit.	100	88	93
Describe in detail results of an examination of the ocular fundi including specific references to the disc, vessels and presence/absence of hemorrhages and exudates.	63	87	76
Explain to the patient the objectives of treatment and the results of noncompliance, even if the patient is asymptomatic.	100	91	95
Assess by history and/or physical exam the extent of brain, heart, vascular, and renal damage.	76	87	82
Describe "body habitus" and "metabolic state."	48	74	62
Reduce blood pressure within 3 months.	89	89	89
Provide incremental therapy when using phenobarbitol or mild tranquilizers (including alpha-methyldopa, reserpine), diuretics, hydralazine, propanalol or guanethidine.	91	92	92
Results of palpation and auscultation of abdomen for masses and bruits.	63	91	78
Provide a patient with past or present heart failure with a 3-gram-or-less sodium diet and detailed instruction.	67	75	71

TABLE B.3 (*CONTINUED*)
Essential Criteria for Hypertension

Criteria Designated Essential by CACS Panel	Percent of Private Physicians Designating Item Essential[1]		
	GP	IM	Both
If a patient is on guanethidine, obtain supine and erect BP readings at each visit.	52	90	73
Hospitalize patient if there is evidence of aldosteronism, renovascular hypertension, coarctation, or adrenal tumor.	63	85	75
Determine presence/absence of the following: visual disturbance, nocturia, angina, muscle cramps and sweating.	75	91	84
Assess or obtain results of assessments of serum renin or aldosterone in patient with muscle weakness, cramps, nocturia or a serum K level of less than 3.5 or when K falls significantly on a "salt load" when off diuretics.	22	64	45
Provide careful instructions to patient on side effects of drugs prescribed; emphasize postural hypotension with ganglionic blockers and the possible occurrence of depression with reserpine, if appropriate.	83	90	87
Perform or obtain results of a thyroid function test if there is a possibility of thyrotoxicosis.	100	100	100
Check peripheral vessel pulsations.	47	90	71
If diuretics are prescribed, assess serum electrolyte balance 6 months after initiation of therapy, then annually with blood sugar.	72	54	62
Instruction in sensible living habits: i.e., reducing alcohol intake and smoking, weight reduction and prudent exercising, if appropriate.	94	92	93
Number of Sample Physicians	32	39	71

[1] This topic was not applicable to pediatricians.

TABLE B.4
Essential Criteria for Urinary Tract Infection

Criteria Designated Essential by CACS Panel	Percent of Private Physicians Designating Item Essential[1]		
	GP	IM	Both
Describe frequency and character of urination.	83%	95%	90%
Describe location of pain and relationship to urination.	84	87	86
Note all known drug allergies.	63	70	67
Include results of abdominal exam including description of kidneys and bladder.	72	74	73
Include results of dip-stick and sediment exam of a clean-voided or glass-catheter-collected urine specimen.	94	84	88
Obtain results of urine culture if patient has had previous infection or is not responding to therapy.	72	92	83
Obtain results of IVP if recurrent and patient has kidney involvement (unless patient is pregnant).	85	87	86
Include diagnosis of underlying cause of recurrent UTI.	87	92	90
Prevent recurrences.	69	69	69
Do not use chloramphenicol.	67	69	68
Provide patient with explanation as to why medications are prescribed.	66	82	75
If cystitis, explain the benign, self-limiting nature of the disease with high frequency of recurrence.	62	51	56
If the patient has an upper tract infection, explain seriousness of a kidney infection as well as the good prognosis when adequate studies are done to exclude abnormalities.	72	82	77
Prescribe the following medications: sulfonamides, tetracycline, ampicillin, nitrofurantoin, and/or cephalosporins. Give others only if specifically indicated by the culture.	97	89	93
Hospitalize patients for high fever, toxicity, unremitting vomiting or sepsis.	84	100	93
Prescribe two weeks of medication for the first acute infection.	68	45	55
If reflux is present, medicate until resolved.	41	31	36
Arrange for a minimum of one follow-up visit one week after completion of antibiotic therapy.	28	38	33
Note from physical exam the presence/absence of CVA tenderness.	83	90	87
Refer for and obtain findings from cystoscopy for recurrent infection.	69	72	71
Explain to the patient the need for continued medical surveillance.	56	49	52

TABLE B.4 (CONTINUED)
Essential Criteria for Urinary Tract Infection

Criteria Designated Essential by CACS Panel	Percent of Private Physicians Designating Item Essential[1]		
	GP	IM	Both
Prescribe a minimum of a 6-week course of medication for a relapse or a recurrent infection.	54	41	47
Indicate onset, duration and progress of the signs and symptoms.	81	90	86
Inquire about previous urological problems and treatment.	56	87	73
Perform tuberculin skin test for persistent sterile pyuria.	59	54	56
If structural abnormalities are present, explain them to the patient.	50	69	60
Instruct the patient to call if signs of allergic reaction to drugs are experienced (e.g., fever, chills, back pain) or if relief of symptoms is not experienced in 5–7 days.	91	85	88
If drugs prescribed which change the color of the urine, explain this to the patient.	69	64	66
Instruct the patient to maintain an adequate intake of fluids.	88	80	84
Inquire about presence of chills and fever; check the patient's temperature.	78	82	80
Number of Sample Physicians	32	39	71

[1]This topic was not applicable to pediatricians.

TABLE B.5
Essential Criteria for Pharyngitis (Adult and Pediatric)

Criteria Designated Essential by CACS Panel	Percent of Private Physicians Designating Item Essential			
	GP	IM	PED	All
Record date of onset.	90%	90%	83%	88%
Provide detailed description of pharynx and tonsils.	90	92	94	92
Describe tympanic membrane and ear canals.	68	72	82	74
If enlarged cervical nodes or severe exudates are present, note results of cardiac auscultation and abdominal palpation (LTC & young adults).	76	89	76	81
Pharyngeal culture.	64	89	92	82
Perform CBC and mono test if enlarged spleen, diffuse adenopathy or membranous exudates are present.	97	100	66	89
Prescribe 10 days of penicillin, bicillin or erythromycin when streptococcal (culture positive for strep); tetracycline and sulfa are acceptable if patient is allergic to any of the above.	100	97	96	98
Check for enlarged cervical nodes.	81	82	93	85
Inquire about rheumatic fever.	74	87	48	72
Explanation of need to complete full course of therapy.	72	85	92	83
Note presence/absence of cough or fever.	81	87	81	83
Inquire about similar previous illness.	55	NA	46	51
Check for presence of skin rash (if child).	55	NA	76	65
Statement as to whether viral or bacterial.[1]	—	—	—	—
Appropriate treatment to eradicate strep when present.[1]	—	—	—	—
Culture/treat family if appropriate.[1]	—	—	—	—
Number of Sample Physicians	33	39	29	101

[1]Not included in Criteria Checklist.

TABLE B.6
Essential Criteria for Otitis Media (Pediatrics, 0–12 Years)

Criteria Designated Essential by CACS Panel	Percent of Private Physicians Designating Item Essential[1]		
	GP	PED	Both
Use analgesics to relieve pain.	65%	62%	63%
Follow patient until infection resolved or referral made.	93	100	97
Clear up infection in 10–14 days.	93	90	91
Treat with ampicillin, bicillin, penicillin (unless allergic) for no less than 7 days.	93	93	93
Provide instructions to patient/parent on duration and dosage of medication.	93	100	97
Provide instructions for follow-up.	97	100	98
Refer to ENT for sinus complications such as mastoiditis, cellulitis, etc.	90	61	75
Perform detailed exam of tympanic membranes and auditory canals.	100	100	100
Describe condition of pharynx and tonsils.	97	100	93
Record onset and duration of symptoms.	82	83	82
Include notation of past and/or present hearing problems.	78	84	81
Describe symptoms.	100	97	98
Prescribe oral decongestants.	60	59	59
Restore any hearing loss.	83	86	84
Take appropriate steps to prevent chronic ear disease.	86	86	86
Number of Sample Physicians	27	29	56

[1]This topic was not applicable to internists.

TABLE B.7
Essential Criteria for Pediatric Abdominal Pain

Criteria Designated Essential by CACS Panel	Percent of Private Physicians Designating Item Essential[1]		
	GP	PED	Both
Describe in detail the duration, type and character of the pain including circumstances at onset, periodicity, and comparison with previous pain.	88%	100%	94%
Note abdominal tenderness, rebound, and guarding.	100	100	100
Rule out surgical emergency by abdominal palpation, urinalysis and CBC; refer when appropriate.	100	100	100
Obtain urine culture for signs and symptoms of urinary tract infection.	92	100	96
Perform LFT when dark urine, liver tenderness or jaundice present.	96	100	98
Sickle cell prep if black. (Inoperative)[2]	62	54	58
Positive/negative findings of physical exam of throat and lungs.	79	83	81
Inquire about recent respiratory and recent urinary tract infection.	78	86	82
Inquire about changes in bowel patterns or appearance of stool.	88	100	94
Culture stool for blood, ova, and parasites if indicated by history.	75	76	76
Provide a working or final diagnosis at first visit.	88	93	91
Obtain stool culture if chronic diarrhea present.	64	86	76
Discuss possible causes and need for tests and procedures with patient/parent.	83	90	87
Number of Sample Physicians	25	29	54

[1]This topic was not applicable to internists.
[2]Data on race could not be obtained from records.

TABLE B.8
Essential Criteria for Well-Child Examination (Infant, Birth—2 Years)

Criteria Designated Essential by CACS Panel	Percent of Private Physicians Designating Item Essential[1]		
	GP	PED	Both
Description of pregnancy and delivery.	75%	93%	85%
Record head and chest circumference and length and weight at birth.	75	93	85
Medical history and description of the family.	78	89	84
Obtain head size at each examination.	50	100	77
Record height and weight at each examination.	87	93	90
Provide immunizations according to AAP schedule.	91	100	96
Perform tuberculin skin test by 12th month.	67	79	74
Record negative/positive findings of systems review.[2]	74	83	79
Description of home environment.	50	54	52
Perform urinalysis, PKU.	67	80	74
Description of elimination patterns.	50	69	60
Description of sensory, motor, and social development.	67	79	74
Description of crying patterns (behavior).	70	71	70
Develop supportive relationship with parents.	78	86	82
Description of eating patterns.	78	90	84
Description of response to separation from parents.	35	37	36
Number of Sample Physicians	24	29	53

[1] This topic was not applicable to internists.
[2] EENT, red reflex, chest, heart, abdomen, genitalia, extremities, reflexes, hips, areas of common herniation, peripheral pulses; include general remarks on behavior.

TABLE B.9
Essential Criteria for Well-Child Examination (Preschool, 2–7 Years)

Criteria Designated Essential by CACS Panel	Percent of Private Physicians Designating Item Essential[1]		
	GP	PED	Both
Record negative/positive findings of systems review.[2]	83%	100%	92%
Obtain height and weight for each examination.	83	96	90
Describe speech, sensory, and motor development.	90	90	90
Describe social development and interpersonal relationships.	61	93	78
Check vision if patient is over 3 years of age.	34	52	44
Develop supportive relationship with parents.	78	89	84
Assess parents' concerns over physical or psychological problems and provide guidance where appropriate.	83	83	83
Description of eating pattern.	52	83	69
Provide guidance to parents on appropriateness of child's attending Nursery School (3–4 years of age).	26	48	38
Provide guidance on nutrition and feeding.	70	90	81
Check coordination and attention span.	36	69	54
Check blood pressure if patient is over 3 years of age.	35	63	50
Do hemoglobin and hematocrit.	44	50	47
Description of elimination patterns.	79	56	66
Perform urinalysis.	83	90	87
Number of Sample Physicians	24	29	53

[1]This topic was not applicable to internists.
[2]Hips, common areas of herniation, genitalia, visual disorders, feeding problems, failure to thrive, speech and hearing problems, family and/or social problems, scoliosis, hyperkinesis.

Leadership Opinion Questionnaire
Leader Behavior Descriptor Questionnaire

Appendix C

I. Office Practice (Physician) Leadership Opinion Questionnaire

This questionnaire has been developed to collect data on administrative behavior. We have modified it to apply to the various settings under study in our research project.

This part of the interview process should take only ten minutes of your time. Please read each question carefully. Then, select and circle the response that first occurs to you. Please do not linger over each item and ask questions only if you must.

All the information you give us will be held in absolute confidence. Statistical analyses are done on aggregates of scores which are computerized so that individual identification is not possible.

I.D. No. _____

Interviewer _____

Date _____ Time _____

WOULD YOU DESCRIBE YOURSELF AS A PERSON WHO:

* Encourages overtime work. (1) often (2) fairly often (3) occasionally (4) once in a while (5) very seldom.
* Encourages others to try out new ideas. (1) often (2) fairly often (3) occasionally (4) once in a while (5) very seldom.
* Rules with an iron hand. (1) always (2) often (3) occasionally (4) seldom (5) never.
* Criticizes poor work. (1) always (2) often (3) occasionally (4) seldom (5) never.
* Talks about how much should be done. (1) a great deal (2) fairly much (3) to some degree (4) comparatively little (5) not at all.
* Encourages slow-working people to work harder. (1) often (2) fairly often (3) occasionally (4) once in a while (5) very seldom.

Based on LOQ/LBDQ developed by Fleishman, et al. (1955).

• Assigns people to particular tasks. (1) always (2) often (3) occasionally (4) seldom (5) never.
• Asks that people under you follow to the letter standard routines and procedures. (1) always (2) often (3) occasionally (4) seldom (5) never.
• Offers new approaches to problems. (1) often (2) fairly often (3) occasionally (4) once in a while (5) very seldom.
• Puts the office's (hospital's, clinic's, O.P.D.'s, E.R.'s, etc.) welfare above the welfare of any employee. (1) always (2) often (3) occasionally (4) seldom (5) never.
• Insists that you be informed on decisions made by staff under you. (1) always (2) often (3) occasionally (4) seldom (5) never.
• Lets others do their work the way they think best. (1) always (2) often (3) occasionally (4) seldom (5) never.
• Stresses being ahead of other office practices (hospitals, groups). (1) a great deal (2) fairly much (3) to some degree (4) comparatively little (5) not at all.
• 'Needles' people under you for greater effort. (1) always (2) often (3) occasionally (4) seldom (5) never.
• Emphasizes meeting of deadlines. (1) always (2) often (3) occasionally (4) seldom (5) never.
• Decides in detail what shall be done and how it shall be done by staff. (1) always (2) often (3) occasionally (4) seldom (5) never.
• Meets with staff at regularly scheduled times. (1) always (2) often (3) occasionally (4) seldom (5) never.

I.D. No. _____

OFFICE PRACTICE ONLY

• Sees to it that staff are working up to capacity. (1) always (2) often (3) occasionally (4) seldom (5) never.
• Refuses to compromise a point. (1) always (2) often (3) occasionally (4) seldom (5) never.
• Does personal favors for people. (1) often (2) fairly often (3) occasionally (4) once in a while (5) very seldom.
• Speaks in a manner not to be questioned. (1) always (2) often (3) occasionally (4) seldom (5) never.
• Asks for more than staff can get done. (1) often (2) fairly often (3) occasionally (4) once in a while (5) very seldom.
• Helps people on staff with their personal problems. (1) often (2) fairly often (3) occasionally (4) once in a while (5) very seldom.
• Stands up for those on staff under you, even though it makes you unpopular. (1) always (2) often (3) occasionally (4) seldom (5) never.
• Insists that everything be done your way. (1) always (2) often (3) occasionally (4) seldom (5) never.
• Rejects suggestions for change. (1) always (2) often (3) occasionally (4) seldom (5) never.
• Changes the duties of staff without first talking it over with them. (1) often (2) fairly often (3) occasionally (4) once in a while (5) very seldom.
• Resists changes in ways of doing things. (1) always (2) often (3) occasionally (4) seldom (5) never.
• Refuses to explain your actions. (1) often (2) fairly often (3) occasionally (4) once in a while (5) very seldom.

II.   Office Practice (Staff)
Leader Behavior Descriptor

This questionnaire has been developed to collect data on administrative behavior. We have modified it to apply to the various settings under study in our research project.

This part of the interview process should take only ten minutes of your time. Please read each question carefully. Then, select and circle the response that first occurs to you. Please do not linger over each item and ask questions only if you must.

All the information you give us will be held in absolute confidence. Statistical analyses are done on aggregates of scores which are computerized so that individual identification is not possible.

I.D. No.   _____

Job Title _____

Interviewer   _____

Date _____   Time _____

WOULD YOU DESCRIBE DR. _____ AS A PERSON WHO:

- Encourages overtime work.   (1) often   (2) fairly often   (3) occasionally   (4) once in a while   (5) very seldom.
- Encourages others to try out new ideas.   (1) often   (2) fairly often   (3) occasionally   (4) once in a while   (5) very seldom.
- Rules with an iron hand.   (1) always   (2) often   (3) occasionally   (4) seldom   (5) never.
- Criticizes poor work.   (1) always   (2) often   (3) occasionally   (4) seldom   (5) never.
- Talks about how much should be done.   (1) a great deal   (2) fairly much   (3) to some degree   (4) comparatively little   (5) not at all.
- Encourages slow-working people to work harder.   (1) often   (2) fairly often   (3) occasionally   (4) once in a while   (5) very seldom.
- Assigns people to particular tasks.   (1) always   (2) often   (3) occasionally   (4) seldom   (5) never.
- Asks that people under him/her follow to the letter standard routines and procedures.   (1) always   (2) often   (3) occasionally   (4) seldom   (5) never.
- Offers new approaches to problems.   (1) often   (2) fairly often   (3) occasionally   (4) once in a while   (5) very seldom.
- Puts the office's (hospital's, clinic's, O.P.D.'s, E.R.'s, etc.) welfare above the welfare of any employee.   (1) always   (2) often   (3) occasionally   (4) seldom   (5) never.
- Insists that he/she be informed on decisions made by staff under him/her.   (1) always   (2) often   (3) occasionally   (4) seldom   (5) never.
- Lets others do their work the way they think best.   (1) always   (2) often   (3) occasionally   (4) seldom   (5) never.
- Stresses being ahead of other office practices (hospitals, groups).   (1) a great deal   (2) fairly much   (3) to some degree   (4) comparatively little   (5) not at all.

- 'Needles' people under him/her for greater effort.   (1) always   (2) often   (3) occasionally   (4) seldom   (5) never.
- Emphasizes meeting of deadlines.   (1) always   (2) often   (3) occasionally   (4) seldom   (5) never.
- Decides in detail what shall be done and how it shall be done by staff.   (1) always   (2) often   (3) occasionally   (4) seldom   (5) never.
- Meets with staff at regularly scheduled times.   (1) always   (2) often   (3) occasionally   (4) seldom   (5) never.

I.D. No. _____

OFFICE PRACTICE ONLY

- Sees to it that staff are working up to capacity.   (1) always   (2) often   (3) occasionally   (4) seldom   (5) never.
- Refuses to compromise a point.   (1) always   (2) often   (3) occasionally   (4) seldom   (5) never.
- Does personal favors for people.   (1) often   (2) fairly often   (3) occasionally   (4) once in a while   (5) very seldom.
- Speaks in a manner not to be questioned.   (1) always   (2) often   (3) occasionally   (4) seldom   (5) never.
- Asks for more than staff can get done.   (1) often   (2) fairly often   (3) occasionally   (4) once in a while   (5) very seldom.
- Helps people on staff with their personal problems.   (1) often   (2) fairly often   (3) occasionally   (4) once in a while   (5) very seldom.
- Stands up for those on staff under him/her, even though it makes him/her unpopular.   (1) always   (2) often   (3) occasionally   (4) seldom   (5) never.
- Insists that everything be done his/her way.   (1) always   (2) often   (3) occasionally   (4) seldom   (5) never.
- Rejects suggestions for change.   (1) always   (2) often   (3) occasionally   (4) seldom   (5) never.
- Changes the duties of staff without first talking it over with them.   (1) often   (2) fairly often   (3) occasionally   (4) once in a while   (5) very seldom.
- Resists changes in ways of doing things.   (1) always   (2) often   (3) occasionally   (4) seldom   (5) never.
- Refuses to explain his/her actions.   (1) often   (2) fairly often   (3) occasionally   (4) once in a while   (5) very seldom.

(If office practice, stop here)

Selected Items from Organizational Characteristics Interview Schedule

APPENDIX D

Selected Items from Organizational Characteristics Interview Schedule
(Chapter 6)

Table No.	Question
6.1	What percent of the patients that you see in your office would you consider—on the basis of occupation, education and income—to be of lower, middle or upper socioeconomic status: (a) _____ % lower? (b) _____ % middle? (c) _____ % upper?
6.2	If a patient cannot speak English is there someone on the staff who can interpret for them? (a) _____ yes (b) _____ no If yes, what language(s) are spoken by this (these) person (people)?
6.3	Is the physician's home phone number listed? (Responses were checked by research assistant.)
6.4	Information on specialty and number of years in practice were obtained from the AMA physician biographical tape and Connecticut State Licensing files. Practice size was ascertained from the number of patient visits on the two-week patient log.
6.5	What do the patients you see complain about? _____ unsatisfactory telephone communications _____ long waits for care _____ billing errors _____ parking problems _____ lack of consideration shown to them _____ other
6.6	Who handles these complaints? _____ office manager/administrator _____ nurse _____ physician/clinic chief _____ medical assistant _____ other particular member of staff

Table No.   *Question—continued*

_____ physician and/or any staff
_____ no one; not applicable (i.e., no staff)
_____ other

6.7   Who do staff complain about?
_____ out-dated telephone equipment
_____ friction among personnel that interferes with work
_____ overwork
_____ too little pay
_____ insufficient fringe benefits
_____ too much work after hours
_____ doctor not delegating enough responsibility
_____ frequent absences of certain staff
_____ no avenue for complaint and/or suggestions of staff members
_____ poor working conditions
_____ other

6.8   How does staff feel about the present patient load (volume)?
_____ desire fewer patients
_____ comfortable with patient load
_____ could handle more

6.9   Are patients seen
_____ by appointment
_____ on a first-come first-serve basis?
If by appointment, how much time is allocated (given) for a regular office visit (in minutes)? _____

6.10   What proportion (percent) of your patients, do you believe, come in for trivial complaints?

6.11   Information regarding personnel was obtained from office manager or other senior staff person and was supplemented by the observations of the research assistant.

6.12   How are the following tests and procedures done?

	Staff	Physician	Pt. Referred or Specimen Sent Out
ECG	_____	_____	_____
Hemoglobin	_____	_____	_____
Hematocrit	_____	_____	_____
Sed Rate	_____	_____	_____
Urinalysis	_____	_____	_____
BP	_____	_____	_____
Temp	_____	_____	_____
Height and Weight	_____	_____	_____
Routine Immunizations	_____	_____	_____
Other Injections	_____	_____	_____

6.13   Information obtained by observing the layout of the office.

6.14   (Hand respondent sheet and offer help as needed.)

Which of the following do you feel is most detrimental to productivity? (Choose the pertinent items and rank from one to five, most detrimental to least detrimental.)

a) _____ Increasing paper work (paper work piles up)
b) _____ Poor appointment planning
c) _____ Errors in billing
d) _____ Problems with third party payment
e) _____ Slow payment on insurance claims
f) _____ Steadily rising overhead
g) _____ Inadequate facilities
h) _____ Low collection ratio
i) _____ Low utilization of X-ray and lab facilities
j) _____ Misfiled financial and medical records
k) _____ Poorly prepared examination and treatment rooms
l) _____ Frequent absences of staff members
m) _____ Frequent emergencies (taking doctor out of office)
n) _____ Inability of aides to cover for each other
o) _____ Slow or inefficient training of new staff personnel
p) _____ Other(s): _____
q) _____ _____
r) _____ _____
s) _____ _____

Appendix E

Characteristics of the Patient Population

APPENDIX E

Characteristics of the Patient Population

PATIENT SAMPLE: PRESENTING COMPLAINT

The Patient Log, an instrument which was instituted in each of the hospital and private practice sites for a two-week period, was the source of information on the patient sample involved in the study. Staff in the respective settings had been instructed to record the reason for the patient visit in the patient's own words whenever possible. The resulting data on presenting complaint was coded in order to provide an overview of the types of diseases and problem areas that were handled on a regular basis by private and hospital practitioners.

The most difficult problem connected with describing the physicians' workload was the selection of an appropriate coding index. An early decision to use the coding scheme developed by the National Ambulatory Medical Care Survey (NAMCS) was aborted because private practice staff tended to record their own or the physician's impression of the illness—usually a working diagnosis—rather than the patient's interpretation. Working diagnoses were also prevalent in the hospital emergency room and clinic logs. The Hurtado and Greenlick classification scheme (1971) was carefully considered, but it seemed unnecessarily complex for this research. It was finally decided that a modification of the Hospital Adaptation of the International Classification of Diseases (Second Edition) would be best suited to our purposes. A group of hospital medical records librarians familiar with modified H-ICDA were recruited to code the presenting complaints for the 30,000 patients logged.

Tables E.1 and E.2 demonstrate the results of this coding by diagnostic or procedure categories for all private practice and hospital patients respectively. The distribution of presenting complaints is further broken down by specialty and individual hospital.

Table E.1 shows that Diseases of the Circulatory System (11.3 percent), Diseases of the Respiratory System (11 percent), Signs, Symptoms and Ill-Defined Conditions (16.6 percent) and Special Admissions and Examinations without Complaint or Reported Diagnosis (31.1 percent) accounted for 70 percent of presenting complaints for private practice patients. Higher frequencies were expected for several categories, particularly Diseases of the Digestive System and Diseases of the Genitourinary System. Very few Connecticut general practitioners seemed to be treating female patients for Delivery and Complications of Pregnancy. It should be mentioned that routine office visits, check-ups, and well-exams are included in the category Special Admissions and Examinations Without Complaint or Reported Diagnosis. The table also presents these data by primary specialty of the physician; a large proportion of these well-exams occurred in pediatrics (43.8 percent). Patients with Diseases of the Circulatory System were more apt to visit internists (19.3 percent) than general practitioners (10.5 percent). An alternative explanation is that internists were more apt to classify these problems as circulatory than other practitioners.

A comparison between Tables E.1 and E.2 indicates that fewer cases of Endocrine, Nutritional and Metabolic Diseases were logged in hospitals (1.5 percent) as compared with private practices (5.5 percent). Diseases of the Circulatory System represented only 3 percent of the hospital work load as compared with 11.3 percent for private practices; Diseases of the Respiratory System appeared more often in hospital logs (14.6 percent versus 11 percent). Signs, Symptoms, and Ill-Defined Conditions were more prevalent in the hospital settings (24.2 percent versus 16.6 percent for private practice) and, as might be expected, many more patients presented with Injuries and Adverse Effects in hospital clinics and emergency rooms (23.9% versus 4.3%). The relatively small percentage for Special Admissions and Examinations Without Complaint or Reported Diagnosis (13.2 percent versus 31.1%) stems from the fact that hospitals are somewhat more careful in recording reason for visit, as they are required to do so by third-party payers.

Results shown in the hospital tabulations may be colored by the problems of data collection encountered in one large hospital setting (Hospital D; see Appendix A for further detail). Table E.2 also indicates a rather low incidence of Diseases of the Respiratory System in this hospital (6.2 percent) and a much more frequent occurrence of Signs,

TABLE E.1

Patients' Presenting Complaints, as Reported by Private Practice Physicians, by Diagnosis, Symptom or Procedure, and by Physician Specialty
(Percentage Distribution)

Diagnostic or Procedure Category	General Practice	Internal Medicine	Pediatrics	All Specialties
I Infective and Parasitic Diseases (001–136)	1.9	2.7	3.0	2.1
II Neoplasms (140–239)	.9	1.6	—	.8
III Endocrine, Nutritional and Metabolic Dis. (240–279)	7.2	6.9	.2	5.5
Diabetes Mellitus (250)	2.2*	4.4	.1	2.5
Obesity (277)	4.2	1.1	.1	2.3
IV Blood and Blood-Forming Organs (280–289)	.4	.7	—	.5
V Mental Disorders (290–318)	2.2	3.0	.2	2.0
Neuroses (310)	2.0	2.5	—	1.7
VI Nervous System and Sense Organs (320–389)	2.3	2.8	4.6	3.0
Otitis Media (381)	.8	.6	3.8	1.4
VII Circulatory System (390–458)	10.5	19.3	.1	11.3
Essential Benign Hypertension (401)	6.9	11.4	—	7.0
Chronic Ischemic Heart Disease (412)	.9	3.3	—	1.5
VIII Respiratory System (460–519)	14.0	7.6	9.8	11.0
Acute Nasopharyngitis (460)	2.3	.7	.8	1.5
Acute Pharyngitis (462)	1.4	1.4	2.5	1.6
Acute Tonsillitis (463)	1.5	.4	1.4	1.1
Acute URI of multiple or unspecified sites (465)	5.5	1.3	2.8	3.5
IX Digestive System (520–577)	1.3	3.0	.2	1.6
X Genitourinary System (580–629)	1.8	2.2	.3	1.6
XI Deliveries and Complications of Pregnancy, Childbirth, and the Puerperium (631–678)	—	—	—	—
XII Skin and Subcutaneous Tissue (680–709)	3.0	2.2	2.0	2.3
Other eczema and dermatitis (692)	1.1	.7	1.0	1.0

TABLE E.1 (*CONTINUED*)
Patients' Presenting Complaints, as Reported by Private Practice Physicians, by Diagnosis, Symptom or Procedure, and by Physician Specialty (Percentage Distribution)

Diagnostic or Procedure Category	General Practice	Internal Medicine	Pediatrics	All Specialties
XIII Musculoskeletal System and Connective Tissue (710–739)	2.4	3.8	.1	2.6
Rheumatoid arthritis and allied conditions (712)	—	1.3	—	.5
Arthritis or polyarthritis, unspecified (715)	.9	1.0	—	.7
Synovitis, bursitis and tenosynovitis (731)	1.0	.6	.1	.7
XIV Congenital Anomalies (740–759)	—	—	—	—
XV Diseases Peculiar to Newborn Infants (760–768)	—	—	—	—
XVI Signs, Symptoms and Ill-Defined Conditions (770–796)	16.3	16.7	17.6	16.6
Symptoms referable to other organs of special sense (772)	.6	.4	1.8	.8
Symptoms referable to heart and vessels (774)	1.5	2.5	.3	1.6
Symptoms referable to mouth, pharynx and larynx (777)	11.1	.8	3.4	1.8
Other symptoms referable to respiratory system (779)	.6	.3	1.4	.7
Symptoms referable to abdomen and peritoneum (780)	1.3	1.7	.8	1.3
Symptoms referable to skin and subcutaneous tissue (786)	1.1	.8	1.3	1.1
Symptoms referable to limbs and joints (788)	1.3	.9	.3	1.0
Other symptoms referable to musculoskeletal syst. (781)	1.3	1.4	.2	1.1
Other general symptoms (792)	2.1	2.5	3.5	2.5
Observation and evaluation without need for further medical care (793)	1.2	2.1	2.4	1.7

XVII Injuries & Adverse Effects (800–999)	5.6	3.1	3.6	4.3
Unspecified injuries (919)	1.3	.2	.3	.7
XVIII Special Admissions and Examinations without Complaint or Reported Diagnosis (1000–1086)	26.9	21.3	56.9	31.1
Medical exam. of indiv. (1000)	18.7	15.0	43.8	22.7
Special investigations and exams (1001)	2.5	1.9	4.3	2.7
Medical and surgical aftercare (1015)	2.5	1.8	1.8	2.1
Prophylactic vaccinations and innoculations (1081)	.9	1.1	3.4	1.5
Desensitization to other vac. and innoculations (1082)	1.1	.4	1.6	1.0
XIX Not Ascertained				
TOTAL PERCENT**	100.0	100.0	100.0	100.0
Number of Cases	7632	6086	4584	18302

*Contacts in individual three digit codes counted in major category (e.g., contacts with diabetes mellitus counted in percentage of contacts with Endocrine, Nutritional, and Metabolic Diseases).

**Percentages may not total 100 percent because of rounding error.

TABLE E.2

Patients' Presenting Complaints, as Reported by Hospital Physicians by Diagnosis, Symptom or Procedure, and by Hospital
(Percentage Distribution)

Diagnostic or Procedure Category	Hospital A	Hospital B	Hospital C	Hospital D	Hospital E	All Hospitals
I Infective and Parasitic Diseases (001–136)	3.2	3.5	4.6	1.0	4.5	2.8
Diarrheal Disease (009)	2.2	.8	1.7	.1	3.2	1.2
II Neoplasms (140–239)	.5	.8	.4	.9	.4	.6
III Endocrine, Nutritional and Metabolic Dis. (240–279)	1.9	5.2	1.4	1.3	.5	1.7
Diabetis Mellitus (250)	1.3	4.1	.7	.8	.4	1.1
IV Blood and Bloodforming Organs (280–289)	.2	.7	.2	.4	.1	.3
V Mental Disorders (290–318)	3.5	2.8	1.9	.9	2.2	1.8
Neurosis (310)	1.7	.5	.8	.1	1.3	.6
Alcoholism (313)	1.3	1.6	.4	.5	.6	.7
VI Nervous System and Sense Organs (320–389)	1.7	5.9	3.5	3.1	3.9	3.4
Otitis Media (381)	.8	4.6	2.0	2.0	1.5	2.0
VII Circulatory System (390–458)	4.3	7.2	3.2	2.4	4.6	3.5
Essential Benign Hypertension (401)	1.4	5.0	.4	1.2	.4	1.3
VIII Respiratory System (460–519)	12.0	26.2	28.2	6.2	11.9	15.2
Acute Nasopharyngitis (460)	.8	6.0	1.2	2.2	.1	1.9
Acute Pharyngitis (462)	1.9	1.9	1.5	.2	1.0	1.0
Acute Tonsillitis (463)	1.5	3.2	.9	—	2.8	1.0
Acute URI of multiple or unspecified sites (465)	3.4	9.2	12.1	.4	3.7	5.0

Influenza (470)	1.1	1.2	5.4	—	.2	1.7
Pneumonia, organism and type not specified (486)	.8	2.0	1.1	.3	1.0	.8
Bronchitis, unqualified (490)	—	—	1.8	—	—	.5
Asthma (493)	1.4	1.2	1.4	2.5	—	1.7
IX Digestive System (520–577)	2.4	1.6	3.0	1.6	4.8	
X Genito-urinary System (580–629)	3.6	2.4	4.0	2.1	2.5	
Other diseases of urinary tract (599)			.4	.7	.4	
XI Deliveries & Complications of Pregnancy, Childbirth and the Puerperium (631–678)	1.1	1.3			.8	.7
XII Skin & Subcutaneous Tissue (680–709)	.4	—	.5	.1		
Other exzema and dermatitis (692)	2.2	3.3	2.5	2.3	4.0	.5
XIII Musculoskeletal System and Connective Tissue (710–739)	.9	1.8	.4	.3	1.0	.9
XIV Congenital Anomalies (640–759)	.7	.5	1.5	.2	2.2	.2
XV Diseases Peculiar to Newborn Infants (760–768)	—	.1	.3	—	—	—
XVI Signs, Symptoms and Ill-Defined Conditions (770–796)	—	—	—	33.6	—	
Symptoms referable to heart and vessels (774)	20.2	17.2	13.2		7.6	22.5
Other symptoms referable to cardiovascular	3.8	1.7	2.0	2.2	.3	2.2

TABLE E.2 (CONTINUED)
Patients' Presenting Complaints, as Reported by Hospital Physicians by Diagnosis, Symptom or Procedure, and by Hospital (Percentage Distribution)

Diagnostic or Procedure Category	Hospital A	Hospital B	Hospital C	Hospital D	Hospital E	All Hospitals
XVI Signs, Symptoms and Ill-Defined Conditions (770–796) (Continued) and lymphatic system (775)	1.1	.2	.4	.7	.2	.6
Symptoms referable to nose and sinus (776)	1.1	.4	.6	.4	.9	.6
Symptoms referable to mouth, pharynx and larynx (777)	.1	—	.2	1.7	—	.8
Symptoms referable to respiratory dysfunction (778)	1.9	1.4	.3	1.4	.7	1.1
Other symptoms referable to respiratory system (779)	.1	.5	—	.4	—	.2
Symptoms referable to abdomen and peritoneum (780)	4.2	3.2	2.7	5.2	1.7	3.9
Symptoms referable to limbs and joints (788)	1.6	1.8	.3	2.4	.1	1.5
Other symptoms referable to musculoskeletal syst. (789)	2.2	1.3	1.4	1.9	2.0	1.8
Other general symptoms (792)	1.3	1.3	1.3	5.5	.7	3.0
Observation and evaluation without need for						

further medical care (793)	—	—	.2	3.8	—	1.6
XVII Injuries and Adverse Effects (800-999)	38.3	7.5	21.0	23.4	46.0	25.3
Musculoskeletal injuries of ankle and foot (845)	.2	—	1.0	.2	2.6	.6
Concussion (850)	.2	—	—	—	1.2	.1
Other and unspecified laceration of head (873)	4.1	.8	2.1	2.0	4.1	2.4
Other, multiple and unspecified open wounds of head, neck and trunk (879)	.2	—	.2	1.5	.3	.7
Open wound of hand, except finger(s) alone (882)	1.9	.4	.8	.9	1.8	1.0
Open wound of finger(s) (883)	3.1	.2	1.4	.9	4.3	1.6
Superficial injury of face, neck and scalp (910)	.7	—	.4	1.9	.2	1.0
Superficial injury of hip, thigh, leg & ankle (916)	.2	.2	.2	1.6	.1	.8
Unspecified injury (919)	17.0	2.8	2.7	2.3	.5	4.2
Contusion of trunk (922)	.4	—	.4	.2	1.1	.3
Contusion of upper limb (923)	.2	—	1.1	—	3.8	.7
Contusion of lower limb (924)	.3	—	.8	.1	3.2	.6
Contusion of multiple & unspecified sites (925)	.1	.2	.2	—	1.4	.2
Foreign body in eye and adnexa (930)	1.2	.2	—	.4	1.0	.4

TABLE E.2 (*CONTINUED*)

Patients' Presenting Complaints, as Reported by Hospital Physicians by Diagnosis, Symptom or Procedure, and by Hospital (Percentage Distribution)

Diagnostic or Procedure Category	Hospital A	Hospital B	Hospital C	Hospital D	Hospital E	All Hospitals
XVIII Special Admissions and Examinations without complaint or reported diagnosis (1000–1086)	4.8	15.1	10.6	19.3	4.1	13.3
Medical examination of individuals (1000)	1.4	6.6	5.5	13.2	1.5	7.9
Special investigations and examinations (1001)	.8	2.1	.4	.9	.1	.8
Antepartum observation (1006)	.1	—	.2	1.0	—	.5
Medical and surgical aftercare (1015)	1.1	2.9	1.4	1.0	2.0	1.4
XIX Not ascertained	—	—	—	.8	—	.3
TOTAL PERCENT*	100.0	100.0	100.0	100.0	100.0	100.0
Number of Cases	1,664	1,200	3,302	5,195	1,139	12,500

*Percentages might not total 100 because of rounding error.

Symptoms and Ill-Defined Conditions (33.6 percent). A thorough inspection of the cells will reveal still other anomalies.

SOCIO-DEMOGRAPHIC CHARACTERISTICS

Assignment of Census Tract Codes to Patient Population.

The Patient Log was also used to collect data on patient age, sex, and residence. Nearly 30,000 patients visiting hospitals or private practices were assigned census tract numbers on the basis of their addresses. The source of information for the census tract codes was a printout available from the state university that listed street address and corresponding tract numbers for every area of the state which has already been tracted. Areas which had been assigned census tract codes were assigned town code numbers, but these could not be used in some of the secondary analyses because of the clear lack of homogeneity of socio-demographic characteristics within a town or township.

Social Area Classification.

Strictly speaking, social area analysis applies to a specific typology proposed and outlined by Shevky, Bell, and Williams (1949, 1955). The concept has since been extended to include a number of multi-variate refinements (e.g., factor analysis) to the basic taxonomical problem of forming clusters of similar units in social space (e.g., individuals, tracts, cities). Social area analysis uses information gained from selected census tract characteristics to classify populations according to various dimensions such as Socio-Economic Status (SES). The underlying assumption is that persons living in one type of social area tend to differ systematically in terms of socio-economic characteristics, attitudes, and behavior from persons living in other types of social areas. In the present study, various census tract data such as age, education and income have been grouped by means of factor analysis. Once a census tract has been assigned a factor score, it is treated as a homogeneous area: any patient living within this tract is assumed to have the characteristics that the factor represents. Shevky and Bell (1955, p. 20) define social area as follows:

we view a social area as containing persons with similar social positions in the larger society. The social area, however, is not bounded by the geographical frame of reference, as is the natural area, nor by implications concerning the degree of interaction between persons in the local community, as is the subculture. We do claim, however, that the social area generally contains persons having the same living level, the same way of life, the same ethnic background; and we hypothesize that persons living in a particular type of social area would systematically differ with respect to characteristics, attitude and behavior from persons living in another type of social area.

Timms (1971, p. 1) supports this view of the interrelationships between residential and social differentiation:

The urban community is neither an undifferentiated mass nor a haphazard collection of buildings and people. In the residential differentiation of the city the urban fabric comes to resemble a "mosaic of social worlds." Similar populations cluster together and come to characterize their areas.

Tyron (1955) adds that, although census tracts do not always exhibit complete internal homogeneity, individuals classified within a social area experience an essentially similar social and psychological environment.

FIGURE E.1
Definitions of Variables Used in Social Area Analysis

Variable	Description
FACTOR I SOCIO-ECONOMIC CHARACTERISTICS	
High Education	Percent of population with 16 or more years of education.
Professional Occupations	Percent of work force in professional/managerial occupations.
High Income	Percent of families earning $5,000 or more per annum.
Blue Collar	Percent of work force in blue collar occupations.
Low Education	Percent of population with 8 or less years of education.
Child	Percent of population aged 5 years or under.
FACTOR II RACE AND RESOURCE CHARACTERISTICS	
Black	Percent Black.
Low Income	Percent of families earning $3,999 or less per annum.
FACTOR III AGE AND ETHNICITY CHARACTERISTICS	
Aged	Percent of population aged 60 years and over.
Foreign	Percent of population of foreign stock.
Child	Percent of population aged 5 years or under.

Procedure Used to Derive Social Areas.

A total of 624 tracts, representing the combined population of ten Standard Metropolitan Statistical Areas (SMSAs) in Connecticut, were employed as the reference group from which social areas were constructed. On the basis of previous research (Duncan and Reiss 1956), ten aggregate tract characteristics were chosen to be included in the factor analysis. These variables are operationally defined in Figure E.1.

The results of the principal component analysis (a variant of the general factor analytic method) are shown in Figure E.2. It is clear that three distinct factors emerged from the data. The first factor is labelled Socio-Economic Status (SES) and has high positive factor loadings on High Education (.953), Professional Occupations (.917) and High Income (.838), and high negative loadings on Blue Collar (−.892), Low Education (−.801) and Child (−.447). The second factor is labelled Race and Resources (RR) and has high positive loadings on proportion of Blacks (.840) and Low Income (.814). The third and final factor is Age and Ethnicity (AE) which has high positive loadings on proportion of Aged (.858) and Foreign Stock (.760), and high negative loadings on Child (−.679). Together these three factors account for approximately 82 percent of the total variance.

Computation of the Factor Scores.

Factor scores for each tract in the reference group were computed from the appropriate combination values as suggested by the factor analysis. The Socio-Economic Status score for each tract was computed

FIGURE E.2
Summary Tabulation of Results of Rotated Factor Analysis on
Socio-Demographic Variables Showing Factor Loadings

Variable No. & Name	Factor Names		
	Socio-economic Status (SES)	Race Resources (RR)	Age/Ethnicity (AE)
1 High Ed.	(.953)	0.0	0.0
2 Prof.	(.917)	0.0	0.0
3 High Inc.	(.838)	−.342	0.0
4 Blue Collar	(−.892)	.264	0.0
5 Low Ed.	(−.801)	.351	.281
6 Black	−.272	(.840)	0.0
7 Low Inc.	−.364	(.814)	0.0
8 Aged	0.0	0.0	(.858)
9 Foreign	−.256	−.375	(.760)
10 Child	(−.447)	0.0	(−.679)

by adding the tract's score on variables 1 (High Education), 2 (Professionals) and 3 (High Income); subtracting the tract's score on variables 4 (Blue Collar), 5 (Low Education) and 10 (Child); and dividing the total by 6 (i.e., the number of variables used to compute this first factor):

$$SES = (Var1 + Var2 + Var3) - (Var4 + Var5 + Var10)/6$$

Race and Resources were computed by adding each tract's score on variables 6 (Black) and 7 (Low Income), and dividing by 2:

$$RR = (Var6 + Var7)/2$$

Age and Ethnicity were computed by adding each tract's score on variables 8 (Aged) and 9 (Foreign), subtracting the score on variable 10 (Child), and dividing by 3:

$$AE = (Var8 + Var9) - (Var10)/3$$

Following the computation of factor scores for all tracts in the reference group, these scores were standardized using the following linear transformations:

Transformed score = 50 + 10 (Original Score)

This transformation resulted in scores ranging from approximately 0 to 100, with a mean of 50 and a standard deviation of 10. It did not change the shape of the original distribution of factor scores or the relative distance between scores. The transformation was used to facilitate definition and interpretation of social areas. Scores were categorized into one of three distinct social areas:

Area 1   The low group comprised all tracts which had scores falling one standard deviation or more below the mean on any of the three factors.

Area 2   The middle group included all tracts with scores between one standard deviation below the mean and one standard deviation above the mean of the reference group.

Area 3   The high group was the classification for all tracts with scores greater than one standard deviation above the mean.

Before including these characteristics in the secondary analyses, accompanying the previously described attributes of physicians and organizations, we investigated differences in care received by hypertensive patients from different social areas within this practice area. It was expected that patients coming from Area 1 would receive poorer care than patients from Areas 2 and 3. No differences were shown. However, there might have been differences if a less rudimentary analytic strategy had been used. At this point in the study, dwindling project resources did not permit further exploration of the relationship between patient social area and provider performance. Socio-demographic variables were not included in the AUTOGRP analyses.

Results of Physician Performance by Components of Care

TABLE F.1
Compliance with Criteria for *Adult Abdominal Pain*
(Percentage of Patients for Whom Criteria Were Met)

Criterion Item	Private Practice				Hospital				Both Settings			
	GP	IM	PED	All	GP	IM	PED	All	GP	IM	PED	All
HISTORY												
Type of Pain	13%	15%	—	14%	58%	32%	15%	42%	21%	19%	15%	20%
Persistent Pain	18	41	—	30	62	60	77	61	26	45	77	37
Constant Pain	15	26	—	21	18	21	—	19	16	25	—	21
Onset of Pain	42	56	—	49	88	84	85	86	51	62	85	57
Affecting Factors	26	39	—	33	19	39	38	31	25	39	38	32
Current Events	13	25	—	20	25	45	23	36	15	30	23	23
Food & Drugs	19	38	—	29	32	38	—	34	21	38	—	30
Location of Pain	65	69	—	67	55	80	69	69	63	72	69	68
Radiation	13	16	—	15	17	29	8	23	14	19	8	16
Other Points of Pain	20	25	—	23	42	31	62	37	24	27	62	26
Fever	7	16	—	12	16	48	38	35	9	23	38	17
Nausea	22	35	—	29	46	62	8	53	27	41	8	34
Vomiting	14	34	—	25	70	75	54	72	25	43	54	35
Hematemesis	6	10	—	8	40	43	31	41	12	18	31	15
Dyspepsia	10	8	—	9	—	17	—	9	8	10	—	9
Diarrhea	17	39	—	29	42	54	54	49	22	42	54	33
Melena	6	21	—	14	18	46	8	33	8	26	8	18
Stool Character	22	31	—	26	32	25	23	28	24	29	23	27
Stool Appearance	5	17	—	11	21	19	8	20	8	17	8	13
Rectal Bleeding	4	15	—	10	15	21	—	18	6	17	—	11
Previous Pain	49	50	—	50	52	53	38	52	50	51	38	50
Hx of Surgery	28	32	—	30	41	30	15	34	30	32	15	31
Hx of Studies	31	40	—	35	17	32	46	26	28	38	46	34
Hx of Inquiries	14	10	—	12	17	13	—	7	11	10	—	11
Relationship of Pain to Menses[1]	61	59	—	60	84	70	69	76	66	62	69	64

PHYSICAL EXAMINATION											
Temperature	23	21	22	85	82	100	84	35	35	100	35
Pulse	20	34	28	76	85	100	82	31	45	100	39
Blood Pressure	46	70	58	89	83	100	86	54	72	100	64
Chest Exam	27	47	38	50	73	100	65	32	53	100	43
Abdominal Tenderness	46	61	54	80	90	85	86	52	68	85	61
Abdominal Guarding	13	26	19	48	50	69	50	19	31	69	26
Abdominal Rebound	14	25	20	50	55	69	53	21	31	69	27
Abdominal Masses	17	30	24	43	57	—	49	22	36	—	29
Abdominal Distension	15	11	13	18	31	—	24	16	15	—	15
Visual Inspection of Abdomen	6	7	7	30	27	77	30	10	12	77	12
Bowel Sounds	10	21	16	50	51	8	49	18	27	8	23
Pelvic Exam[1]	45	36	40	70	63	62	66	50	62	62	45
Rectal Exam	14	25	20	34	33	23	33	17	27	23	23
DIAGNOSTIC TESTS											
Urinalysis	25	28	27	35	37	—	34	27	30	—	28
Occult Blood	1	7	4	7	12	—	9	2	8	—	5
CBC	19	31	25	48	47	54	48	25	34	54	30
ASSESSMENT											
Working Diagnosis	49	69	60	100	99	100	99	58	76	100	68
Final Diagnosis	24	19	21	63	45	15	51	31	25	15	28
MANAGEMENT											
Medication[1]	96	99	97	70	96	100	86	91	98	100	95
New Appointment	13	39	27	26	42	69	36	15	40	69	29
Number of Sample Cases	93	119	212	35	111	7	153	128	230	7	365

[1] Scores inflated due to application of System One scoring; does not affect summary scores on performance factors.

TABLE F.2
Compliance with Criteria for Chest Pain
(Percentage of Patients for Whom Criteria Were Met)

Criterion Item	Private Practice				Hospital				Both Settings			
	GP	IM	PED	All	GP	IM	PED	All	GP	IM	PED	All
HISTORY												
Chest Pain	100%	85%	—	92%	100%	100%	100%	100%	100%	90%	100%	94%
Chest Fullness	3	3	—	3	8	2	—	3	3	3	—	3
Chest Ache	19	—	—	9	8	6	—	6	18	2	—	8
Chest Pressure	3	9	—	6	8	12	—	11	3	10	—	7
Chest Cramps	—	3	—	2	8	2	—	3	1	3	—	2
Gas	5	18	—	12	8	—	—	2	6	11	—	9
Difficulty Breathing	3	33	—	18	33	54	—	48	7	40	—	26
Location of Chest Pain	60	69	—	65	67	87	50	81	61	75	50	69
Radiation	26	46	—	36	58	51	—	51	30	48	—	40
Onset	54	72	—	64	92	84	50	85	59	77	50	69
Mode of Onset	23	34	—	28	33	26	—	26	24	31	—	28
Duration	21	36	—	29	67	43	—	47	27	39	—	34
Frequency	6	41	—	24	25	38	—	34	9	40	—	27
Quality	25	37	—	31	25	53	—	46	25	43	—	35
Aggravated by Body Position or Motion	17	30	—	24	—	24	—	19	15	28	—	22
Aggravated by Exercise or Physical Activity	19	55	—	37	17	28	—	25	18	45	—	34
Aggravated by Stress and/or Anxiety	9	25	—	17	—	8	—	6	8	19	—	14
Aggravated by Time of Day	9	16	—	13	—	9	—	7	7	14	—	11
Aggravated by Respiration or Swallowing	5	12	—	8	25	26	—	25	8	17	—	13
Diaphoresis	20	18	—	19	33	47	—	42	22	28	—	25
Nausea	16	19	—	18	42	44	—	42	20	28	—	24
Vomiting	3	16	—	9	42	46	—	43	8	26	—	18
Cough	13	18	—	15	58	31	100	39	19	22	100	22
Dyspnea	13	32	—	23	25	51	—	44	15	39	—	29

Hemoptysis	3	—	—	1	—	—	20	—	15	—	2	7	—	5
Fever	3	8	—	5	—	17	20	50	20	50	4	12	50	9
Chills	—	6	—	3	—	17	17	50	18	50	2	10	50	7
Dizziness	19	18	—	19	—	8	17	—	16	—	19	18	—	18
Syncope	—	6	—	3	—	—	6	—	6	—	1	6	—	4
Dysphagia	5	3	—	4	—	8	4	—	3	—	5	4	—	4
Eructation	—	9	—	4	—	—	4	—	5	—	1	7	—	5
Abdominal Pain	3	12	—	7	—	25	23	—	23	—	5	16	—	11
History of Previous Experience	45	57	—	51	—	17	68	—	55	—	41	60	—	52
History Diagnosis for Previous Problems	25	47	—	36	—	8	52	—	42	—	23	49	—	37
Treatment for Previous Problems	20	35	—	28	—	—	48	—	36	—	17	40	—	30
History Nitroglycerine Prescribed	11	26	—	19	—	—	26	—	19	—	10	26	—	19
History Nitroglycerine Effect	9	27	—	18	—	8	19	—	16	—	9	24	—	18
History Prior Restrictions	11	14	—	13	—	—	9	—	7	—	10	12	—	11
Acceptance of Prior Restrictions	3	14	—	9	—	—	4	—	7	—	3	11	—	8
Occupation	35	49	—	42	—	83	70	100	74	100	42	56	100	51
Past Chest Injury	10	13	—	11	—	17	10	—	11	—	11	12	—	11
Smoking History	20	60	—	40	—	25	30	—	28	—	20	49	—	37
PHYSICAL EXAMINATION														
Temperature	19	3	—	11	—	100	61	100	70	100	30	24	100	27
Pulse	23	39	—	31	—	92	92	100	92	100	32	58	100	47
Respiration	5	10	—	8	—	58	49	100	53	100	12	24	100	20
Blood Pressure	68	97	—	83	—	92	92	100	92	100	71	95	100	85
Heart Rhythm	29	53	—	41	—	58	71	—	66	—	33	60	—	48
Description of Appearance	3	20	—	12	—	58	70	50	67	50	11	38	50	27
Description of Emotional State	3	21	—	12	—	42	40	—	39	—	8	28	—	19
Fundoscopic Exam	5	13	—	9	—	17	29	—	25	—	7	18	—	13
Description of Sputum	3	—	—	1	—	17	10	—	11	—	4	4	—	4
Neck Veins Distended	11	25	—	18	—	25	41	—	36	—	12	31	—	23
Cervical Nodes	8	6	—	7	—	25	21	—	21	—	10	11	—	11
Relation of Pain to Movement of Neck	3	9	—	6	—	8	21	—	18	—	4	13	—	9
Chest Wall Tenderness	5	11	—	8	—	8	8	—	8	—	5	10	—	8
Location of Apex Beat	—	12	—	6	—	25	19	—	19	—	3	14	—	10
Murmurs	19	58	—	39	—	67	71	50	69	50	25	63	50	47

TABLE F.2 (CONTINUED)
Compliance with Criteria for Chest Pain
(Percentage of Patients for Whom Criteria Were Met)

Criterion Item	Private Practice				Hospital				Both Settings			
	GP	IM	PED	All	GP	IM	PED	All	GP	IM	PED	All
PHYSICAL EXAM (Continued)												
Gallops	13	41	—	27	33	53	—	47	16	45	—	33
Rubs (friction, pleural, pericardial)	16	29	—	22	33	37	—	35	18	32	—	26
Auscultation of Chest	39	59	—	49	83	84	100	85	45	68	100	59
Percussion of Chest	9	37	—	23	33	41	—	38	12	38	—	27
Auscultation of Abdomen	8	28	—	18	33	38	50	37	11	32	—	23
Organ Size	3	36	—	20	42	53	100	53	8	42	50	29
Masses	3	32	—	18	25	50	100	47	5	38	100	25
Status Venous Circulation of Legs	8	22	—	15	42	42	—	41	12	29	—	22
Status Arterial Circulation of Legs	10	20	—	15	33	43	—	40	13	28	—	22
DIAGNOSTIC TESTS												
ECG	54	92	—	73	75	86	—	81	56	90	—	75
Hematocrit	3	41	—	22	33	48	—	43	7	43	—	28
Urinalysis	14	40	—	27	33	26	—	26	16	35	—	27
ASSESSMENT												
Final Diagnosis	30	28	—	29	83	74	100	77	37	44	100	42
Working Diagnosis	50	82	—	66	100	90	100	92	56	85	100	73
FOLLOW-UP												
Is condition improving?[1]	57	61	—	59	67	48	50	52	58	56	50	57
Is problem yielding to Medication?[1]	44	58	—	51	67	56	50	58	47	58	50	54
Number of Sample Cases	29	33	—	62	12	58	2	72	41	91	2	134

[1]Scores inflated due to application of System One scoring; does not affect summary scores on performance factors.

TABLE F.3
Compliance with Criteria for *Hypertension*
(Percentage of Patients for Whom Criteria Were Met)

Criterion Item	Private Practice				Hospital				Both Settings			
	GP	IM	PED	All	GP	IM	PED	All	GP	IM	PED	All
HISTORY												
Visual Disturbance	6%	20%	—	14%	50%	36%	50%	38%	6%	21%	50%	15%
Angina	9	32	—	22	50	47	100	49	9	33	100	23
Nocturia	5	17	—	12	50	20	50	22	6	18	50	13
Muscle Cramps	—	—	—	—	—	—	—	—	—	—	—	—
Weakness	—	—	—	—	—	—	—	—	—	—	—	—
Abnormal Sweating	6	21	—	14	50	27	—	28	6	21	—	15
Urinary Tract Disease	—	—	—	—	—	—	—	—	—	—	—	—
Cushing's Syndrome	—	—	—	—	—	—	—	—	—	—	—	—
Thyrotoxicosis	—	—	—	—	—	—	—	—	—	—	—	—
Aldosteronism	—	—	—	—	—	—	—	—	—	—	—	—
Oral Contraceptives[1]	76	85	—	81	100	66	100	69	76	84	100	80
Family History of Hypertension	9	27	—	19	25	39	50	39	9	28	50	20
Family History of Neurologic Disease	5	11	—	8	25	12	50	13	5	11	50	9
Family History of Cardiovascular Disease	11	32	—	23	25	34	50	34	11	32	50	24
Family History of Renal Disease	4	9	—	7	25	12	50	14	4	9	50	7
PHYSICAL EXAMINATION												
BP Readings under 6 Weeks	31	30	—	30	50	50	50	50	31	31	50	31
BP 6th Week	25	21	—	23	25	39	—	37	25	22	—	24
BP, Arms, Legs, Supine, Erect	1	12	—	7	25	9	—	9	1	11	—	7
BP, Time	—	—	—	—	—	—	—	—	—	—	—	—
Current Weight	68	73	—	70	75	72	100	73	68	73	100	71
Ocular Disc	7	26	—	18	50	43	—	42	7	28	—	19
Retinal Vessels	7	17	—	13	75	47	—	47	7	19	—	14
Hemorrhages	—	6	—	4	50	31	—	32	—	8	—	5
Exudates	—	7	—	4	50	—	26	27	—	8	26	5

TABLE F.3 (CONTINUED)
Compliance with Criteria for Hypertension
(Percentage of Patients for Whom Criteria Were Met)

Criterion Item	Private Practice				Hospital				Both Settings			
	GP	IM	PED	All	GP	IM	PED	All	GP	IM	PED	All
PHYSICAL EXAM (Continued)												
Cardiac Sounds	25	46	—	37	50	67	50	66	25	48	50	38
Heart Size	4	19	—	12	25	42	—	40	5	20	—	14
Murmurs	13	35	—	26	75	79	50	78	14	38	50	28
Pulmonic Rales	27	56	—	44	100	77	50	77	28	58	50	45
Abdominal Masses	8	34	—	23	50	49	—	48	8	35	—	24
Abdominal Bruit	1	8	—	5	50	29	—	28	2	10	—	6
Deep Tendon Reflexes	3	22	—	14	100	46	—	48	4	23	—	15
Peripheral Pulses	5	25	—	16	75	51	—	51	6	27	—	18
Peripheral Edema	7	25	—	17	25	60	—	56	7	27	—	19
DIAGNOSTIC TESTS												
Urinalysis	34	55	—	46	75	67	—	66	34	56	—	47
BUN	15	36	—	27	75	70	100	71	15	38	100	28
Creatinine	5	9	—	7	25	41	100	42	5	11	100	8
Hemoglobin	14	35	—	26	75	65	100	66	14	37	100	28
Hematocrit	14	38	—	27	75	70	100	71	14	40	100	29
Serum Electrolytes	—	—	—	—	—	—	—	—	—	—	—	—
Chest X-ray	14	36	—	27	50	71	100	70	15	38	100	28
ECG	16	50	—	35	75	70	100	71	16	51	100	37
Uric Acid	47	56	—	52	100	67	100	70	47	56	100	53
MANAGEMENT												
Weight Reduction	29	40	—	35	25	36	—	34	29	40	—	35
Low Sodium Diet Prescribed	7	28	—	19	25	48	—	46	7	29	—	20
Low Sodium Diet Instructions	—	—	—	—	—	—	—	—	—	—	—	—
Urinary Treatment	—	—	—	—	—	—	—	—	—	—	—	—
Angina, 12 months	33	35	—	34	75	52	100	54	33	36	100	35
Nocturia, 12 months	32	30	—	31	75	47	100	50	32	32	100	32

	1	2	3	4	5	6	7	8	9	10	11	12
Muscle Cramps, 12 months	32	100	31	32	50	100	47	75	31	—	30	32
Sweating, 12 months	31	100	29	32	50	100	47	75	30	—	28	32
Fundoscopic, 12 months	36	100	38	33	62	100	60	75	33	—	37	33
Chest Exam, 12 months	47	100	51	42	68	100	66	75	46	—	50	42
Neurologic Exam, 12 months	33	100	34	32	52	100	50	75	33	—	33	32
Edema, 12 months	35	100	38	32	58	100	56	75	34	—	36	32
Urinalysis, 12 months	11	—	13	9	10	—	11	—	11	—	13	9
BUN, 12 months	—	—	—	—	—	—	—	—	—	—	—	—
Creatinine, 12 months	—	—	—	—	—	—	—	—	—	—	—	—
ECG, 12 months	—	—	—	—	—	—	—	—	—	—	—	—
Explanation of Objectives	—	—	—	—	—	—	—	—	—	—	—	—
Explanation of Consequences	—	—	—	—	—	—	—	—	—	—	—	—
Explanation of Importance	—	—	—	—	—	—	—	—	—	—	—	—
Side Effects	2	100	3	1	2	100	2	100	2	—	3	1
BP at this Visit	62	100	64	58	74	100	72	75	61	—	64	58
BP, 12 months	74	100	75	74	89	100	90	75	74	—	74	74
Visual Disturbance, 12 months	33	100	34	32	52	100	49	75	33	—	33	32
ANF, Repeat	29	—	25	32	46	—	43	—	28	—	25	31
BP, Every Visit	8	100	8	7	9	100	10	100	7	—	8	7
Chest X-ray, Repeat	42	100	44	39	66	100	63	100	41	—	43	38
ECG, Repeat	48	100	51	44	69	100	66	100	47	—	50	43
Urinalysis, Repeat	56	—	57	55	68	100	66	100	56	—	56	55
BUN, Repeat	42	100	42	41	70	100	67	75	41	—	41	41
Creatinine, Repeat	33	100	33	35	61	100	59	100	32	—	31	34
Electrolytes, Repeat	43	100	43	41	81	100	80	100	41	—	41	41
Blood Sugar, Repeat	59	100	61	57	82	100	80	75	58	—	59	57
Scheduled Follow-up	82	100	82	83	94	—	95	—	82	—	81	83
Visual Disturbance, Follow-up	2	—	3	1	3	—	3	—	2	—	3	1
Angina, Follow-up	8	—	10	4	8	—	9	—	8	—	10	4
Nocturia, Follow-up	2	—	3	2	3	—	4	—	2	—	2	2
Muscle Cramps, Follow-up	2	—	3	2	2	—	4	—	2	—	2	2
Weakness, Follow-up	2	—	3	1	7	—	8	—	—	—	2	1
Sweating, Follow-up	1	—	1	—	5	—	5	—	—	—	—	—
BP Reading, Follow-up	68	—	70	67	54	—	58	25	69	—	70	67

TABLE F.3 (CONTINUED)
Compliance with Criteria for Hypertension
(Percentage of Patients for Whom Criteria Were Met)

Criterion Item	Private Practice				Hospital				Both Settings			
	GP	IM	PED	All	GP	IM	PED	All	GP	IM	PED	All
MANAGEMENT (Continued)												
Ocular Disc, Follow-up	—	1	—	1	—	—	—	—	—	1	—	1
Retinal Vessels, Follow-up	—	—	—	—	—	—	—	—	—	—	—	—
Hemorrhages, Follow-up	—	3	—	2	—	5	—	5	—	3	—	2
Exudates, Follow-up	—	3	—	2	—	5	—	5	—	3	—	2
Cardiac Sounds, Follow-up	7	6	—	7	—	4	—	4	7	6	—	7
Heart Size, Follow-up	1	2	—	1	—	—	—	—	1	2	—	1
Murmurs, Follow-up	4	6	—	5	—	10	—	9	4	6	—	5
Pulmonic Rales, Follow-up	11	25	—	19	—	23	—	21	11	25	—	19
Abdominal Masses, Follow-up	1	8	—	5	—	5	—	5	1	8	—	5
Abdominal Bruit, Follow-up	—	—	—	—	—	1	—	1	—	—	—	—
Peripheral Pulses, Follow-up	2	4	—	3	—	5	—	5	2	4	—	3
Number of Sample Cases	265	389	—	654	4	98	2	104	269	487	2	758

[1] Scores inflated due to application of System One scoring; does not affect summary scores on performance factors.

TABLE F.4
Compliance with Criteria for Urinary Tract Infection
(Percentage of Patients for Whom Criteria Were Met)

Criterion Item	Private Practice				Hospital				Both Settings			
	GP	IM	PED	All	GP	IM	PED	All	GP	IM	PED	All
HISTORY												
Pain with Description	31%	59%	—	44%	53%	69%	100%	66%	34%	62%	100%	49%
Onset of Pain	12	37	—	23	40	43	100	43	15	39	100	28
Location of Pain	28	44	—	35	33	63	100	56	28	50	100	40
Pain related to urination?	4	32	—	16	20	29	100	28	6	31	100	19
Frequency of urination	28	56	—	40	60	55	—	55	32	55	—	44
Onset and Description of Frequency	9	30	—	18	27	36	—	33	11	32	—	22
Other Signs and Symptoms Present	51	70	—	60	93	88	100	90	56	76	100	67
Onset, Other Signs and Symptoms	28	32	—	30	67	60	—	60	33	41	—	37
Signs and Symptoms More Severe	6	11	—	8	—	6	100	6	5	10	100	8
Signs and Symptoms No Longer Present[1]	100	100	—	100	100	100	100	100	100	100	100	100
Drug Allergies	21	20	—	20	53	48	100	50	25	29	100	27
Chills	8	21	—	13	7	13	100	11	7	18	100	13
Fever	7	32	—	18	13	15	100	16	8	26	100	18
Vaginal Discharge	8	10	—	9	13	14	100	16	9	11	100	10
Color[1]	100	100	—	100	100	100	100	100	100	100	100	100
Turbidity[1]	98	100	—	99	100	94	100	96	98	98	100	98
Clarity[1]	100	100	—	100	93	96	100	96	99	99	100	99
Blood in Urine	9	30	—	18	27	20	—	22	11	27	—	19
History Urologic Problem	51	64	—	57	33	43	—	40	49	57	—	53
Hospitalized for Urologic Problems	29	37	—	33	—	14	—	10	25	30	—	27
Surgery for Urologic Problems	19	25	—	22	20	7	—	5	17	19	—	18
Drug Treatment for Urologic Problems	13	29	—	20	20	21	—	21	14	27	—	20
Pregnant	29	52	—	39	40	55	100	52	30	53	100	42
Recurrent Episode?	17	17	—	17	7	13	—	11	15	16	—	16
PHYSICAL EXAM												
Temperature	19	34	—	26	87	73	100	77	28	47	100	38
Abdominal Exam	39	65	—	50	80	88	100	86	44	73	100	59

TABLE F.4 (CONTINUED)
Compliance with Criteria for Urinary Tract Infection
(Percentage of Patients for Whom Criteria Were Met)

Criterion Item	Private Practice				Hospital				Both Settings			
	GP	IM	PED	All	GP	IM	PED	All	GP	IM	PED	All
PHYSICAL EXAM (Continued)												
Description of Kidneys[1]	100	100	—	100	100	100	100	100	100	100	100	100
Description of Bladder	6	11	—	8	13	21	—	19	7	14	—	11
CVA Tenderness	13	42	—	26	47	44	—	44	17	43	—	30
DIAGNOSTIC TESTS												
Urinalysis	71	71	—	71	100	96	100	97	74	79	100	77
Sediment Exam	33	67	—	48	100	89	100	92	41	74	100	58
Urine Culture	41	38	—	39	53	82	—	73	42	52	—	47
MANAGEMENT												
Sulfonamides	9	15	—	12	13	7	—	9	10	13	—	11
Tetracycline[1]	100	100	—	100	100	100	100	100	100	100	100	100
Ampicillin	8	16	—	11	27	27	—	27	10	20	—	15
Nitrofurantoin[1]	100	100	—	100	100	100	100	100	100	100	100	100
Cephalosporins[1]	100	100	—	100	100	100	100	100	100	100	100	100
Azogantrisin	26	8	—	18	33	6	—	13	27	7	—	17
Azogantanol[1]	100	100	—	100	100	100	100	100	100	100	100	100
Urised[1]	100	100	—	100	100	100	100	100	100	100	100	100
Why Medications	13	15	—	14	20	29	—	26	13	20	—	17
Explain common, benign nature of disease	100	94	—	97	100	90	100	93	100	93	100	96
Need Continued Surveillance	4	6	—	5	27	23	—	23	7	11	—	9
Advise Extra Fluids	2	15	—	8	47	21	—	28	7	17	—	12
Call if reaction to drug[1]	100	100	—	100	100	95	100	97	100	98	100	99
Call if fever, chills, back pain[1]	100	100	—	100	100	95	100	97	100	98	100	99
Call if not well in 5–7 days[1]	100	95	—	98	87	85	100	85	98	92	100	95

FOLLOW-UP

Follow-up Scheduled?	60	68	—	63	73	70	100	72	61	69	100	65
Visit 1 week post treatment with antibiotics	14	11	—	13	—	18	—	13	12	13	—	13
Patient Asymptomatic[1]	74	63	—	69	40	51	100	49	70	59	100	64
Number of Sample Cases	35	34	—	69	15	58	1	74	50	92	1	143

[1] Scores inflated due to application of System One scoring; does not affect summary scores on performance factors.

TABLE F.5
Compliance with Criteria for *Pharyngitis*
(Percentage of Patients for Whom Criteria Were Met)

Criterion Item	Private Practice				Hospital				Both Settings			
	GP	IM	PED	All	GP	IM	PED	All	GP	IM	PED	All
HISTORY												
Chief Complaint	75%	93%	80%	81%	100%	99%	98%	99%	77%	95%	81%	83%
Cough	14	31	18	19	38	51	44	45	17	35	20	22
Fever	21	37	50	36	40	49	71	53	23	40	52	38
Rheumatic Fever	8	8	5	7	1	7	7	5	8	8	5	7
Recurrent Infection	36	54	68	52	7	12	29	15	33	45	64	48
Hx of Smoking[1]	44	28	94	61	51	24	83	50	45	27	93	59
Allergy Hx[1]	47	27	94	61	65	45	93	65	49	30	94	62
Rhinorrhea	4	15	5	7	1	18	18	13	3	16	7	7
Hoarseness	1	4	3	2	3	3	2	3	1	3	3	2
Vomiting[1]	67	87	14	50	57	80	51	65	66	86	17	52
PHYSICAL EXAM												
Temperature	42	53	14	33	97	97	92	96	48	62	21	41
Skin Rash[1]	63	84	14	48	51	84	33	59	62	84	16	49
Ear Canal	7	38	33	24	59	59	76	64	12	42	37	29
Tympanic Membranes	7	38	33	24	59	59	77	64	12	42	37	29
Pharynx	36	78	72	59	97	99	97	98	42	82	74	64
Tonsils	36	78	73	60	97	99	97	98	42	82	75	64
Cervical Nodes	14	53	29	28	35	66	54	53	16	56	31	31
Diffuse Adenopathy	1	13	1	4	1	5	8	5	1	11	2	4
Cardiac Auscultation[1]	39	60	15	34	44	85	60	65	39	65	19	37
Abdominal Palpation[1]	37	64	12	33	41	68	75	62	38	65	18	36
DIAGNOSTIC TESTS												
Pharyngeal Culture	36	74	84	63	56	62	68	62	38	72	82	63
CBC	5	16	6	8	3	10	16	10	5	15	7	8
Mononucleosis Test	1	10	3	4	1	2	4	3	1	8	3	4

MANAGEMENT												
Tetracycline[1]	93	98	100	97	97	99	98	98	93	98	100	97
Sulfa[1]	98	100	100	99	100	99	97	99	98	100	100	99
Penicillin	54	52	54	54	47	37	32	39	54	49	52	52
Bicillin	—	—	1	*	9	5	4	6	16	1	1	1
Erythromycin	16	11	10	13	9	3	2	4	16	9	9	12
Other Medication	38	51	27	36	66	64	61	64	41	54	30	40
Concern for Strep Infection	—	2	—	*	—	7	11	6	—	3	1	1
Need for Culture	1	5	—	1	—	7	7	5	1	5	1	2
ASSESSMENT												
Working Diagnosis	38	57	64	53	97	99	98	98	44	66	67	58
Final Diagnosis	37	38	48	42	84	85	88	85	42	48	52	47
FOLLOW-UP												
Follow-up Scheduled?	15	23	26	21	46	48	46	47	18	28	28	24
Second Culture Taken?[1]	94	89	83	89	97	88	92	92	94	89	84	89
Notation About Family if Strep	—	2	3	2	—	—	4	1	0	1	3	2
Number of Sample Cases	206	126	311	643	68	106	84	258	274	232	395	901

*Value of less than .5 percent.

[1]Scores inflated due to application of System One scoring; does not affect summary scores on performance factors. For Hx of Smoking and Allergy Hx, only scores for pediatricians are inflated; for Vomiting, Skin Rash, Cardiac Auscultation and Abdominal Palpation, only scores for internists are inflated.

TABLE F.6
Compliance with Criteria for *Otitis Media*
(Percentage of Patients for Whom Criteria Were Met)

Criterion Item	Private Practice				Hospital				Both Settings			
	GP	IM	PED	All	GP	IM	PED	All	GP	IM	PED	All
HISTORY												
Chief Complaint Regarding Ear	72%	100%	63%	65%	85%	87%	81%	82%	75%	90%	66%	68%
Date of Onset	27	—	36	34	70	73	68	69	38	54	40	40
Ear Drainage	10	50	6	7	—	7	9	7	8	18	6	7
Other Present Respiration Illnesses and Symptoms	31	—	45	43	70	87	90	86	41	64	51	50
Location of Pain	59	100	54	55	70	87	82	80	61	90	57	59
Past Ear Infections	47	—	57	55	15	7	27	22	39	5	53	49
Hearing Problems	3	—	6	6	—	—	2	1	3	—	6	5
Adenoidectomy	7	—	4	5	—	—	—	—	5	—	4	4
Myringotomy	—	—	3	3	—	—	—	—	—	—	3	2
Swimming	—	—	4	3	—	—	7	5	—	—	4	4
Penicillin Allergy	7	—	15	14	65	87	54	61	21	64	20	22
PHYSICAL EXAM												
Description of Auditory Canal	3	—	2	2	—	—	4	3	3	—	2	2
Tympanic Membrane Characteristics	7	—	2	2	—	—	—	—	5	—	2	2
Stappes or Ossicles Visible	—	—	1	1	5	—	8	6	1	—	2	2
Pharynx Description	17	—	7	8	25	13	12	15	19	10	8	9
MANAGEMENT												
Ampicillin	—	—	—	—	—	—	—	—	—	—	—	—
Penicillin	—	—	—	—	—	—	—	—	—	—	—	—
Sulfa	80	100	92	91	80	53	62	64	80	66	88	86
Analgesics Prescribed	95	100	80	82	85	60	54	61	93	71	76	78
Oral Decongestants	90	100	74	76	75	80	63	68	86	85	72	75
Duration and Dosage of Medication	93	100	70	73	25	40	27	28	76	56	64	65
Follow-up Directions	—	—	7	6	25	13	17	18	6	10	8	8
Was there a referral to a specialist?	—	—	—	—	—	—	—	—	—	—	—	—

ASSESSMENT Working/Final Diagnosis	88	89	100	79	95	94	100	95	87	88	100	73
FOLLOW-UP												
Is hearing normal?	3	3	—	—	*	1	—	—	3	4	—	—
Follow-up	3	4	—	—	—	—	—	—	—	3	—	—
First Follow-up Visit	5	5	5	10	16	11	7	40	2	3	—	—
First Follow-up Improvement of Signs and Symptoms[1]	75	75	66	80	48	49	53	40	81	79	100	93
Second Follow-up Improvement of Signs and Symptoms[1]	96	95	100	100	93	90	100	100	96	96	100	100
Asymptomatic First Follow-up[1]	88	90	66	80	52	55	53	40	95	95	100	93
Asymptomatic Second Follow-up[1]	98	98	100	97	95	95	100	90	98	98	100	100
Signs and Symptoms Worse First Follow-up[1]	89	91	61	82	57	64	47	40	95	95	100	97
Signs and Symptoms Worse Second Follow-up[1]	98	98	100	95	96	94	100	100	98	98	100	97
Mention Signs and Symptoms First Follow-up[1]	80	80	56	82	54	61	40	40	85	83	100	97
Mention Signs and Symptoms Second Follow-up[1]	96	96	100	100	96	94	100	100	97	96	100	100
No Change, First Follow-up[1]	87	88	66	82	59	65	53	40	92	92	100	97
No Change, Second Follow-up[1]	97	96	100	100	96	94	100	100	97	96	100	100
Number of Sample Cases	393	330	17	46	134	99	15	20	259	231	2	26

*Value of .5 percent.

[1]Scores inflated due to application of System One scoring; does not affect summary scores on performance factors.

TABLE F.7
Compliance with Criteria for *Pediatric Abdominal Pain*
(Percentage of Patients for Whom Criteria Were Met)

Criterion Item	Private Practice				Hospital				Both Settings			
	GP	IM	PED	All	GP	IM	PED	All	GP	IM	PED	All
HISTORY												
Type of Pain	60%	74%	60%	61%	89%	67%	86%	85%	67%	71%	67%	67%
Persistent Pain	35	74	60	50	58	87	86	75	41	79	67	57
Constant Pain	21	47	28	27	26	27	36	31	22	39	30	28
Date of Onset	46	74	57	54	89	87	93	91	51	79	67	64
Affecting Factor	18	74	11	19	47	27	48	44	25	54	21	26
Previous Pain	47	21	30	37	16	13	41	27	39	18	33	34
Pattern	14	21	5	10	—	—	9	4	11	12	6	9
Relief of Pain	11	—	—	5	5	7	5	5	9	3	1	5
Vomiting	23	53	29	28	84	60	77	77	38	56	42	42
Recurrent Vomiting	7	26	13	12	58	47	34	45	20	35	19	21
Hematemesis	4	—	11	7	42	27	18	29	13	11	13	13
Pattern Change	7	47	35	24	37	20	36	34	15	36	35	27
Appearance of Stool	—	21	17	10	37	20	34	33	9	20	22	16
Change in Stool Appearance	—	—	11	5	32	13	18	23	8	6	13	10
Parasites	—	—	5	3	—	—	2	1	—	—	5	2
Chronic Diarrhea	7	—	16	11	16	27	9	14	10	11	14	12
Rectal Bleeding	—	—	5	3	5	7	2	4	1	3	5	3
Respiratory Symptoms	8	—	11	9	26	47	32	32	13	20	16	15
Urinary Symptoms	11	47	15	16	5	7	30	16	9	30	19	16
Current Events	—	74	24	18	16	13	18	16	4	48	23	17
Pica	—	—	—	—	—	—	2	1	—	—	1	1
Foreign Substance Ingested	—	—	—	—	—	—	5	2	—	—	1	1
Food Cause of Pain?	—	—	—	—	—	—	5	2	—	—	1	1
PHYSICAL EXAMINATION												
Jaundiced	5	—	15	9	11	13	36	23	6	6	20	13
Lungs Normal	25	47	33	30	47	53	59	54	30	50	40	37

Pharynx Normal	34	41	38	26	53	61	53	42	27	33	26	21
Tonsils Normal	21	27	32	11	34	43	40	21	15	21	26	7
Abdomen Distended	13	19	18	4	24	36	7	16	8	13	26	—
Abdomen Tenderness	52	48	83	49	89	93	60	95	38	32	100	33
Abdominal Rebound	40	31	65	43	71	66	53	84	28	19	74	29
Abdominal Guarding	35	33	53	33	68	64	53	79	22	21	53	18
Abdominal Masses	25	20	21	30	34	43	13	32	21	12	26	30
Rectal Exam	19	29	27	6	22	39	27	—	17	25	26	7
DIAGNOSTIC												
Urinalysis	32	45	15	21	27	36	—	26	33	48	26	19
Stool Blood Test	1	1	6	—	4	5	13	—	—	—	—	4
Parasite Test	1	—	—	3	—	—	—	—	2	3	—	—
Stool Culture	2	4	3	—	3	7	—	5	1	3	—	—
Urine Culture	3	5	—	1	8	11	7	—	—	—	26	—
Liver Function Test	2	2	18	—	3	7	—	—	2	—	—	—
Upper GI Series	2	1	6	—	2	2	7	—	—	7	—	7
Blood Chemistry	1	—	3	—	2	—	13	5	6	—	—	15
Additional X-rays	7	8	3	7	8	11	7	—	—	7	—	7
Barium Enema	1	—	11	—	2	2	7	—	—	—	—	—
CBC	19	17	—	24	27	32	27	21	17	12	—	15
ASSESSMENT												
Working Diagnosis	55	57	55	54	96	93	93	100	40	44	26	38
Final Diagnosis	17	22	25	10	42	59	60	16	8	8	—	8
MANAGEMENT												
Referral	18	10	15	28	28	39	—	26	14	11	26	28
Consultation	13	18	14	7	32	36	33	26	5	56	—	—
Symptomatic Therapy	65	57	89	67	74	61	73	89	61	3	100	60
Discussion of Condition	4	7	3	—	9	18	7	—	1	—	—	—
Discussion of Tests	1	1	3	—	2	2	7	—	—	—	—	—
FOLLOW-UP												
Repeat Urinalysis	5	2	3	9	1	—	7	—	7	3	—	12
Repeat Urine Culture	3	1	3	5	2	2	7	—	3	—	—	7

TABLE F.7 (CONTINUED)
Compliance with Criteria for Pediatric Abdominal Pain
(Percentage of Patients for Whom Criteria Were Met)

Criterion Item	Private Practice				Hospital				Both Settings			
	GP	IM	PED	All	GP	IM	PED	All	GP	IM	PED	All
FOLLOW-UP (Continued)												
Repeat Stool Testing	—	—	3	1	—	7	2	2	—	3	3	2
Liver Function Repeat	—	—	3	1	—	7	—	1	—	3	2	1
Referral Follow-up	7	26	—	5	47	—	5	21	17	15	1	9
Emergency Room Referral	7	26	4	7	16	13	7	11	9	21	5	8
Number of Sample Cases	20	4	32	56	19	10	34	63	39	14	66	119

TABLE F.8

Compliance with Criteria for *Well-Child Examination* (Infant)

(Percentage of Patients for Whom Criteria Were Met)

Criterion Item	Private Practice				Hospital				Both Settings			
	GP	IM	PED	All	GP	IM	PED	All	GP	IM	PED	All
HISTORY												
Description of Pregnancy	11%	—	71%	68%	—	—	56%	56%	11%	—	70%	67%
Type of Delivery	21	—	73	70	—	—	83	83	21	—	74	71
Head Circumference at Birth	14	—	66	63	—	—	74	74	14	—	66	64
Chest Circumference at Birth	8	—	43	40	—	—	12	12	8	—	40	38
Height at Birth	75	—	84	83	—	—	76	76	75	—	83	82
Weight at Birth	82	—	95	94	—	—	90	90	82	—	95	94
Sensory and Motor Development	5	—	53	50	—	—	71	71	5	—	55	52
Social Development	—	—	19	18	—	—	27	27	—	—	19	18
Bowel Pattern	—	—	28	27	—	—	50	50	—	—	30	28
Urination	—	—	2	2	—	—	11	11	—	—	2	2
Crying Behavior	3	—	4	4	—	—	4	4	3	—	4	4
Feeding Behavior	31	—	58	57	—	—	87	87	31	—	61	59
Sleeping Behavior	3	—	28	27	—	—	47	47	3	—	30	29
Response to Separation from Parents	—	—	2	2	—	—	3	3	—	—	2	2
Family Description	13	—	10	10	—	—	10	10	13	—	10	10
Family Hx of Illness and Deaths	7	—	12	12	—	—	25	25	7	—	13	13
Living Situation	10	—	4	4	—	—	34	34	10	—	6	6
PHYSICAL EXAMINATION												
Head Size	—	—	55	52	—	—	79	79	—	—	57	54
Height	67	—	97	95	—	—	97	97	67	—	97	95
Weight	92	—	98	98	—	—	98	98	92	—	98	98
Eyes	—	—	16	15	—	—	54	54	—	—	19	18
Ears	3	—	18	17	—	—	60	60	3	—	21	20
Nose	5	—	16	15	—	—	54	54	5	—	19	18
Throat	3	—	15	14	—	—	59	59	3	—	18	18
Chest	5	—	15	14	—	—	67	67	5	—	19	18

TABLE F.8 (CONTINUED)
Compliance with Criteria for *Well-Child Examination* (Infant)
(Percentage of Patients for Whom Criteria Were Met)

Criterion Item	Private Practice				Hospital				Both Settings			
	GP	IM	PED	All	GP	IM	PED	All	GP	IM	PED	All
PHYSICAL EXAM (Continued)												
Heart	5	—	18	17	—	—	64	64	5	—	22	21
Abdomen	5	—	15	15	—	—	67	67	5	—	20	19
Genitalia	—	—	18	17	—	—	32	32	—	—	19	18
Extremities	5	—	20	19	—	—	41	41	5	—	21	20
Reflexes	—	—	10	9	—	—	38	38	—	—	12	11
Hips	—	—	2	2	—	—	15	15	—	—	3	3
Common Areas of Herniation	—	—	—	—	—	—	7	7	—	—	1	1
Peripheral Pulses	—	—	—	—	—	—	12	12	—	—	1	1
Behavior in General	16	—	15	15	—	—	41	41	16	—	17	17
DIAGNOSTIC TESTS												
Urine PKU	—	—	18	17	—	—	12	12	—	—	17	16
Hemoglobin/Hematocrit	—	—	11	10	—	—	12	12	—	—	11	10
Tuberculin Test	84	—	88	88	—	—	91	91	84	—	88	88
ASSESSMENT												
Detection of Abnormality	11	—	18	17	—	—	40	40	11	—	19	19
More Than One Abnormality	—	—	—	—	—	—	—	—	—	—	—	—
FOLLOW-UP												
Follow-up Done	—	—	—	—	—	—	—	—	—	—	—	—
Guidance Re: Feeding	—	—	—	—	—	—	—	—	—	—	—	—
Guidance Re: Discipline	—	—	—	—	—	—	—	—	—	—	—	—
Guidance Re: Toilet Training	—	—	—	—	—	—	—	—	—	—	—	—
Guidance Re: Appetite	—	—	—	—	—	—	—	—	—	—	—	—
Was This Visit Scheduled?	54	—	40	41	—	—	93	93	54	—	45	45
Guidance to Parent Re: Behavior	—	—	—	—	—	—	—	—	—	—	—	—
Immunization Schedule Met	76	—	97	96	—	—	95	95	76	—	97	96
Number of Sample Cases	21	—	445	476	—	—	125	125	21	—	580	601

TABLE F.9
Compliance with Criteria for *Well-Child Examination* (Preschool)
(Percentage of Patients for Whom Criteria Were Met)

Criterion Item	Private Practice				Hospital				Both Settings			
	GP	IM	PED	All	GP	IM	PED	All	GP	IM	PED	All
HISTORY												
Bowel Pattern	6%	—	23%	22%	—	—	24%	23%	6%	—	23%	22%
Urination Pattern	—	—	19	18	—	—	14	14	—	—	19	18
Feeding Pattern	14	—	38	37	—	100	24	27	14	100	38	37
Concern over Physical or Behavioral Problems	6	—	21	20	—	100	24	27	6	100	21	20
Speech Development	—	—	26	25	—	100	38	41	—	100	26	25
Sensory Development	8	—	5	5	—	—	19	18	8	—	5	5
Motor Development	8	—	25	24	—	100	33	36	8	100	25	24
Social Development and Interpersonal Relationships	—	—	35	33	—	100	33	36	—	100	35	33
PHYSICAL EXAMINATION												
Blood Pressure	47	—	80	79	—	100	67	68	47	100	80	78
Height	53	—	97	95	—	100	95	95	53	100	97	95
Weight	53	—	97	95	—	100	95	95	53	100	97	95
Height/Weight Percentile	16	—	43	42	—	100	67	68	16	100	44	42
Coordination	—	—	6	5	—	—	19	18	—	—	6	6
Attention Span	—	—	1	1	—	—	—	—	—	—	1	1
Vision	14	—	38	37	—	100	29	32	14	100	38	37
Eyes	8	—	22	22	—	100	86	86	8	100	23	23
Ears	—	—	22	21	—	100	95	95	—	100	23	22
Nose	8	—	17	16	—	100	71	73	8	100	18	17
Throat	19	—	19	19	—	100	95	95	19	100	20	20
Chest	8	—	16	16	—	100	95	95	8	100	17	17
Heart	8	—	22	21	—	100	90	91	8	100	23	22
Abdomen	8	—	16	15	—	100	95	95	8	100	17	16
Genitalia	—	—	20	19	—	—	52	50	—	—	21	20

TABLE F.9 (CONTINUED)
Compliance with Criteria for Well-Child Examination (Preschool)
(Percentage of Patients for Whom Criteria Were Met)

Criterion Item	Private Practice				Hospital				Both Settings			
	GP	IM	PED	All	GP	IM	PED	All	GP	IM	PED	All
PHYSICAL EXAM (Continued)												
Extremities	8	—	21	20	—	100	62	64	8	100	21	21
Reflexes	—	—	10	9	—	—	71	68	—	—	10	10
Hips	—	—	1	1	—	—	5	5	—	—	1	1
Common Areas of Herniation	—	—	2	2	—	—	—	—	—	—	2	2
Peripheral Pulses	—	—	—	—	—	—	14	14	—	—	1	1
Behavior in General	—	—	15	14	—	100	57	59	—	100	15	15
DIAGNOSTIC TESTS												
Urinalysis	—	—	40	39	—	—	19	18	—	—	40	38
Hematocrit	—	—	12	11	—	—	38	36	—	—	12	12
Hemoglobin	11	—	5	6	—	—	38	36	11	—	6	6
Tuberculin Test	11	—	78	75	—	100	81	82	11	100	78	75
ASSESSMENT												
Detection of Abnormality[1]	100	—	100	100	—	100	100	100	100	100	100	100
MANAGEMENT												
Follow-up Done	—	—	—	—	—	—	—	—	—	—	—	—
More than One Follow-up	—	—	—	—	—	—	—	—	—	—	—	—
Was This Visit Scheduled?	71	—	43	44	—	100	95	95	71	100	44	45
Reference to Dental Care	—	—	3	3	—	—	10	9	—	—	3	3
Reference to School	—	—	18	17	—	—	—	—	—	—	17	17
Guidance Re: Social Development	—	—	2	2	—	—	—	—	—	—	2	2
Number of Sample Cases	13	—	320	333	—	1	21	22	13	1	341	355

[1] Scores inflated due to application of System One scoring; does not affect summary scores on performance factors.

Appendix G

Observation Checklist

APPENDIX G

Observation Checklist

OBSERVATIONS
PHARYNGITIS AND OTITIS

Physician I.D.# _____   Patient Sex: _____
Visit begins: _____   Patient Age: _____
Visit ends: _____   Date of Visit: _____

HISTORY

_____ chief complaint(s) elicited
_____ time(s) of onset
_____ cough
_____ fever (record exact temperature if known)
_____ chills
_____ inquires about history of rheumatic fever (accept sore throat followed by joint pain)
_____ is this a recurrent infection
_____ inquires about history of weight trouble or heart murmur
_____ smoking history (age 17 or older)
_____ history of allergy (patient or family) including drug reactions (17 or older)
_____ presence of rhinorrhea
_____ presence of hoarseness
_____ presence of nausea (age 16 or younger)
_____ presence of vomiting (age 16 or younger)
_____ history of frequent strep infections (age 16 or younger)
_____ history of unusually frequent or severe respiratory infections
_____ earache

PHYSICAL EXAMINATION

1. General

   _____ temperature   _____ head circumference
   _____ pulse   _____ chest circumference
   _____ blood pressure   _____ length
   _____ respirations   _____ inspection of skin
   _____ height   _____ general appearance
   _____ weight   _____ other: (describe) ——

OBSERVATION: PHARYNGITIS continued;

2. HEENT
_____ external eye exam (pupils, conjunctivae and sclerae, eom's, fields)
_____ fundus exam
_____ visual acuity using Snellen Chart
_____ otoscopic ear exam
_____ gross test for aural acuity
_____ tuning fork test of hearing
_____ protrude tongue
_____ inspection of nose, mouth, throat
_____ other: (describe) _____

3. Neck
_____ palpation of carotid
         pulse   _____ palpation of trachea for
                                                      mobility and tug
_____ passive motion of
         head (assessment of
         neck stiffness)   _____ palpation of thyroid
_____ other: (describe) _____

4. Nodes
_____ palpation of neck and
         head   _____ palpation of inguinal
                                                      region
_____ palpation of
         supraclavicular fossa   _____ palpation of axillae
_____ other: (describe) _____

5. Chest and Back
_____ inspection for deformity, abnormal motion
_____ percussion of back for tenderness (fist percussion)
_____ palpation of back for muscle spasm
_____ inspection/palpation of chest expansion
_____ percussion of diaphragmatic motion with respiration
_____ other: (describe) _____

6. Lungs
_____ finger percussion of lung fields (front and back)
_____ auscultation of lung fields (front and back)
_____ other: (describe) _____

7. Heart
_____ palpation of heart   _____ percussion of cardiac
                                                      borders
_____ auscultation of heart   _____ other: (describe) ___

8. Abdomen
_____ inspection of abdomen
_____ auscultation of abdomen

OBSERVATION: PHARYNGITIS continued;

_____ palpation and bimanual palpation of abdomen in all quadrants, at times instructing patient to breathe deeply

9. Extremities
   _____ inspection (for venous or skin changes)
   _____ palpation for edema
   _____ palpation of pulses (brachial, radial, dorsalis pedis, posterior tibial, anterior tibial, popliteal or femoral)
   _____ other: (describe) _____

10. Neurological
   _____ *Cranial nerves* (partially covered by HEENT)—eye movements, visual fields and acuity, fundus exam, corneal reflex or jaw strength, grin, wrinkle forehead, hearing tests, gag reflex, shrug shoulders or turn head against resistance, stick out tongue.
   _____ *Sensory*—pinprick, cotton swab, tuning fork, position of fingers and toes with eyes closed.
   _____ *Motor*—muscle strength (grasp hands, move against resistance).
   _____ *Coordination*—rapidly alternating movements, finger to nose, heel to skin, standing with eyes closed and feet together.
   _____ *Reflexes*—biceps, triceps, knee jerk, ankle jerk, plantar.
   _____ other: (describe) _____

SPECIAL EXAMINATIONS

_____ throat culture
_____ CBC
_____ CBC with differential
_____ mononucleosis (heterophil agglutination)
_____ viral titres
_____ urinalysis
_____ EKG
_____ CXR
_____ sinus films

REFERRAL

_____ none
_____ routine return appointment with same physician
_____ return appointment with same physician for same problem

THERAPY

_____ none
_____ oral decongestant
_____ tetracycline
_____ sulfa
_____ penicillin
_____ bicillin
_____ erythromycin
_____ other: (describe) _____

OBSERVATION: PHARYNGITIS continued;

PATIENT EDUCATION

_____ patient or family instructed in what to do if chief complaint worsened
_____ patient or family instructed in what to do if new complaints appeared
_____ diagnosis or _differential diagnosis_ discussed with patient or family
_____ patient told consequences he might suffer if not properly diagnosed or treated
_____ patient told why culture was needed
_____ treatment explained to patient or family
_____ need to complete full course of medicine discussed with patient or family
_____ other: (describe) ————————————————————————

References

Advance Data from Vital and Health Statistics. October 12, 1977. U.S. Department of Health, Education and Welfare, No. 12.

Armstrong, J. and Soelberg, P. 1968. "On the interpretation of factor analysis." *Psychological Bulletin* 70:361.

Bales, R. F. 1970. *Personality and interpersonal behavior.* New York: Holt Rinehart and Winston.

Brook, R. H. and Appel, F. A. 1973. "Quality-of-care assessment: choosing a method for peer review." *New England Journal of Medicine* 288:1323.

Brook, R. H., Davies-Avery, A., Greenfield, S., et al. 1977. "Assessing the quality of medical care using outcome measures: an overview of the method." *Medical Care* Supplement 13.

Buckley, W., 1968. "Society as a complex adaptive system," in W. Buckley, ed., *Modern systems research for the behavioral scientist.* Chicago: Aldine.

Campbell, D. T. and Fiske, D. W. 1959. "Convergent and discriminant validation by multi-trait-multi-method matrix." *Psychological Bulletin* 56:81.

Christoffell, T. and Loewenthal, M. 1977. "Evaluating the quality of ambulatory health care: a review of emerging methods." *Medical Care* 25:877.

Clark, D. A.; Kroeger, H. H.; Altman, I.; Johnson, A. C.; and Sheps, C. G. 1965. "The office practice of internists: IV. Professional activities other than care of private patients." *Journal of the American Medical Association* 194:177.

Clute, K. F. 1963. *The general practitioner: a study of medical education and practice in Ontario and Nova Scotia.* Toronto: University of Toronto Press.

Dalkey, N. C. 1967. *Delphi.* California: Rand Corporation.

Delbecq, A. L.; Van de Ven, A.; and Gustafson, D. H. 1975. *Group techniques for program planning: a guide to Nominal Group and Delphi processes.* Glenview, Ill.: Scott, Foresman and Co.

Donabedian, A. 1968. "Promoting quality through evaluating the process of patient care." *Medical Care* 6:181.

Duncan, O. D. and Reiss, A. J., Jr. 1956. *Social characteristics of urban and rural communities.* New York: John Wiley and Sons.

Fessel, W. J. and Van Brunt, E. E. 1972. "Assessing the quality of care from the medical record." *New England Journal of Medicine* 286:134.

Fine, E. G. 1978. The front line of medicine: a study of private practitioners in Connecticut. Unpublished dissertation. New Haven, Yale University.

Fleishman, E.; Harris, E. F.; and Burtt, H. E. 1955. *Leadership and supervision in industry*. Bureau of Educational Research Monograph No. 33. Columbus: Ohio State University.

Friedson, E. 1975. *Doctoring together: a study of professional social control*. New York: Elsevier Scientific Publishing Co.

Gonella, J. S. Presentation. PSRO II Workshop. May 18, 1977. Stratford, Connecticut.

Greenfield, S.; Lewis, C. E.; Kaplan, S. H.; et al. 1975. "Peer review by criteria mapping: criteria for diabetes mellitus—the use of decision-making in chart audit." *Annals of Internal Medicine* 83:761.

Groves, J. E. 1978. "Taking care of the hateful patient." *New England Journal of Medicine* 298:883.

Hackman, J. R. and Lawler, E. E., III. 1971. "Employee reaction to job characteristics." *Journal of Applied Psychology Monograph* 55:259.

Hackman, J. R. and Oldham, G. R. 1976. "Motivation through the design of work: test of a theory." *Organizational Behavior and Human Performance* 16:250.

Hays, W. L. 1971. *Statistics*. 2nd ed. New York: Holt, Rinehart, and Winston.

Helmer, O. 1967. *Analysis of the future: the Delphi method*. California: Rand Corporation.

Herzberg, F. 1966. "One more time, how do you motivate employees?" *Harvard Business Review* 66:53.

Hopkins, C. E.; Hetherington, R. W.; and Parsons, E. M. 1975. "Quality of medical care: a factor analysis approach using medical records." *Health Services Research* 10:199.

Hurtado, A. V. and Greenlick, M. R. 1971. "A disease classification system for analysis of medical care utilization, with a note on symptom classification." *Health Services Research* 6:235.

Katz, D. 1970. "The motivational basis of organizational behavior." in V. H. Vroom and E. L. Deci, eds. *Management and motivation*. Baltimore: Penguin Books.

Katz, D. and Kahn, R. L. 1966. *The social psychology of organizations*. New York: John Wiley and Sons.

Kendall, P. L. and Selvin, H. C. 1957. "Tendencies toward specialization," in R. W. Merton; G. G. Reader; and P. L. Kendall, eds. *The student physician*. Cambridge: Harvard University Press.

Kessner, D. M. 1973. "Assessing health quality—the case for tracers." *New England Journal of Medicine* 288:189.

Lawler, E. E., III and Porter, L. 1967. "Antecedent attitudes of effective managerial performance." *Organizational behavior and human performance,* 2:122.

Lawrence, P. R. and Lorsch, J. W. 1969. *Organization and environment—managing differentiation and integration*. Homewood, Ill.: Richard D. Irwin.

Lyons, T. F. and Payne B. C. 1974. "The relationship of physicians' medical recording performance to their medical care performance," *Medical Care* 12:714.

"Leading diagnoses and reasons for patient visits." March, 1970. *National Therapeutic Drug Index Review,* 1:15.

Lee, R. I. and Jones, L. W. 1933. *The fundamentals of good medical care*. Chicago: University of Chicago Press. Publications of the Committee on the Costs of Medical Care: No. 22.

Lembcke, P. A. 1967. "Evolution of the medical audit." *Journal of the American Medical Association* 199:111.

Lewis, C. E. 1974. "The state of the art of quality assessment—1973." *Medical Care* 12:799.

Makover, H. B. 1951. "The quality of medical care: methodology of survey of the medical groups associated with the Health Insurance Plan of New York." *American Journal of Public Health* 41:824.

March, J. G. and Simon, H. A. 1970. "Motivational constraints: the decision to participate." in V. H. Vroom and E. L. Deci, eds. *Management and motivation.* Baltimore: Penguin Books.

McClain, J. O. 1970. "Aids to utilization review: a decision problem in a hospital setting." Ph.D. Dissertation, Yale University.

Mills, R.; Fetter, R. B.; Riedel, D. C.; and Averill, R. 1976 "AUTOGRP: an interactive computer system for the analysis of health care data." *Medical Care* 14:603.

Morehead, M. 1967. "The medical audit as an operational tool." *American Journal of Public Health* 57:1643.

National Ambulatory Medical Care Survey: Background and Methodology: Vital and Health Statistics; Data Evaluation and Methods Research Series 2, No. 61, DHEW Publications No. (HRA) 76-1335.

National Center for Health Statistics. 1974. *Health resources statistics, 1974.* Washington, D. C.: U.S. Department of Health, Education and Welfare, DHEW Publication (HRA) 75-1509.

Nelson, A. 1977. "The role of the PSRO's," in Egdahl, R. H. and Gertman, P. M., eds., *Quality health care,* Germantown, Md.: Aspen Systems.

Nie, N. H.; Hall, C. H.; Jenkins, J. G.; Steinbrenner, K.; and Bent, D. H. 1975. *Statistical package for the social sciences.* 2nd ed. New York: McGraw-Hill.

Parker, A. 1974. "The dimensions of primary care: Blueprints for change," in S. Andreopoulos, ed. *Primary care: where medicine fails.* New York: John Wiley and Sons.

Parsons, T. 1951. *The social system.* Glencoe, Ill: The Free Press.

———. 1975. "The sick role and the role of the physician reconsidered." *Milbank Memorial Fund Quarterly* 53:257.

Payne, B. C. 1967. "Continued evolution of a system of medical care appraisal." *Journal of the American Medical Association* 201:536.

Payne, B. C. and Lyons, T. F. 1972(a). *Method of evaluating and improving personal medical care quality—episode of illness study for Hawaii medical association.* Ann Arbor: University of Michigan.

———. 1972(b). *Method of evaluating and improving personal medical care quality— office care study for Hawaii medical association.* Ann Arbor: University of Michigan.

"The pediatrician in private practice." June, 1972. *National Therapeutic Drug Index Review* 3:12.

Peterson, O. L.; Andrews, L. P.; Spain, R. S.; and Greenberg, B. G. 1956. "An analytical study of North Carolina general practice 1953–1954." *Journal of Medical Education* 31: Part 2.

Rhee, S. -O. 1976. "Factors determining the quality of physician performance." *Medical Care* 14:733.

Riedel, D. C. and Fitzpatrick, T. B. 1964. *Patterns of patient care: a study of hospital use in six diagnoses.* Ann Arbor: The University of Michigan.

Schwab, D. P. and Cummings, L. L. 1970. "Theories of performance and satisfaction: a review," *Industrial Relations* 9:408.

Shevky, E. and Bell, W. 1955. *Social area analysis: theory, illustrations, application and computational procedures.* Stanford: Stanford University Press.

Shevky, E.; Bell, W.; and Williams, M. 1949. *The social areas of Los Angeles: analysis and typology.* Los Angeles: University of California Press.

Shortridge, M. H. 1974. "Quality of medical care in an outpatient setting." *Medical Care* 12:283.

Starfield, B. and Scheff, D. 1972. "Effectiveness of pediatric care: the relationship between processes and outcome." *Pediatrics* 49:547.

Szasz, T. S. and Hollender, M. H. 1956. "A contribution to the philosophy of medicine: the basic models of doctor-patient relationship." *Archives of Internal Medicine* 97:585.

Thompson, H. C. and Osborne, C. E. 1974. "Development of criteria of quality assurance of ambulatory child health care." *Medical Care* 12:807.

Timms, D. 1971. *The urban mosaic.* Cambridge: Harvard University Press.

Triandis, H. C. 1959. "A critique and experimental design for the study of the relationship between job productivity and job satisfaction." *Psychological Bulletin* 56:309.

Tyron, R. C. 1955. *Identification of social areas by cluster analysis.* University of California Publications in Psychology, Vol. 8, No. 1.

Vroom, V. H. and Yetton, P. W. 1973. *Leadership and decision-making.* Pittsburgh: University of Pittsburgh Press.

Wagner, E. H.; Greenberg, R. A.; Imrey, P. B.; et al. 1976. "Influence of training and experience on selecting criteria to evaluate medical care." *New England Journal of Medicine* 294:871.

Yuchtman, E. and Seashore, S. E. 1967. "A system approach to organizational effectiveness." *American Sociological Review.* 32:891.

Index

About the Authors

Ruth Lyn Riedel was Research Director of the Connecticut Ambulatory Care Study. She is currently on the faculty of the Graduate Program in Health Services Administration and Planning and is Project Director of the Western Network for Continuing Education in Health Administration at the University of Washington, Seattle. Donald C. Riedel is Professor and Chairman, Department of Health Services, School of Public Health and Community Medicine, University of Washington, and was formerly Professor and Director of the Center for the Study of Health Services, Institution for Social and Policy Studies, Yale University. He is author and coauthor of numerous publications in the field.